KENNETH WILLIAMS

KENNETH WILLIAMS

A Biography

Michael Freedland

WEIDENFELD AND NICOLSON · LONDON

First published in Great Britain in 1990 by
George Weidenfeld and Nicolson
91 Clapham High Street, London SW4 7TA

British Library Cataloguing in Publication Data
Freedland, Michael
    Kenneth Williams: a biography
    1. Great Britain. Entertainments. Williams,
Kenneth, 1926–1988
    I. Title
    791.092

    ISBN 0–297–79701–8

Printed and bound in Great Britain by
The Bath Press Ltd, Avon

For Fiona, Dani and Jonathan
Who have grown to maturity while their father has
proudly watched – and listened, and wondered

Contents

Illustrations

Acknowledgements

This has been a complex task, writing a book about such an extraordinarily complex personality. But it would have been impossible without the help of so many people who knew the real Kenneth Williams and were willing and in most cases very happy to share their thoughts with me. To them, I am extremely grateful – as I am to those who supplied me with information but who didn't want to be quoted as having done so.

At the top of the list of those who unsparingly provided time and help, must undoubtedly be Ken's mother, the indomitable 'Lou' and his charming sister Pat. It wasn't an easy task for them, particularly since it began very soon after his death and the wounds were raw. But they spent hour after hour, week after week with me and I am very much in their debt. Pat also lent me letters and photographs from the family albums.

Letters provide a great source of information to any biographer and having them so willingly provided by others who knew Ken well, like Michael Codron, Sir Clement Freud, Annette Kerr and Val Orford is also gratefully acknowledged – as is the time they gave me for interviews. Richard Pearson, an actor I have always greatly admired, supplied me with photographs too, as did Val Orford and these are more appreciated than can easily be said. There were pictures very generously supplied by Peter Rogers and Gerald Thomas, who both also spent much time with me, and I thank them both for all their help. The task was also made much easier for me by the kindness and co-operation of Ken's literary heir, Michael Anderson, a man who must be recommended to any talented performer looking for a good agent.

Dozens of others spent time with me in interviews, Among those I wish to heartily thank are:

Simon Brett, Gyles Brandreth, Charles Brodie, Brenda Bruce, Kenneth Connor, Beverly Cross, Barry Cryer, the Marchioness of Dufferin and Ava, Peter Estall, Fenella Fielding, Liz Frazer, Bamber Gascoigne, Sheila Hancock, Anita Harris, David Hatch, David Jacobs, Sue Krisman, John Lahr, Jennie Linden, Michael Margolis, Miriam Margolyes, Ian Messiter, David Nathan, Nanette Newman, Derek Nimmo, Hugh Paddick, Nicholas

Parsons, Geoffrey Paul, Lance Percival, Bill Pertwee, Leslie Phillips, Andrew Ray, Sylvia Reed, Manny Robinson, Peter Shaffer, Joan Sims, Peter Spence, Nigel Tewkesbury, Barry Took, Timothy West, Richard Wilcox and Barbara Windsor.

They made all the difference to my work.

My thanks, too, for the enormous kindness David Roberts, editorial director at Weidenfeld, has shown me. His patience really has been amazing. My editor, Amanda Harting, has been as close to the ideal occupant of that position as any I have ever come across.

Finally, without the support of my wife, Sara, I could never have attempted it. She knows how I feel.

Michael Freedland
London, 1990.

Introduction

Kenneth Williams was not an international star. Cross the Atlantic and few will know the name. In his native Britain – a country he was never happy to leave – he was the antithesis of the showbiz personality. He was a combination of show-off and virtual recluse.

Yet in the age of the megastar who exists by virtue of the fact that to succeed at all, you have to be as easily recognized by people eating with chopsticks in Hong Kong, drinking borsht in Moscow, enjoying a hamburger in New York and a plate of fish and chips in London, Williams was again an aberration. At home, he *was* a star – the kind who would bring taxi drivers shuddering to a halt as they saw him cross the road, who could send up the figures for a radio or TV show simply by saying, 'Stop messing about'.

His is a complicated story because he was a complicated person. The man who was the mainstay of the 'Carry On' film empire was perhaps the most erudite comic actor this country has ever known. He wrote avidly – as seriously and as conscientiously as he read the works of Shaw or Ibsen or as he could discuss the current world crisis or *The Decline and Fall of The Roman Empire*. Yet few of his own writings said very much about him.

Until now, the book on Kenneth Williams has remained closed. People who say they knew him well, did so from their own necessarily limited perspective. His fellow radio personality and close friend, Derek Nimmo, put it perfectly when he said that he metaphorically kept all his friends in separate rooms – and none of them knew what was going on in the room next door. It was sometimes more than a metaphorical room. Being ensconced with him in a particular place was to have a wall built around you, even if you couldn't see it.

This, therefore, is an attempt to bring the walls down.

ONE

The Caledonian Road in Islington has in recent years developed a kind of snob appeal – a market area where intellectuals and stockbrokers do their Saturday shopping and where prospective antique dealers queue up for the chance of getting a new shop. It's the centre of a district which has come to symbolize that new word 'gentrification'.

In 1926, it was very different. Not cockney in the true literal sense of the word, although if the wind was blowing in the right direction and the ringers were particularly loud, one might just, theoretically, hear the bells of Bow. Islington was as working class as the traders selling whelks and cockles and mussels. The people travelling to the road, the traders and the customers, would talk about 'going up the Caly'.

Just down the road were King's Cross and St Pancras Stations – and again, if the wind were blowing fiercely, the smoke from the trains lingered in the air. Pentonville Prison was just before the stations. Gentrification was a long way off.

It wasn't a great deal more gentrified in Marchmont Street, although the barrow boys weren't there and as close as Caledonian Road had been to Pentonville, so Marchmont Street was near to London University. Russell Square, hub of the Duke of Bedford's estate and where the authors who made up the Bloomsbury Set would walk, was even closer.

None of that mattered very much to Charlie Williams. He had once been a van driver with what was then the London, Midland and Scottish Railway, an occupation that some might have thought more in the line of the rough-edged (and probably rough-centred) Charlie, newly released from First World War army service. But by this time, he was manager of a small ladies' hairdressing shop in Marchmont Street and his only concern was that one day it would be his own. His wife Louisa had much the same sort of ambition. She used to wash the hair of his customers and take the money in the till, hoping as much as they did that she would get the change right.

Charlie was very fussy, or very particular, as people like him used to say.

When he and Louisa took the bus that brought them from Marchmont Street to their home at Bingfield Street, off the Caledonian Road, he would bemoan the standards of the world. After all, he *had* been a soldier in World War I. On the mantlepiece in the two-room flat was a photograph showing Private Williams flanking his commanding officer in the Royal Berkshire Regiment – given its charter on the field 'by the King himself, God bless him'. Charlie had been invalided out of the Army, a victim – although it bought his ticket for 'Blighty' – of trench fever. But he remembered the standards the Army had taught him for the rest of his life.

There were standards that you didn't easily forego. A man had to be a man, to earn his living. And even if you were a girl, you had to learn a trade. He didn't represent the popular stereotype of a ladies hairdresser. He spoke as he found, he would probably say, which was why he would as likely tell a customer that if she wanted her hair dyed, she'd look like one of those ladies who thronged Russell Square Underground station without any intention of buying a ticket. No effeminate chatter, no jewels. His own hair was short back and sides and that's the way every real man should have it.

His daughter Pat knew about his standards of good clean living by the time she was at school. 'You'd better learn a trade when you leave,' he told her from the earliest days.

She seems to have better recall of these days when she helped her mother look after the new baby who was born in the flat at Bingfield Street, on February 22, 1926 – 2.30 on a Monday afternoon. Louisa Williams would never forget that date. How could she? It was, after all, early closing day and Charlie was at home, too. She was confined to her bedroom at the flat with a midwife in attendance. So was her mother-in-law.

It was an easy birth. She adored the son who was born that day. 'I knew I'd love him right from the start,' she was to tell me. 'Oh, he was lovely. He wasn't very big, but he had lovely skin. He was pale. He had lovely curly hair.' She called the baby Kenneth – Kenneth Charles – out of deference to Charlie her husband. 'But Kenneth was the name I liked. Kenneth Charles sounded nice.' Even so, he would almost always be called simply 'Ken' in the Williams household. Charlie called him 'The boy' and 'The boy' he stayed until Charlie died. He was also Louisa's boy, even if she didn't call him that herself. 'I was glad I had a boy because I always wanted one,' she told me. 'I think boys are much better than girls. I think they have more feeling.'

It is more apparent now than it was then that this was not an ideal marriage. The Williamses weren't exactly a love match and Charlie was to suspect before very long, that even as a little baby, Kenneth was the one male in Louisa's life for whom she really cared. Pat readily admits that he was the favourite.

There are people who never really leave the places where they are born. The old story that they can be taken out of the slums but the slums will never be removed from them couldn't be said of Kenneth Charles Williams, even if Bingfield Street, working class though it undoubtedly was, was not in the least bit a slum. He left it in spirit probably even before his parents decided to give up the flat and move into rooms at the Marchmont Street shop.

Charlie, too, liked the idea of having a son. He would take him to football matches with him, wouldn't he? Well, no, perhaps he wouldn't. Give young Kenneth a ball to play with and he'd look at it with a kind of disdain and make his way to Pat's dolls. That suited Pat quite well. 'I was more interested in playing football than I was in the dolls,' she would tell me. Charlie was less than impressed with that. It wasn't what nature decreed. He would spend the rest of his life vainly trying to come to terms with the situation and reconciling his own firmly-held beliefs with the facts life had served him.

Louisa showed not the slightest sympathy with her husband's views. 'My Ken' was a beautiful boy and he plainly loved his mother very much. He seemed to do as he was told and she knew that when she let loose her caustic wit along with her cockney accent – 'She's all kid gloves and no drawers' – he'd appreciate it without (heaven forbid) any sexual connotation being allowed to register. Louisa was always ready for the kind of quip that a generation earlier would have guaranteed her a place as a small-time Marie Lloyd in a music hall; perhaps even low down on the bill at Collin's, Islington's proudest variety theatre, where you could sit in the balcony for tuppence.

But for the moment she wasn't interested in show business from a professional point of view. Charlie certainly wasn't, although going into a pub was one of his choicest diversions, even if – as we shall see – he would sometimes seek some kind of subterfuge to go there. The pub sing-song and the knees-up was as much part of the cockney way of life as a plate of bangers and mash.

'The only thing Dad ever did for us,' Pat now recalls, 'was to insist that we had a reasonably good education and we learned a trade – the fact that I myself got expelled from school was besides

3

the point. But I wish he had been softer with us. I never remember his reading us a bedtime story.'

Louisa looked upon her responsibilities as chiefly to bring up her children, clean in body and clean in mind. The first was taken care of personally. No dirty necks or black spots behind the ears for her children. Ken seems to have accepted it to the point of having a desire for cleanliness positively floating in his bloodstream – it would stay there with the red and white corpuscles for the rest of his life. 'Even as a little boy,' Pat now remembers, 'if he got some jam on his fingers, he would say, "Erh..." as if it was something revolting and go and wash his hands. He couldn't bear it.' And since the children almost always had bread and jam to eat when they came home from school at the end of the day, that routine of the disdain and the immediate wash would follow as surely as the sunset.

'We always had to take our clothes off at night and put them straight on a hanger. The dirty clothes had to go straight into a linen basket.'

Charlie insisted on another requirement from his children: they had to perfect their handwriting. Both Pat and Ken were expected to copy the alphabet, time after time, letter after letter, until he was satisfied that they had reached perfection. Both of them would have reason in later years to thank him for that, despite the apparent drudgery of it all.

And although the Williamses weren't particularly religious, they insisted that the children go to Sunday school. This concentrated on Bible stories which the youngsters took to with about as much enthusiasm as a trip to the dentist but because it happened at the same time every week, the sheer regularity of it dulled both the terror and the boredom.

Both were sent out to King's Cross Wesleyan Sunday school, opposite St Pancras Station. They went at the same time every Sunday – and each of them was given a penny for the collection. Pat would decide not to go and Ken kept *her* penny as hush money. 'He'd buy sweeties with it,' she recalled. They had an arrangement. After Sunday school, Ken would meet his sister, tell her the details of the text under discussion and then go home. She'd play cricket or football with the boys.

Ken needed to tell Pat what they had learned that day so that she could answer the cross-examination of her father. 'What did they teach you today?' their parents would ask. Pat would be ready with the latest details of the story of Joseph and his coat of many colours – aided by the text card every pupil used to bring home. Ken contrived to get hold of two, one for him, one for his sister.

Ken was not above using a little blackmail and sometimes after one of her absences from Sunday school, Pat seemed to be doing a great deal of washing up while her brother sat in his room playing his gramophone and reading his books. 'If you don't do it all,' he'd tell his sister, 'I'll tell Mummy you didn't go to Sunday school.' The story would go on for the rest of the week.

As a small boy, Ken joined the Wolf Cubs, as the junior scouts were known at the time. He didn't stay long. In fact, he was thrown out of their camp. 'He should never have joined in the first place,' says Pat. 'He wasn't the kind of person who was happy in a crowd.'

Ken and the Akela were not the best of friends and he was very unhappy. 'There were flies and people blowing off,' recalls Louisa today.

The breaking of wind and its prevention were to become one of Kenneth Williams's main passions in life, according to his sister. His father had a similar preoccupation with that anatomical body function. He had a phrase for it that became permanently etched in the Williams youngsters' childhoods. 'Who's cut the cake?' he'd ask. At this camp, there was just too much cake-cutting for young Ken. He wanted no part of it and the camp leaders wanted no part of him, either.

But he had tried to fit in, to make the necessary arrangements – which went awry mainly because young Kenneth didn't know enough of the facts of life. It was just before a Cubs camp that a parcel arrived addressed to a 'Miss K. Williams'. That mystified the family, since the only 'Miss' was a Miss *P*. Williams. Ken saw it and said, 'Oh, yes, I've been waiting for this' and darted up to his room.

He came downstairs a little later with a pale blue and a pale pink sanitary towel in his hands. He asked his mother: 'What are these supposed to be?' 'Oh,' she demanded, sternly and looking very flustered, 'where did *you* get them from?' The emphasis on the 'you' was intended to inform him that he had no business knowing about such merchandise, let alone handling it.

Ken was surprised by the reaction, but was determined not to be flustered. 'I saw an advertisement,' he said, 'for towels ... As I'm going away to camp with the Cubs for the weekend and you're always moaning about my making the towels dirty, I thought I'd get two new ones of my own and I wouldn't have to take yours.' He was seven years old at the time. Ken started to cry, Charlie demanded: 'What the bleeding hell is going on here?' and all poor Louisa could stammer was, 'I'll tell you later. I'll tell you later.' His mother took charge of the offending objects and Ken went to his last camp.

Long ago, the Williams family had come from Wales. Their basic Methodism – very basic indeed, as it turned out, since neither of the two adults did much about going inside a church – was one of the relics of that past. Nevertheless, given the right mood or the appropriate occasion, Charlie would feign deep piety and remind his offspring that 'God can see you, if nobody else can.' Charlie's strict Methodism was framed by his own specific needs and regulations. Somehow or other, he managed to convince himself – if nobody else – that his adherence to the faith was via a group whose own rules did not stipulate the abhorrence of alcohol every other Methodist was expected to accept.

'We told the children to believe in God,' recalls Louisa now without trying to convey any great conviction on her own part. Sending the kids to religious instruction seemed to be enough to appease their consciences.

Certainly, it wasn't enough to come between them and their families, all of whom seemed to enjoy a tipple as their means of seeing the good that God can bring to the world. There were, for instance, the two grand-mothers': matriarchs whose word could not be breached – that is, without the help of a glass of stout.

Louisa Morgan had been left motherless at the age of four and her father, Henry, married a woman named Ellen Cod. Ellen ill-treated the young Louisa and her sisters Edith and Daisy, beat them and tormented them, but even when Louisa was grown up and married to Charlie and then a mother herself, Ellen was treated as mother and grandmother – except in one vital detail. No one referred to her by either title. To the family, she was always Tin Lizzie. No one has been able to explain a reason for the title, unless it was the way the whalebones in her corset would ping when she sat down.

Louisa and her family were the only ones who stayed in contact with the erstwhile Ellen Cod, partly because the Williamses and Tin Lizzie lived close to each other. 'She was a right old drunkard,' Pat remembered. 'She would get so drunk, she'd fall down and get carted off to hospital, with blood streaming down her face.' It happened so often that Charlie and Louisa could contemplate virtually buying a season ticket to the hospi-tal to which she would be taken with alarming regularity. 'She was always around – and just a pain in the arse to us all. You had to hide the booze whenever she was here.'

Grandma Williams was less of a fixture in Charlie's and Lou's home. She herself lived 'up the Caly' with her youngest daughter (Charlie was her eldest child). She, too, liked her booze. Years later, when she was in her eighties, she lived near Pat, and her granddaughter was treated to some of her exploits – like asking for a brandy in the pub where she usually only bought herself the familiar stout; or persuading the younger

6

woman to part with a tin of fruit or a bag of coal, which she couldn't afford on her pension.

If there were doubts about the pedigree of any of the other residents of 'the Caly', Grandma Williams was pure cockney − and, recalls Pat, 'shaped like a cottage loaf': all hips and bust, with grey wispy hair tied back in a bun. Her language was calculated to make a visiting sailor run home to his mother. Every sentence began with a 'bleeding' this or a 'bloody' that. 'Hail, rain or shine − ice so that you could hardly walk − she'd be round at the pub as soon as it opened, and sit there until it closed, when she'd go home to make herself something to eat. Then, at half-past-five, she'd be back in there again.'

Louisa didn't have time for a great deal of entertainment herself. But she *had* got reasonably close to it, and in later years despite her earlier reluctance was to boast that she could have been a star, given half the chance.

She would demonstrate her artistic skills for the benefit of her children − like singing 'Are you Lonesome Tonight?' (years before Elvis Presley and even Al Jolson ever sang it in public) while she scrubbed the floor around the kitchen table on which Ken had been placed. She always got the words wrong, he later remembered, but she sang it just the same as though the work had been specially commissioned for her.

She used to be a laundress, working for the grand-sounding Madame Louise's French Laundry in Museum Street, a stiff-collar's throw from Marchmont Street. What she liked best about the job was the chance to walk through London, wheeling the wicker basket filled with the clothes of people she would never meet − unless they happened to walk past the door as she was talking to a maid at the tradesmen's entrance.

It was a fun life for a poor girl, as much fun for her friend Gladys as for herself, because Gladys would get a ride on top of the basket. One day, an axle broke and a wheel spun down the road. Only the far-sightedness of a passing policeman saved the day and Louisa's job. He took a hat pin from a flowergirl and got the girls going again, although their boss was less than happy. As a mark of revenge, she sent them out again − this time to the Oxford Music Hall, where Daisy Dormer, creator of *After The Ball* was so impressed with the way Louisa had pressed her linen that she offered her a job as her dresser. Louisa said no, but always regretted it and for years afterwards dreamed of what might have been in a showbiz world that was to be hers only vicariously through her Ken.

Instead, she met Charlie. By that time, she was working behind the counter of an Express Dairy café. Charlie came in to order a Welsh rarebit – and before long was deciding that Louisa herself was a rare bit of enticement for a young fellow like himself. Once they married, and after the children had reached the age when they could be left, she went to work in the shop with him.

By the time he was managing the salon, Charlie was showing a degree of enterprise that wasn't always evident. He had anticipated the unisex hair salons two generations before they appeared on every London high street and she was now brought in to attend to the men's hair, washing a window cleaner's locks one moment and a postman the next.

Her favourite customers were the train drivers who had either just knocked off work or were on the way to clocking in at St Pancras or King's Cross. Being with them was like taking a magic carpet ride. They might be on their way to Bradford or Manchester or even Edinburgh, but when they told their stories of journeys on the footplate, it was as if they were on their way to Hong Kong or New York. She was a Londoner through and through, but she rarely saw much even of the City surrounding their little corner of the earth.

Charlie saw more and, through him, so did his children, even if Pat now realizes that there was method in the apparent madness of giving up his Sunday afternoons for their benefit. They were outings to which they were told to look forward all week. 'If you're good,' the two Williams youngsters were advised, 'Dad will take you out on Sunday.'

The journeys were usually the same. 'He would 'cart us all around the City,' remembers Pat. 'And we thought it was terrific.'

One moment, they were at the Bank of England – 'This is the Old Lady of Threadneedle Street,' said Charlie with the sense of pride only a Londoner can have in his native city, and with an additional feeling of achievement in being able to instruct his children. 'And this old inn was in Dickens's books.' He took them on journeys around the historical sites, on the surface more valuable to the children's learning processes than school ever was – as Ken was to say, his education was practically non existent.

At the Monument, Charlie would describe in great detail how the Great Fire of London broke out. Kenneth in particular was greatly impressed with that. He loved history and hearing about historical characters. 'But,' says Pat, 'that was when we would suddenly find ourselves outside a public house.' 'I'll just nip in here for a moment,' he would say. 'Just to have a pint.' He would bring them out a glass of fizzy sugary lemonade and a packet of crisps. And then it would continue the same way around the corner.

8

'It wasn't until years later that I realized what a crafty old bugger he was,' says Pat. 'He pretended to take us around the historical buildings of London, but it was just a jolly old pub crawl. I knew more about the pubs of Wapping than I ever learned about the Great Fire of London.' If Ken told him he wanted to see a particular statue or building, it would be another excuse for a pub crawl – more glasses of lemonade, more packets of crisps. At the end of the day, Ken would ask: 'Well, where's that statue, then?' 'Oh, Christ,' said Charlie, I'll take you next week.' And next week, again they would discover the drafty exterior of some other East End pub.

They enjoyed those days, though, Pat and Ken. 'It's because we were out, simply that,' Pat now says. 'During the week, there weren't the opportunities.' Charlie worked on Saturdays, and Sundays were the only times that the children got to see him.

Occasionally, they were allowed out on their own – but only if they were very good, had done their homework and their chores. Pat had to scrub out the shop and Ken had to polish his father's shoes, just as he had to clean his own.

All the time, Charlie was hoping that his Kenneth would find, as if by some kind of magic, a hitherto latent interest in playing football. He hadn't shown it at Manchester Street Junior School, the educational establishment near King's Cross where he first displayed his interest in reading and history.

It was apparent that both children disliked their father although his widow now disputes that. She agrees with her daughter, though, that the kindest thing that could be said about the relationship between Charlie and his son was that they didn't have a relationship at all – of any kind that seemed to matter.

Charlie would dearly have loved to have looked forward to the day when Ken would go on one of those pub crawls with him, to be able to say to Louisa – or 'Lou' as everyone was by now calling her – 'Just going out with the boy'. But even at this early stage, he knew that was a kind of pie that was going to stay in the sky. Pat went out with him on her own occasionally. Ken stayed with Lou. 'They were virtually inseparable,' says Pat. None of that would have mattered to Charlie, though, if he could have been sure that, even though they weren't together, Ken was good at sports. But that was even less likely than the pub crawl.

The nearest he had come to sport was playing what he and Pat called 'OG' for 'our game', in which Ken would show his new-found talent for impersonating relatives whom they had visited or who had come to the flat.

In those days – in fact, until she was twelve and he was nine – they shared a bedroom together, little twin beds neatly placed close to each other. They would talk and play OG for as long as they thought the coast would remain clear. 'We'd better shut up,' one of them would say. 'The old man'll be home soon.' The 'old man', then in his early forties, used to work very late each night and by the time he had shut up the shop and caught his bus from Marchmont Street to 'the Caly', it was later still.

And then things changed. The owner of the hairdressers' shop died. The wife offered it to Charlie – after all he had run it successfully enough, so there was no question that he could make a go of it. The problem was that Charlie didn't have the money. But Louisa's brother did and he lent him the cash.

It meant, however, a tightening of belts and not just the ones that Charlie would strop when he gave his male customers a shave. Williams was not the sort of man who would allow himself to get into long-term debt. To reduce the financial outlay, the family moved into the empty flat above the shop and the basement below, which had been used for storing the lotions and other equipment which a hairdresser needs to proceed with his professional activities. Now the storage would have to be accommodated elsewhere. The family would eat in the basement, in a kitchen-come-dining-room-cum lounge. There was a three-room flat at the very top of the building, which was to be rented out, as were two other rooms downstairs. Louise did the housework for the entire building, as well as continuing as shampoo girl and keeper of the till.

'She worked very, very hard,' Pat remembers. 'She kept the whole of the house clean, did all of the washing and everything else in the morning and then worked in the shop in the afternoon. She really was a goer, my mum.' On the other hand, 'the old man would fall out of bed, sit down and eat his breakfast and go to the shop when he was ready.'

It wasn't an easy move. Living accommodation always seemed as if it had to be secondary to the shop, and Ken was less than happy that it was, even though he was never noisy about it – which was more than could be said about Pat, who was far more defiant.

'Ken hated the shop,' Lou told me. 'He would walk right through as quickly as he could to get upstairs. He didn't want anything to do with hairdressing. All he cared about was his reading, writing and listening to his gramophone, his classical records.' Ken also had a large stamp collection, which was perhaps the only 'regular' small boy thing that he did. 'He was a very quiet boy, always wanting to be on his own. I never worried about that. I used to think that it was his life and if he enjoyed it that way, it was up to him.' He very occasionally made new friends at school. Lou remembers a little black girl he used to bring home in the afternoons. 'Everyone was talking about them. She was a sweet girl.'

If there was something to worry about, it was young Ken's complexion. He was terribly pale and that which had been so attractive in a baby now gave cause for concern. Lou took him to several doctors. They all told her the same thing: 'Don't worry – it's just the way he is.'

It may not have been easy living above and below the shop, but Lou kept it as clean as a brand new hairpin in an unopened box. The bedrooms were upstairs and the kitchen and dining room which were in the basement could be seen through the gratings, then as much part of the London scene as the chimney sweeps and flower girls of the day.

But the shop was Charlie's whole life. When the time came, thirty years later, to give it all up, he was a lost man. The important thing to come out of all this for the Williams children was that they no longer shared a room – and that meant the end of OG, 'although we did play it over the washing up,' Pat recalls.

In those games, Pat was always herself. Ken took over the role of whoever he considered suitable for the role he was now taking on. Pat dreamed of having a red, open MG sports car. 'Right,' said Ken, 'you've got your MG and I'm driving. I'm Uncle Bill.' Another occasion, Pat would have to play herself to Ken's Auntie Alice. If imitation is the sincerest form of flattery, the Morgan and Williams clans were being flattered constantly. It was the birth of the Kenneth Williams who played with other people's voices the way his schoolmates played with a football.

He liked the Manchester Street school, near the Regent Cinema, what is now Camden Town Hall. 'He didn't complain much,' remembers his mother. But, as Pat says, he was a loner. Apart from the black girl, he had one friend. That friend for much of his school life now was Freddie Berry. 'He walked to school with Freddie, played on the way to and from home at lunchtime with Freddie' – always the same 'pretend' games, their own kind of OG.'

Ken would imagine he and Freddie were scaling the 'unclimbable' Everest. 'I'm the leader of the mountaineers,' said Ken. 'You'll be my packhorse.' 'And,' says Pat, 'Freddie used to take all this.' 'Berry,' instructed Ken, 'go and do what I told you...' and Freddie would do it. Then he'd start on Pat. 'I'd tell him to go and jump in the lake.'

OG to Ken was always more than just a game. In a way, it was a philosophy. To himself, he was never just an 'ordinary' boy called Kenneth Williams living above and below a hairdressing salon in Marchmont Street. In his mind, he was a prince. Nor was it just a childhood fantasy. He last told Pat about that belief on the Boxing Day before his death, more than half a century later. 'He always believed that there must have been some mix up along the line that made him Charlie Williams's son, instead of the son of some king.' Neither Charlie nor Lou ever knew about that. 'I fell about,' said Pat, 'but he was quite serious.'

'He always thought that everything was beneath him and he should have been living in some grand style.'

At school, he was a good pupil, shining in English and history as well as art. Mathematics was more of a drawback, but in the way that he was to perfect in the years to come, he wouldn't allow that fact to interfere with what he considered to be the more necessary things in life.

Charlie became stricter than ever. He wasn't happy with the thought of his children playing OG, even if the washing up did get done in the process. No, that was not enough for Charlie, who was growing more strict with every day that passed. One can understand why he was so strict, he worked a long day trying to make a living in circumstances that weren't easy. The Army had taught him a sense of discipline that he dearly wanted his children to take into account along with the work ethic.

He insisted on both children polishing their shoes every night now, and he would inspect their work, including the instep between the heel and the sole, which had to be as bright and shiny as the toecaps. When they came home from school, necessity meant that they had to walk through the shop – if Charlie could have arranged it differently, he would have done, because he didn't like mixing business with family. So they were not allowed to talk to him when they came in – merely to make sure that Kenneth raised his cap politely when he said 'Good afternoon' to each customer, giving them the kind of courtesy they probably never received anywhere else. If they lingered over the shampoo basin, there was one certain comment from Charlie: 'Hop it'.

'He was always very insistent that we were polite, had good table manners and spoke properly and learnt a trade. To him, it didn't matter if we didn't work at it, but we should have something to fall back upon,' said Pat.

There was a constant conflict in Lou's mind between her love of her Ken and what had to be loyalty to Charlie. 'Why don't you leave him alone?' she'd constantly ask the father of the family as he laid down his own definition of the law. When both children complained to her about his demands, she would try to soften them. 'Just forget it,' she'd say, 'I'll have a word with him.'

But Ken took no notice. He wasn't an emotional child. He allowed the water to run down his back like a duck on the lake in the nearby park.

Nevertheless, both children had to know that their father's word was law when it came to the important things in life. 'Dad was dogmatic,' Pat recalled. 'He was a Victorian bastard. When you were under his roof, you did as he told you.'

In truth, Charlie expected a lot of his two children – seemingly for little in return. He almost never gave them gifts. One day, however, he did. 'Come here, son,' he said to Kenneth. 'What do you want?' the boy asked. 'I've got a present for you.' He handed over a parcel, big enough to make any small boy's heart race that little bit faster.

Ken rushed to undo the paper and produced a pair of football boots. He held them up by the laces as though there was a dead rat in his hands, the tail just about the only part he could bear to touch. 'And what,' he asked, 'am I supposed to do with these?' He wasn't so much shocked as contemptuous of the thought of being expected to play a game like that. 'Put them on your feet, you silly bugger,' said Charlie. 'And get out and play football, get out with the boys.'

'I don't play football,' said Ken, disdainfully. He dropped the boots in their box and left them on a shelf at the end of the living room before going back to his books and records. 'The man went mad,' says Pat now.

She recalls looking at the boots longingly. If a girl could play football – and she could and did – then she should be allowed to wear football boots, but she wasn't.

The boots stayed on a shelf, a monument to his father's total lack of understanding of what his son was made of. He left it at that for a time, ego bruised a bit (as he wished his son might be, playing a real boy's game) but leaving it alone. Then he gave Kenneth another present. A few days earlier, Ken had been involved in a fight at school – picked on as an easy target by boys who enjoyed bullying a great deal more than Charlie would have wished his Ken to enjoy football.

The boy undid *this* parcel a little more cautiously – as he was right to do. This time, Charlie had bought him a pair of boxing gloves. They went on the shelf next to the football boots. It wasn't that Charlie had some perverse desire to see his son hurt. He just couldn't understand

13

why he didn't want to play football or get involved in a boxing match. If he had the right equipment, surely he would love to play? The fact was that Kenneth didn't have the right equipment and his father couldn't buy it for him.

He was – in his father's eyes at least – woefully unmechanical. One year, Pat recalls, 'he got a beautiful Meccano set for Christmas – a great big one. *I* spent hours playing with it. He played with my dolls. I was intrigued with it, but Ken didn't want to know.'

When it came to school sports, it was hell on earth for him. 'He wouldn't have wanted to get his hands dirty, playing rugby. Good God, no.'

Louisa understood it and was delighted to hear a gramophone playing scratchy records in her Ken's room and know that when he had done his homework he was reading.

'He always had a book in his hands,' Louisa recalled for me. 'Though *what* he was reading I never really knew. He just liked to read. I didn't think there was anything strange in that. I didn't want him to be more manly than he was. I didn't think he was being a Cissy. There are just some boys who like sport and some who don't. I didn't object to him not being interested in it. You couldn't *make* him interested. He wouldn't like rugby. It would have been too rough.'

Charlie wasn't disturbed by Ken's behaviour, but he certainly was disappointed.

Ken was never funny at home, Louisa says. 'When he came in, he would walk straight through the shop and go into his room to read and listen to his classical records.'

He and Pat would talk incessantly – usually about family matters; about an uncle who was ill, how strangely Charlie behaved, 'the sort of thing most brothers and sisters would talk about.' And they did crossword puzzles between them. 'He was good at them,' said Pat. 'If I came up with the right answer, he'd get annoyed.' So he would try to impress – by using long words. That, too, would be something he wouldn't easily grow out of.

At school, it was as hard to convince his teachers that they shouldn't consider him for team games as it was to persuade his father. Louisa didn't allow it to worry her, however. Ken was going to be his own man, she was sure. And he had another friend whom she liked, a boy named Wreyford Palmer. He, too, was a fellow conspirator in OG – a game that usually consisted of acting out a kind of Prisoner of Zenda routine in which Ken was always king and Palmer always prime minister. Theirs was an army without privates, but as many a theatrical writer and producer discovered before and has since, there's a lot more colour in people in officers' uniforms. It was the beginning of the fantasy world Kenneth Williams was destined to inhabit long before others would see him in it.

Only once did that fantasy appear to be dangerous. It became so important to Ken that it took over his life, waking and sleeping. One night, he walked in his sleep – while dreaming of fighting a battle to the death on behalf of his own kingdom. He started heaving what he believed were rocks at his enemies. What he really was doing was throwing a flower pot out of the window – which landed on the head of a passing neighbour rejoicing in the name of Florrie Plume. If she hadn't been wearing her tight-fitting felt hat, she was convinced she would have been a goner – or, at least, suffered from concussion. After that episode, she made it very clear to Louisa that she always passed the Williamses' flat on the other side of the road.

When the time for the school play came around, Ken made sure he had a leading part. He told Charlie about it. His father was less than impressed. 'The stage is for Nancies,' he told him.

But he performed in the school play *The Rose And The Ring*, by William Makepeace Thackeray playing a girl, the Princess Angelica. Contemporary photographs show him looking perfectly angelic. He got his best ever school reports for that. 'A boy of talent,' said a teacher. Louisa could only smile and agree. 'I was so proud. I think any mother is proud to see her kids on the stage. I never thought he'd go on and make a career of it, like he did – carry on like he did. He was always entertaining when he was a little boy at school.'

Not many of the other pupils or the staff of the school could have guessed what was in store after *The Rose And The Ring*.

A great deal of the success of this venture was due to Ken's English teacher, Basil Hodges at Manchester Street school. He not only got him interested in literature – to the extent that it would before long become a veritable passion – he demonstrated how poetry was more than another form of story telling, but was an escape route by which thoughts could be expressed, thoughts that wouldn't come out in any other way. He also discovered that it gave him a certain degree of power. The boy who appeared so wimpish in the playground could hold everyone's attention reciting a line of Shakespeare.

A school report recorded that the young Williams was 'quick to grasp the bones of a subject, slow to develop them'. No one seemed to press him too hard to grasp the bones of the poetry to which he was subjected so willingly. Rupert Brooke in those days when, for millions World War I was still a vivid memory inspired him like little else. To the accompaniment of his classical 78s, Brooke and Williams were a virtually inseparable partnership in the after-school hours.

The master assured him he would enjoy acting. The experience lit a pilot light inside. He knew it was up to himself as to whether it would ever catch fire seriously. For the moment, he would content himself with the experience of being on stage at school and doing imitations of the teachers in the playground. Years later, Ken would recall: 'When I did things at school, the other boys would recognize the character. When I did the headmaster, they said, "Cor, that's just like him."'

The other boys at Manchester Street School thought it was wonderful. Once, they gathered in a group around him, giggling as Ken contorted his face, played with his jacket and changed his voice. Suddenly, the group dispersed, the giggling stopped. The head was approaching.

Needless to say, the head himself was less than pleased about it – especially since Ken was now a prefect. 'You must understand what I'm trying to tell you,' he said, 'as a prefect you have certain responsibilities. If you mock teachers, you might succeed in amusing people, but you'll also succeed in undermining your own authority.' Ken nodded in mock agreement. 'Jokes will make you popular,' the head said in a seemingly extraordinarily prescient remark, 'but you won't be taken seriously when you want to be sincere.'

Ken later admitted that he understood nothing of the kind, but he told the teacher that, of course, he did. It was, as he said, more water off a duck's back.

The headmaster obviously had something. Ken fooled about, trying to give the impression that he was strong and in control of all around him. But it hid a sense of deep insecurity.

If Charlie heard about that, he would have been less than impressed. As for Ken's work in the play, he could only sneer that he didn't think much of it. Ken said he was also good at drawing. 'Do cartoons,' Charlie instructed. 'There's money in cartoons,' which probably said a lot for the kind of papers he read. 'I don't do cartoons,' said Ken, as though he had just been handed another pair of boxing gloves.

But Charlie kept up the pace. He was frightened of insecurity and didn't like to contemplate it for his children any more than he wanted it for himself. That was why he was a hairdresser. It was a trade he had learned and knew. He wouldn't be rich, but he could pay his bills and he wanted Pat and Kenneth always to be able to say the same thing.

Years later, Ken admitted he suffered from an inferiority complex which a teacher at his last school, the Lyulph Stanley Central School for Boys, near Great College Street, had diagnosed quite easily.

Ken had passed a scholarship exam to the Parliament Hill School which would later be known as a grammar – they were called secondary schools in those days before the 1944 Education Act – but the Williamses reckoned they couldn't afford the books and uniform he would need and settled for the in-between status of a 'Central'. It didn't make him any better at maths.

Charlie was, naturally, furious about his lack of concern for the only subject that was really important. After all, if you didn't have maths, how could you run a shop? Ken made it very clear that he had no such intention in the first place. Pat, however, was more calculating. She knew there were going to be times when she would need Charlie's support. So she decided to feign an interest (which she never possessed) in what he did. For hours, Pat would linger over wash basins watching Charlie giving Mr Williams's personal service to a customer requiring a shampoo. Before long, she was formally apprenticed.

Ken wanted none of that. The experience of being in a school play was enough to convince him that all those sessions of OG could be turned to some purpose – a job that he enjoyed doing as much as he would be good at it. But Charlie's taunts of the stage being only for 'Nancies' made him realize that in some ways his father was probably right. You couldn't make your living at acting. It was for fun. But like a good audience at a good play, he could fantasize that he was part of it, just the same.

His drawing, however, met with more approval from his father, even if he finally convinced the older Williams that there were simpler ways of making a living out of art than doing cartoons. One day, nevertheless, Charlie and Louisa had a discussion – and Charlie decided. If their boy was good at art, he should train to make a living at it. That, at least, might have been some sort of compensation for not having a son who would go to the pub with him or to the dogs on a Saturday night. Had Ken been that sort of man, they would have been bosom buddies. 'His real dream,' recalls Pat now, 'was still to be able to say to Mum and me, "You girls can do the washing up. Me and the boy are going out." That was Charlie.'

All that would have fitted perfectly into his own structured lifestyle – a style that was never so perfect or so structured as on a Sunday. He would go into the shop in the morning – just 'pottering around' – until lunchtime, which was always followed by a sleep, stretched out in his

17

chair in front of the fire. This ritual was followed by another one, equally regimented. The sleep over, he would have his weekly bath. He would shave, change his shirt and put on his Sunday best suit – and make himself responsible for tea. In that best suit, he would bring in his speciality – a tray of winkle sandwiches.

Sundays were also the day for religion in the Williams household – although the children were the only ones who 'suffered' it. During the week, they always had to say their prayers and, when very small, had to say Grace, too. They stopped that after the Sunday lunch when Charlie asked, 'Who's turn is it to say Grace?' and Ken replied: 'Grace'.

At the age of fourteen, Kenneth left Stanley Central, which was one of the only distinguished-looking establishments in this distinctly undistinguished area of London. It gloried under the name of Mornington Crescent and in recent years was given a sort of fame in an unfathomable radio quiz game. At Charlie's bidding, Kenneth was taken to an interview at the School of Lithography at Bolt Court, near Fleet Street. The street of ink would find a new talent in the young Ken or his father wasn't called Charlie Williams. If he couldn't achieve on a football pitch, Charlie was going to see his son succeed in a drawing office. Louisa was pleased to agree. Her Ken was going to succeed in whatever he did – and if Charlie didn't mind, that was so much the better.

Ken got through his interview and his drawing prowess met the required standards. He was well and truly a Bolt Court boy except that it was 1940 and the school wasn't going to stay in Bolt Court for long. It was being evacuated to Bicester in Buckinghamshire and Ken was moved along with everyone else. The family weren't pleased about it. 'I remember balling my eyes out,' says Pat.

For Lou it was heart-breaking. Ken was the one who would confide in her. 'He used to tell me about the good things and the bad.'

Charlie was of two minds. He didn't want 'the boy' to leave, but wondered whether at last it would make a man of him, at least according to his own definition of what manliness was all about. Ken didn't worry more about his father now than he ever had. There had been a series of lectures from his father before he left. 'Ken took no notice,' Lou recalls today.

'Come on,' Charlie would say, 'I want a word with you.' But, if Ken would say anything at all in response, it would most likely be 'mind your own business'. As Pat remembered : 'He just walked out and we'd laugh.' Now for a time, the laughs stopped at Marchmont Street. Ken was billeted first in the home of a family, but before long he moved to stay with a kind old man called Mr Chisholm, a bachelor. Chisholm was an eccentric, but he made the house in Sheep Street Ken's home, too.

Chisholm didn't want him to play football, but he liked talking about literature to the boy. In this small country town, they got on like a haystack on fire.

They read poetry to each other and Mr Chisholm, a retired veterinary surgeon, let young Ken roam through his surgery. He talked about his patients and the owners of the patients, who seemed to be more sick – and certainly more eccentric – than their charges. But what really impressed Ken were the long verses he was not only able to recite but which he could deliver with the emotion of an Irving. In so doing he would conflict with his housekeeper, a devout Salvationist whom he told to go away and play with her tambourine. It was a totally different atmosphere to the one Ken had known at Marchmont Street and one he enjoyed immensely. If nothing else, it made the acting pilot light glow slightly more encouragingly.

'He used to tell me about Mr Chisholm when we met,' Lou recalls. 'He liked that old man.'

There are those – Pat included – who believe that Ken had a sexual experience while in Mr Chisholm's house, one that affected him ever afterwards. Years later, he told his close friend Andrew Ray that a man interfered with him on a bus. He wasn't shocked by the encounter. In fact, as a hand was placed on his trousers, he found it a very pleasurable experience indeed. 'I thoroughly enjoyed it,' he was to tell Ray.

Certainly, it was at this time that the boy realized that not only was he not concerned about girls, his only sexual interest was in men. But he wasn't going out of his way to show it. From that moment on, it was to be difficult for him to demonstrate physically what he felt – to anyone.

19

TWO

It was a somewhat bewildered Kenneth who suddenly found himself back in London. The Blitz was over, but there were profound changes to life in Marchmont Street by the time his period with Mr Chisholm had finished.

He was only fifteen but at the age when other boys are suffering the torments of growing up – who was it who said that only girls go through a 'difficult' stage, only young female teenagers who get depressed? – Kenneth Charles Williams was facing a life that he hadn't known before. For one thing, Pat, a qualified ladies hairdresser by now, had joined up and was learning to be a wireless operator in the WAAFS, the Women's Auxiliary Air Force. It was the end of an era. Never again would they be quite so close.

They wrote each other letters. His were signed 'Kenny', hers 'Pattie'. They both began to assess their relationship with each other. 'I know I wished he had been my *elder* brother,' she told me. 'Had he been that, it would have been easier to accept things from him. Instead, when he asked me to do things for him, which he did occasionally, it was always the big sister helping the younger brother.'

When Pat returned from leave in October 1943, Ken decided to put his emotions into verse. He posted this poem to Pat's WAAF unit:

> When you were gone –
> And left this place so desolate,
> Devoid of you –
> Is left a face, so sad of late.

He was writing about Lou – or Louie as their mother was sometimes called.

> She sits alone
> Still, pensive, by the fireside,
> Her thoughts recede
> Upon an ever-flowing tide. . . .
> For her love

Like an evergentle, flowing rain
Is stored away –
To greet your coming home again.

Charlie might have bemoaned the fact that his son didn't enjoy playing or going to football, still heartily condemned 'Nancies' as the ones who went into the theatrical profession – which he considered covered every-thing and everyone from seaside concert parties to the starts of *Hamlet* or *Othello* – but he hadn't come to terms with the fact that his son was one of them. Ken on the other hand had. He had enjoyed the encounter at Bicester but even more had welcomed the company of Mr Chisholm who might or might not have initiated him further into homosexuality. (On a different level, he was certainly responsible for getting him on to the start of his career as a draughtsman.)

Nevertheless, at puberty Ken realized his inclinations and the strength of them. He worried about sex, but was not interested in the kind of encounters other boys at Bolt Court fantasized about. When they told him about nights at the pictures and the excitement of holding a girl's breast, he reacted in much the same way as he had to his father's offer of a pair of boxing gloves.

He couldn't be sure what he wanted to make of his future. But learning to be a draughtsman and a graphic artist measured up to his father's requirements and he could see no real reason to disagree. He was also good at it. As Louisa remembered: 'If he saw a picture as a child, he'd be sure to copy it.' He was good to the point that he could probably have had a highly successful joint career as an artist as well as an actor. His father had reason to be very pleased about that, particularly about his quite beautiful handwriting.

Charlie was more glad about that than he cared to admit too often. As Pat said, 'He was quite chuffed by us both. Ken was going to be a draughtsman and I was a hairdresser, who had served my apprenticeship. I think really he was pleased with himself that his two kids had finally learned a trade. Once you learnt your trade, he used to say, I don't care if you never work at it, I just want you to have one.'

All that seems in tremendous contrast with what was before him. Much to the family's surprise – and that of everyone else who knew him – Ken joined the Sea Cadets. In a way, it was a bit of one-upmanship on his part, or at the very least of equal upmanship. All boys wanted to join service organizations at a time when most adult males were in uniform. It provided a sense of maturity. It also seemed to give a leg up for them when it came to being called up at the age of eighteen.

Get into the cadet force of your choice and chances were you might get into the service of your choice, too.

Lou can't fathom how he decided to go into the cadets. It was totally out of character.

Ken fancied wearing bell-bottoms. Pat thinks there was a deeper personal reason. 'Our favourite cousin Bert was in the Navy and was killed while serving. He had greatly influenced Ken.'

There was a more intelligent and more calculating answer – despite his distaste for communal living and being part of a group mentality of any kind. He had heard that one of the best possible jobs in war service was being a map draughtsman planning naval charts. He fancied that. But it is true that Ken also liked the idea of the Sea Cadets uniform – which is why, when Pat came home on leave, they had a photograph taken together, each in their service dress. Ken swivelled his cap around so that you couldn't see the words 'Sea Cadet' on the ribbon.

Of course, he would never have joined the cadets if he hadn't tasted a different atmosphere at Bicester and seen that life didn't revolve around his little bedroom at Marchmont Street. He also had entered the world of commerce. When it came time to leaving Bolt Court, he embarked on an apprenticeship as the very map draughtsman he expected to be the day the manilla envelope containing his call-up papers arrived on his doorstep. That wouldn't be for a few years yet, so he could settle into working for Stanfords, the cartographers in Covent Garden.

He had a neat hand, as his years at school and his letters home had shown. Charlie was secretly proud of him. Louisa unquestionably was thrilled.

It was also the start of what was to prove to be a long friendship with a much older man named Valentine Orford, or Val as he was known in the sales department. The seventeen-year-old Ken and the thirty-eight-year-old Orford talked during lunch breaks and before long were spending evenings and weekends together.

Orford denies any suggestion that Ken regarded him as a sort of father figure, a substitute for the man who was only interested in his hairdressing shop, or going to the pub or the greyhounds. Chisholm had taught him that much older men were interested in poetry. Val Orford confirmed it and talked for hours with Ken about literature and history.

'I never really thought there was anything strange about us being friends and me being so much older,' says Orford today. 'We had a great deal in common and I believe Ken thought I was in my twenties.'

They began to talk when Ken noticed the picture of Stanfords' original shop, opposite Charing Cross station, on Orford's desk. He was assistant to the sales manager at the time and Ken was already drawing maps for paying customers, providing them with routes for days out or details of the countryside they were visiting for rare wartime weekends. The picture on Val's desk was significant. In the foreground, was the statue of Charles I.

'Charles was a hero of mine and I talked about him to Ken, who was fascinated.'

In the meantime, Ken was fascinating the other staff at Stanfords, an office where many of the men had gone off on war service – although for some, working there was a privileged occupation, which gave them military exemption – and where women in dowdy dresses and steel-rimmed spectacles liked nothing better than to tease a youth wearing his suit from the Fifty Shilling Tailors.

Ken, needless to say, gave as good as he got. The cutting Williams wit was beginning to express itself: 'Say you're a woman of the world do you? You wouldn't be in any world I intend drawing.' They were fascinated by his voices. 'I remember one of the women there,' said Orford, 'who when she first heard him couldn't make out whether he was an old man with a young man's voice or a younger man with an older man's voice.'

Ken and Val were cementing their friendship by visiting each other's homes. The older man was even introduced to Charlie – a rare privilege. 'I was a little nervous because I knew Ken's father's reputation,' Orford told me. He also knew what Charlie thought of men who weren't interested in football and boozing. But after he left, Charlie said : 'I like your friend.' Ken later explained that his father always 'judged other men by their handshakes'. In those days, Orford had a vice-like grip.

He had a similar grip, so Ken believed, on literature, particularly on the work of Bernard Shaw, who was by then the grand old man of letters but still alive and active and working from his garden shed, at Ayot St Lawrence, in rural Hertfordshire. Val gave him a collection of Shaw plays to read and St John Ervine's biography of the playwright. He also had a much more important contribution to make to Ken's life. He took him to the theatre for the first time – to see Shaw's *The Doctor's Dilemma*.

It was Ken's own conversion on the road to Damascus, except that this road was called Shaftesbury Avenue. He was in a daze. He talked of nothing else in the Lyons tea shop to which they went after the perform-ance. He thought of nothing else waiting at the bus stop. For the next days at work, there was no other conversation. Young Kenneth Williams was all set to be a bore, but could not have cared less.

It didn't, though, interfere with his work. Val Orford remembers him 'as a draughtsman who was absolutely brilliant – as good as anyone at Stanfords'. Actually, and he deserved credit for this, he was more than just a draughtsman working at a board in a drawing office. He was a litho artist, which meant that he worked, not on paper, but on stone – and drawing everything backwards.

The women working at Stanfords continued to like him, to love him it seemed in some ways. He looked delicate, undernourished and, some of them felt, underloved. They didn't know the strength of the relationship between Ken and Lou, or perhaps they would have switched to another tack, but what they were offering was a kind of mother's love – even the young girls who teased and smiled had no interest in trying to get him into a corner for a moment's sneaked embrace, even at Christmas parties. Already, it was established that Ken's sexual orientation was in other directions and no one seemed to mind.

'He would keep the drawing office in fits,' Orford remembers. When customers asked for maps indicating directions to their homes it was usually a cue for a riposte from Ken – behind their backs, of course. 'If you don't know the way to your own house how can you expect me to tell you.' It was straight out of *Just a Minute*, more than a quarter of a century before that show and Ken's participation in it became part of the week of a goodly portion of the nation.

Meanwhile, Ken himself was happy enough in Val Orford's company, a relationship that puzzled many of their fellow employees and did not seem totally obvious to even Orford himself. 'Heaven knows what a man of my age had in common with a boy of seventeen, but we did. Charles I started it. Somehow, whenever we talked, we would get back to Charles again.' Or about somebody they both knew and whom Ken disliked. 'If he didn't like anyone, he could be extremely rude, cutting and abrasive.' That, too, would later have a familiar ring about it for people with whom Williams worked.

On Saturday afternoons, they would go to the cinema together – followed by a visit to the second-hand bookshops of Charing Cross Road. It was the combination of a new Williams enthusiasm – to some it might have even seemed to be a mania – and its adaptation as part of his general thirst for more literacy and more education.

'He was a reader. I was a reader,' Orford told me. 'I directed his reading. He directed mine.' By then, Ken had read Gibbon's *Decline and Fall of the Roman Empire*. 'We discussed it,' Orford said, much as the girls working at their place would have discussed *Brief Encounter* or the recent re-run of *Gone With The Wind*.

Reading was Ken's main obsession, reading and the things he was seeing in the theatre. The bug of the drama had bitten deep and like deep bites of another kind it started to fester. It wasn't enough merely to see a play or to read about it, he had to be *part* of it. He joined an amateur drama group attached to the Mary Ward Settlement in Tavistock Place, within a spitting distance of Marchmont Street although spitting was decidedly not a habit of the people who worthily attended the players' performances.

In his autobiography, *Just Williams*, Ken describes his performance in Gitry's *Villa For Sale* as being a combination of the style he remembered from hearing the Methodist preachers at his church and that of Charles Laughton. He wore a false moustache to lend him age but it kept falling off. He says in the book that it was his first and only performance for the group. Val Orford, however, distinctly remembers seeing him play Strength for them in the play *Everyman*.

Whichever is true, what is undeniable is that Ken loved the feel of the boards beneath his feet – and the applause of the sparse audience at the end of the performance was something he was not going to forget in a hurry. Again, it was the subject of conversation with Val when they sipped their tea at Lyons either before or after their Saturday afternoon trip to what everyone called 'the pictures'. When in the mood, Ken would also talk to him about poetry. In that he was on his own. 'I wasn't much interested in poetry,' said Orford, 'but he did give me an interest in it, even if it didn't stay with me.'

What did stay with Orford – even if not with Ken – was a great sense of friendship. He said to the older man once: 'You're the first real friend I've ever had.' To him, being with Val was in a way a demonstration of having started to grow up. Having someone so much older around him meant a recognition of his own maturity. Before Orford, the only friends he had ever known – Pat apart – were those at school.

The friendship was, however, to be put to the test: Ken was called up for war service. To imagine anyone less suited to the rigours of military life than Kenneth Williams would be a tough exercise and, indeed, for a time the doctors who examined him were hard put to find reasons to accept him. But the war was not a Mr Atlas contest – or even a *Rambo* one, to put it into the vernacular of the Nineties.

If the notion of a citizens' army were to work at all, and there were those who consistently doubted that it ever would, it had to be an army

– and a navy (which Ken was determined to go into if he had to be part of any service) and an air force – of *every* citizen. For every officer and non-commissioned officer there were hundreds of mere 'men' who did not have to think at all and do no more than they were told. They had to be reasonably fit because they needed to be able to run (hopefully in an advancing mode), but the forces also needed cooks and clerks and drivers (which would not have suited him at all) and fellows who knew how to sew up torn tents. Providing you could stand up straight, read an eye chart moderately well and didn't pass blood when you were handed that demeaning bottle to fill, you were in.

On 22 February 1944, Ken was eighteen. Just a matter of days later he received an invitation – to present himself before a medical board to judge his suitability to serve King and country.

The doctors at the medical board were not convinced about Ken's ability to perform his patriotic duties – simply because of the way he looked. He stood naked before a group of ageing men and the occasional nurse who had to stand by to pick up those for whom the experience was just too much to remain conscious. He looked as though he had been kept on a starvation diet and denied any exercise more strenuous than climbing out of bed in the morning.

He was sent to see a specialist who pronounced the country sufficiently close to crisis point to require Kenneth Williams's attendance at an army camp. No chance of his getting in the Navy, though. Even if he had passed the necessary mental tests for the kind of draughtsmanship work he wanted to do, he could never have made it with the B–2 grading with which he had been honoured.

Just before he left to begin his army career, he and Orford went for their usual Saturday evening outing.

'The one thing I shall always remember when we separated was his final smile,' Val told me. 'And his strong handshake – which I'd have recognized anywhere. No one else had one like it.'

Few other people also had his talent as a map draughtsman. His employers were marking him out as a young man who would go far in their business. His sister is certain that he would never have considered doing anything else – if he hadn't have gone into the Army.

He reported to a camp at Cumberland where he was handed a pile of khaki clothes and a great deal of indignation. For all Lou's affection and concern, Ken was never the conventional idea of a mummy's boy. He was far too independent for that. He had spent too many hours in his bedroom, reading, and too many sessions with Val Orford discussing the theatre for that. But he was a natural butt for the practical jokes of young men from the less picturesque districts of Glasgow.

He hated the idea of undressing in front of his fellow conscripts. The search for modesty only led to a blatant and aggressive response from his barrack-mates. What did he have between his legs, then? Surely it couldn't be a penis? He wouldn't know what to do with it. No. This must be a refugee or escapee from the ATS (the women's Army, the Auxiliary Territorial Service) who really had a vagina and breasts. They joked so much that the modest Williams turned into the outrageous Ken who henceforth not only stopped hiding when it came to undressing but who virtually performed a nightly striptease. It wasn't sexual. There was no evidence to show that he was endeavouring to take any of his fellow soldiers into his bed. He had simply found out the secret of someone who looked and behaved the way he did, establishing himself in this hard, tough world. He was being outrageous. Kenneth Williams was for the first time playing his most popular role – in a routine that could have been called *Carry on Soldier*.

Suddenly, he was popular – and as if to demonstrate that popularity was given a nickname. It wasn't the sort of name that others of his appearance and apparent behaviour were always being given by hardier bullying types thrust together in a strange barrack room. Nobody called him Nancy or Gladys or Fairy. Ken was 'Casey', which was so neutral it was a compliment. Casey for KC, Kenneth Charles.

Casey even began to enjoy army life – although when he went home on leave, Charlie professed to be unimpressed. 'Make a man of you,' he conceded and secretly he was delighted that his son was bound to throw off the effeminate side that had always made him feel so cheated. 'It'll kill him,' he kept repeating. 'It'll kill him – or make a man of him.'

Maybe he could now go to the pub with him and on to Hackney greyhound stadium. But he wasn't letting on. The Border Regiment stationed at Carlisle Castle wasn't the sort of army he was used to – not like the Royal Berkshires, made Royal on the field by the King himself, God bless him.

Ken, needless to say, took that no more to heart than he had all the other things that his father had been saying over the years. If Charlie wasn't exactly beneath contempt, he was certainly not himself above walking away and totally ignoring him. Lou 'ooed' and 'ahhed' at the sight of her son in uniform and shed the occasional tear when he went back to Carlisle again.

She might have noticed that her son was not quite the scrawny youth who had kissed her goodbye as he left for the train to take him to 'the war'. He was filling out a bit and his complexion had more of a colour to it – the right colour, a certain ruddiness that was neither pink nor red but a manly healthy look that owed a great deal to his physical training instructor who was taking no nonsense about a life dedicated to the stage or literature, but was putting him through paces that extended from outdoor obstacle courses to the camp swimming pool.

Hardly surprisingly, the Army also had much more influence on Ken than Charlie had ever had. When his drill instructor handed him a pair of football boots, he couldn't merely hold out the offending foot covering as though they had a bad smell. He had to wear them – and to use them. It didn't mean that he had to *like* wearing them, however. On one of their first outings together, he and the boots had an experience Ken wouldn't easily forget. Another boot on another foot collided with his nose – and broke it. One of his most distinctive features was shaped in that meeting. Until the end of his life, he would have a series of operations to improve its function, none of which would work. Even if he had not hated football before this, the collision would have made his antipathy to the game complete. It also ensured that at the earliest possible opportunity, he would put the taking of exercise firmly behind him. Nevertheless, physical exertion wasn't having a totally negative effect on him.

No 14747886 Williams KC, Private, was doing remarkably well in exploits in which he might have been considered to be totally out of bounds.

Williams earned a new entry in his army file. He was regraded A–1. In the barrack room, there was a certain respect that hadn't been there before. A concert was held to mark the passing out parade of their training battalion – in which his squad came first. Ken delivered an impersonation of Winston Churchill and of the pantomime dame Nellie Wallace. He was the star of the evening – for the first time in his life. And for the first time in his life, he was really happy. Being accepted was desperately important for the man who always maintained and probably believed he was happiest of all as a loner. In May 1944, Private Williams was transferred to the Royal Engineers at Ruabon, Denbighshire, and the survey division. Totally contrary to usual military practice, he was being put in a unit in which he could use his own civilian expertise and draw maps to his heart's content, or rather to the content of his commanding officer.

Charlie Williams heard of his son's new posting with perfectly feigned disgust. 'He *was* disgusted,' recalls Pat in one of her more jovial moods. 'He wanted Ken to join the Royal Berkshires.'

The moustaches on the faces of the officers in the photograph which still stood on his dining-room bureau – taking it down would have been like hauling down the Union Jack – seemed to twitch with their own displeasure. None more than his immediate superior officer. 'There's me,' Charlie would proclaim to the family. 'Behind Captain Dempsey – General now.'

Ken was good at rubbing salt into his father's wounds, the kind that could never have been treated by the Royal Army Medical Corps. '*We* are the *gentlemen* of the Royal Engineers,' he announced – and pointed to the picture with a finger of admonition. '*They*,' he said, 'are the *men* of the Army.' Charlie hated the idea of Pat going into the Air Force just as much. 'A load of poofs there,' he kept telling her. 'Talk about the bloody Brylcream Brigade. Him in the bloody Royal Engineers. You with the pufters in the Air Force.'

By the time Ken arrived at Ruabon, a letter from a waystation at Bradbury, Hereford, arrived at Val Orford's home. It was the first of a virtual library of letters that would cross between them during Kenneth's army service. Each one of the letters was written firmly in the kind of handwriting that would have won him prizes at school. The one strange thing about the letters was that there were three distinct types of hand-writing – one a flowing script written across the page virtually without margins; another using more cramped square characters; the third, large elegant letters in the centre of the page written as if the characters were members of his regiment, standing to attention on parade.

The first letter on 8 May 1944 was a critique of three from Orford himself. The review was a good one. 'You've no idea how marvellous they were. The entertaining narrative, neatly interspersed with funny bits was really most entertaining – you've *NO* idea, *NO* idea how *lovely* it was to read them. I can't say on paper how much I enjoyed them – I'm afraid mine must seem poor in comparison – but there – you must make allowances.'

He then revealed a nasty habit he had developed. He kept wiping his pen on his pullover. There was much talk about work at Stanfords and of a colleague's description of his 'grabbing' food. 'And you say I'd better not start pinching huge amounts at Lyons when in London next with you (I did laugh!!!)'

Not much hint there of the superior literary intellect that friends and acquaintances would say was so obvious. But it did reveal his enthusiasm for putting thoughts on to paper. It also showed something of the change that had come upon him since putting on that uncomfortable, rough ill-fitting khaki uniform.

In many ways, the Army represented Ken's university. His mother says that he hated every minute of Service life, a statement that is not confirmed by the memories of those who were in the 'mob' with him. Certainly, it is not confirmed by those letters.

In a later generation, it is quite likely that he would have gone to university as a 'mature student'. But it wasn't within his thinking.

Pat remembers: 'He hated all the things he had to do. He was a fussy Bill. He only picked what he wanted to do. He still hated communal living.' And yet suddenly, he had been dropped into a communal living atmosphere that he quite unexpectedly found he could cope with incredibly well.

'But he never looked forward to going back to his unit after a leave.' The youth who was so uncomfortable when not alone, who so hated the idea of sharing a room with others, let alone a whole barrack, could write 'the consoling element was realy (*sic*) the companionship of such a decent set of chaps in the barrack room – it helped a lot – just having a cigarrette (*sic*).' His spelling wasn't as good as his handwriting.

Meanwhile, Orford would go and see Lou every so often and Ken wrote expressing his gratitude. He had given his mother 'a sum of money' to buy things he needed. Val himself had bought him a few things. Ken suggested that Lou give him some money for them – 'say £1 – and if you have anything over in change, keep it in case of anything else I want please.' Which goes to demonstrate just how long ago 1944 really was.

On leave, Ken and Orford renewed their friendship in person. Val still remembers the excitement he felt in seeing his younger friend meet him in uniform.

Ken didn't exactly see military action. But he was conscious of what war was about – and how he perceived his enemies to be. He put that perception into one of his poems:

> All their teachings of hate and fear
> All the making of hell on earth,
> To efficiently kill and maim,
> To show now what life is worth.
> Of the charging of man – the cries
> Of horrible oaths on young lips,
> And the silly loose talk, and lies
> And nothing to prove deceit....
> Nothing ... less ... the pain.

He, meanwhile, was able to spend much more time in London. He was transferred to an army map-printing works in Ruislip in outer London and was virtually a civilian. There was practically no military discipline. He worked for officers and sergeants who were educated and even found other men there who knew people working for Stanfords. It was a congenial atmosphere and time, made only more so by the fact that he was constantly dropping hints that he was engaged on highly secret work, which he couldn't possibly divulge. His rapt listeners at the pub he frequented nodded knowingly and bought him another drink. Had he been so minded, the girls would have queued to be with him. There was an aphrodisiac quality about being on a secret list, even if the sex appeal of a Kenneth Williams, aged nineteen wasn't immediately apparent.

There were to be genuine secrets in which he *was* otherwise involved. In mid-April 1945, just three weeks before the war ended, Sapper Williams – he was no longer a private; the Royal Engineers had their own nomenclature for the lowest ranks in the corps – was told to pick up his kit and join a troopship. The secrets were most of all kept from the poor passengers on the journey, a mystery tour if ever there were one. If the brass could have hidden such things from the troops they would surely have done so, but eventually the increasing sunlight and the rising temperature made it clear they were heading for the tropics.

The war in Europe may have been over, but there were still the Japanese to fight and it began to look increasingly likely that this was the enemy personally chosen for him. The journey was not one of the happiest experiences he had known to date. First through the Suez Canal, then to Bombay and an army camp at Karlya which remained for the rest of his life in Ken's memory, largely because of the somewhat foolhardy decision by his sergeant to put him on guard duty. The notion of Kenneth Williams guarding the Empire from the menace of the men who had planned the Bridge on the River Kwai or the Burma Road has a certain irony about it. The truth of the matter was that he was more concerned with protecting himself from mosquitos.

All the newsreels he had seen of German and Japanese dive bombers were as nothing compared to the real-life swoops by these insects which had perfected precision attacks seemingly with him personally in mind. Another sapper had suggested a remedy – smoking. The mosquitos seemed to have read all the health warnings and kept away from burning tobacco. That was not so of a junior officer who saw the dastardly deed – smoking while on guard was decidedly illegal and equally decidedly subject to severe punishment.

Getting out of that punishment was another matter. Ken was desperate. The only thing he could do was act. Called in to answer the charge before his commanding officer, Ken coughed and spluttered – and burst into tears. His remorse was uncontrollable. There was nothing he could do, he said, his visage now resembling nothing less than a wrung-out face flannel. 'I wasn't myself,' he cried over and over again.

Quite clearly the CO wasn't himself either. Instead of sending Ken to the glasshouse, he incarcerated him in the camp hospital between the coolest linen sheets he had ever known – they didn't run to such things in Marchmont Street. Sapper Williams wasn't well.

In May 1945, just two weeks after the end of the war in Europe, he was transferred to Dehra-Dun in Northern India, a posting which he was delighted to note was far away from the fighting with the Japanese, at least far enough away to make combat fairly remote. It was a terrible journey, with Ken trying to get some sleep on the train's luggage rack. Men were taken off with heatstroke and the conversation in the eight-man compartment was not entirely convivial.

He wasn't totally impressed with the people in the town itself. There was a WVS (Women's Voluntary Service) centre which Ken said in another letter to Val Orford seemed to be 'staffed by English people who appear for the most part, to be snobs'. He hastened to add: 'However that is a first impression only and therefore one not to be relied upon.'

But he was impressed by a lot of what he experienced, not least of all, by the fact that they had sheets on their beds and cloths on the tables when they ate and the food was 'extraordinarily good'. Not many soldiers would be able to say that and Ken certainly hadn't said it before then.

There were poetic moods for him, too. During his train journey to Dehra Dun, 'the clouds hung like great golden peaches – each within itself, burnished and glowing in the fading light from gold to silver to grey – to nothingness. And then – a thousand stars to light the way. ... How often as I sat thus, my thoughts receded back to London. To the innumerable sunsets we had seen. I went in thought, sure of every paving stone, to the embankment – leant over the stone balustrade and looked into the water – and saw? – the reflection of us both.'

Most of his letters to Val had a winsomeness about them. 'Good or ill, it is nevertheless a fact that whenever I light a cigarette after a meal,' he wrote in October 1945, 'I think of us and momentarily I glimpse into the past – into a Slaters, a Corner House and most of all Charing Cross. Remember? Always that cigarette before Aurevoir? And then you would go, speeding southward in those horrid electric trains whilst I would walk back through the blackout, along the Strand. I shall always remember that walk back along the Strand – with its motley crowd of Americans, Londoners, prostitutes and – oh! crowds of foreigners, always one could see the 'strumpets' going into or coming out of that glorified boarding house of Mr Lyons, the Strand Palace.'

'Mr Lyons' wouldn't have liked that, but it was part of Ken's journey, through Kingsway and Southampton Row, Theobalds Road and then home. 'Whilst enjoying the luxury of a quiet smoke, I would turn over the day's events in my mind until everything was neatly pidgeon(*sic*)-holed, so to speak.' The heavy curtains would be pulled back, the lights turned off and he could ruminate. That's what he remembered now.

In another letter he recalled times that the two had spent together, an afternoon at the Duchess Theatre when Val didn't even offer him a cigarette and in a particularly revealing passage remembered an American. 'Funny we never saw him again, did we? Who knows what we *might* have done toward cementing the bond between the United Whatsit.'

The problem with the posting was that there was almost nothing for any of the men to do. Ken was ordered to paint a 'quiet room'. He sprayed pink and cream distemper all over the walls and painted the woodwork.

He missed Pat a great deal – was conscious that she was on her way to Australia where she was emigrating and Ken was going to miss her more than ever.

Soon after she had left for Australia, he wrote her a letter from Marchmont Street in reply to one that had chastised him for the kind of farewell he had offered her.

'We didn't say goodbye properly? I s'pose we never do. But here is a reply to your letter – and a sort of literary handshake:

'Yes! We've had our differences – and been intolerant of one another – quarralled (*sic*) I know – in the past – but never doubt – that I loved you. Goodbye dear and smile a little in your prayers when you think of your dearest –
Loving brother. Ken.'

Once again, he wrote a poem about it:

> To one who loves life, more than I can say –
> Who finds a friendship in a single look,
> Whose heart has flown along the starry way....
> Until we meet again, my dearest Pat.

Ken was quite mature as a poet – most of the time. Occasionally, though he did sound as if he were writing for Christmas cards:

> I told my thoughts to the moonbeams
> And fathomless despair.
> I breathed into the wind
> As it blows.
> To the stars, I kiss'd my daydreams
> On shining empty air.
> But shall I tell my heart
> What it knows?

He had already had his attempt at greeting-card verse, for Pat's twenty-first birthday, he wrote:

> This day is unlike any other
> Created alone for you.
> And unworthy words from your brother
> Are sailing from infinite blue.

And for Christmas 1945, there were seasonal greetings – addressed 'To Mum':

> I can remember so many things
> At Christmas time in the year,
> The paper chains in the living room,
> The special note of cheer:
> The holly sprigs, that we used to put
> Round the edge of the picture frames,
> The glow on the red-tiled fireplace,
> The parties and the games. . . .
>
> But most of all I remember you –
> Your laugh, and your ready smile.
> The sound of your voice, replying to
> Our sallies all the while:
>
> I can remember so many things,
> And though I am far away
> I wish you dear – with all my heart
> A happy Christmas Day.

Ken didn't exactly seem the picture of health at Dehra Dun, although there was little seriously wrong with him. He developed nettle rash, was sent to bed dressed overall in the pinkest calamine lotion and given a parcel of soft, cool poplin uniform slacks and blouse to wear. The jeers that had greeted his pink clown act in the barracks earlier on turned to gasps of admiration. When the sergeant-major then presented him with another parcel containing boots made of the softest Indian leather they were positively overwhelmed. It was almost as if they were waiting for him to kiss Ken goodnight. From then on, there were seemingly no holds barred. He no longer worried about seeming effeminate. It didn't bother the other soldiers too much and when they laughed, he laughed.

Before long, he was even wearing socks with flowers on them.

Shirking duties wasn't his only function while at Dehra Dun. He was once again working in a survey office, drawing maps, preparing them for the printers. He enjoyed that enormously. From India, he was sent to Ceylon, the 62 Map Reproduction Section at Kurenegala. He was employed as a clerk for much of the time – with the rank of lance corporal.

He was totally bored by Ceylon. One of the only times in the colony when life was the least bit bearable was when Pat came out to visit him there for a couple of days on her journey to Australia. She had got married – to a man her father liked enormously; which should have put her off him, she now reflects, years after her subsequent divorce. It was a stop on the way that they both welcomed, an opportunity to share grouses about Charlie and to reminisce about the days of OG. Ken's work was not nearly as satisfying.

In another letter to Val Orford – No 82; Ken was nothing if not meticulous with his indexing and filing – he describes an incident in which the officer commanding his unit asked him about the lack of mail. 'Nobody dumps anything in your tray,' Ken replied. 'Nobody dumps anything in your tray. You're only the OC.' As he added: 'OC explodes into laughter. Conversation finished.'

He had to ask a lieutenant about the regimental haircutting contract.

'Sod it,' said the lieutenant.

'Quite, Sir,' Ken replied. 'How many copies will you require?'

As Ken recalled, the conversation proceeded like this: 'Lieut. R: "It is to be submitted in octuplicate."

'Self: "Eh?" (looking purposefully daft).

'Lieut. R (patiently): "Eight copies corporal."

'Self: "Ha." Vanish into my own private office.' At that, the officer commanding lit a cigarette and lent back on his chair. As Ken left the office, there was a crash. The officer had fallen. The lieutenant was laughing louder than anyone at his superior's discomfiture. Ken laughed, too. The war was over. There was little else to worry about.

If it wasn't for the fact that Ken was barely twenty years old and had been one of the last to join up, he might now have been packing his kitbag ready to go back to London.

Ken had done that most dangerous of things in Army life. He volunteered – for an organization that has entered folk lore, Combined Services Entertainment, CSE, for short. If most of military life seemed to exist on the legend that in every private's knapsack was a field-marshal's baton, here it was more likely to be a stick of greasepaint.

When word got back to his father about that, Charlie's reaction was entirely predictable. Instead of making a man of his son, the Army had succeeded in making him a 'poof' – although to be fair, that was never a term he used about Kenneth himself. What he did say was that anything resembling the kind of show people to whom he believed his son was now aligning himself was indecent.

'Oh no,' he didn't believe in that sort of thing, the old man,' Louisa Williams now recalls. 'He thought they were all a load of poofs.' Ken had discussed this with his father a score of times. 'It's just because you don't understand,' Ken told him. 'I don't *want* to understand,' Charlie would reply. It wasn't so much that he didn't want Ken to be involved in them as that, to quote Pat Williams, 'it never entered his world'. This was the 'mob' in which soldiers pranced around like chorus girls both on and off the stage. Even the sergeant called his charges 'Dear', and instructed them to call him 'Terry', never by his rank.

At the end of the summer of 1946, Ken was on a ship again, still not heading home but on the way to Singapore. He described the ship on which the group sailed, the Cameronia as a 'filthy tub'.

Things got better, however, once they were settled in at a transit camp at Nee Soon. He shared a room with a set designer – 'a charming fellow', he wrote to Orford, who has his place 'tastefully furnished with wardrobe, tables etc., card table, desk, and standard lamp and, of course, two delightful spring-mattressed beds.

For Ken, it was to be his entry into professional show business – even though up to that moment, he hadn't really considered ever earning his living doing anything but drawing maps. But he had done his Nellie Wallace and Winston Churchill impressions at a NAAFI concert (The Navy, Army and Air Force Institute provided comfort for the troops, supplemented the cookhouse and offered cigarettes, beer and a few other essentials from home) and his sergeant suggested that he could do worse than volunteer for CSE.

An officer in his unit had confirmed the fact for him. 'Are you a song and dance man, old boy?' he asked. Ken lied that that was precisely what he was. 'I do know that they want a song and dance man,' said the man. It was all Ken needed to know – and the sergeant was the man who put it in motion for him.

The sergeant knew of the organization's existence – and its main purpose in life, to keep the men away from the boredom threshold. What he couldn't have known was that it provided a nursery for so many in the entertainment industry – from Stanley Baxter, newly graduated from the Unity Theatre in Glasgow – to the film director John Schlesinger, both of whom would become firm friends of Ken.

Ken, though, had his pride to think of, which was the primary inspiration to make him succeed. Before going, he had told his mates in Ceylon that he had been invited to go to Singapore to be a star. They had actually cheered him as he left. No such enthusiasm had ever been attached to the name Kenneth Williams. It was like a mellow wine to him, warm, sympathetic, sweet and very addictive.

Ken arrived, but arrival was no guarantee of employment. That would come – or would not come – at the enterprise's own garrison theatre, which may not have been Shaftesbury Avenue but was ready to break more men than a drill sergeant who couldn't always choose the recruits under his control. Here there were auditions and if you failed, there was a hallowed formula. You'd have an incantation recited over you – in three letters, 'RTU'. Ken didn't know what 'RTU' meant. Before long, though, he would.

It was the military equivalent of 'Don't call us, we'll call you.' Except that there wasn't the slightest chance that they would.

Ken had his audition, wearing an army bush hat, similar to the kind that the Australians wore in all climates – minus corks, it must be said – but which as far as the British were concerned was restricted to the tropics. He did an impersonation of the then radio (or perhaps it should be wireless) favourite, Mable Constanduros. He pulled the hat over his ears and asked himself, 'Hello, are you one of Wingate's boys?' 'No,' he replied, 'I'm one of Colgate's girls – and there are my teeth to prove it.'

'Do you do anything else?' Terry asked him. 'I do Churchill.' He did Churchill – and Terry shouted 'RTU'. The letters, he now found, after hearing them recited a dozen times before it was his own time to go on, meant 'Return to unit'. Lance Corporal Williams would go back to his unit with all the others. Just one problem, however. The unit had been disbanded. There were mutterings offstage and it became apparent that the military thespians needed someone to draw their posters for them. Ken, who drew maps, was plainly intended for such a calling. He got the job and reported to the Victoria Theatre for instructions. He did more than that when he got there. One of the cast was ill with malaria, there was no understudy and – it sounds like an early Warner Bros. musical hereafter – would Ken ... step into the breach and read the part? He would? Good.

He read it so well – or at least well enough; at that stage a parrot who had learned the lines would have been cast – that he was given the part of the harassed detective in the production, *Seven Keys to Baldpate*.

The unit virtually took over the theatre. In January 1947, Ken actually had billing in what was described as 'a bright new musical' – in a poster he himself designed – called *High and Low*. The programme notes, showing a very curly-haired extraordinarily young-looking Kenneth Williams, recorded that 'in this production, he has quite a variety of characters to portray.' The programme also noted 'Rather in contrast to his "public" demeanour, Ken's private life revolves mostly around books and "charpoys". He finds the combination of the two both comfortable and instructive.'

Among the parts he played was that of Miss Tasle in the two-handed Noel Coward playlet, *Cat's Cradle*.

It was to be a formative time for Ken. He made friends while working with CSE – particularly with Stanley Baxter. Theirs would prove to be an enduring friendship.

If Kenneth Williams has always seemed something of an ambivalent character, there was nothing more contradictory in his life than his time in the Army. He himself once put it very succinctly: 'I needed someone to knock that rubbish out of me, but to do it with enough love and care and put something in its place. Luckily enough, it was done – of all places – in the British Army.'

He had gone into the service feeling 'very small and inferior'. Now, conscious of his fairly senior status with a real job to do, he was in an element he had never felt drawing his maps at Stanfords and certainly never when arguing with his father in Marchmont Street.

His friendship with Stanley Baxter got better and better. Now they had a double-act together, which increasingly became one of the most popular features of the shows CSE was putting on. He himself liked best his female impersonations. His commanding officer, however, did not.

'You're a disgrace,' the colonel – who smarted at being put in charge of a group of men Charlie Williams would have called 'poofs' – told him. Ken ran into the wings of the theatre and wept.

This did not seem to cause too much trouble among the audiences at the Victoria, who were grateful for all they could get and received the CSE production with as much enthusiasm as they would a new opening on Broadway or Shaftesbury Avenue. Much of the quality may have been sub-seaside concert party standard, but it didn't matter. Kenneth Williams, Stanley Baxter and the others represented relief from a boredom which, incredible though it might seem, at times seemed as dangerous an enemy as the Japanese.

All the material had to be written by officers. That was part of army life. If you had the King's commission, you were judged suitable to write a musical show. One of the writers, a squadron leader who, despite the almost insufferable heat, insisted on wearing a fur flying jacket, produced the opening routine for their latest show – the chorus line number.

The men all but kicked up their legs as they sang 'We're boys of the service ... we're at your service, entertaining YOU. We'll sing songs old and new; fun and laughter if you're blue.'

The routine was performed in front of the OC and a brigadier who had been brought into action as the Army's own censor. Just like the colonel who thought female impersonations were disgraceful, this man took an instant dislike to the chorus line.

'I don't want any filth,' he told them. And the first time he used the word 'Cut' was for the chorus line number. 'Oh, no,' he proclaimed in the same sort of voice he would have used had he been directing the next offensive against the Japanese, 'that won't do. Boys? Boys of the service? No. Too sibilant. like a lot of pansies.' He ordered the lyrics to be changed to 'We're *men* of the service'. The boys sang that they were men, and the brigadier nodded appreciatively.

Once more, he had to be auditioned – this time by the captain who was also producing the show. He was again to do his impersonations, only this time in a show called *Let's Have A Party* at another Victoria Theatre. A week there would be followed by a tour of the country.

Ken seemed happier than he had been for years, perhaps happier than ever in his life. He was fast coming to the conclusion that he would prefer to spend the rest of his life on the stage and if he could do at least as well in the theatre as he had behind his drawing board or lithograph stone, then maps would play little part in his future. He couldn't even contemplate the idea that one day he might want to drive and use one simply as a consumer. He wouldn't want to drive – ever. For a young man who purposely didn't want to know one end of a hammer from

39

the other, a gear stick held unmitigated terrors.

There were other such terrors in his mind, too. No one had any doubt now what Ken's sexual interests were but he was frightened of it all. The man who had been so scared of human contact in his first barrack room wanted no intimate relations that might mean bodily contact. His experience in Bicester may have excited him, but it repelled him just as much. In another letter to Val Orford, (number 105) he wrote: 'I have made a friend – seems an awfully decent chap (straight actor). He is homosexual, but keeps it strictly to himself as far as I am concerned, so I don't mind. I hope very much it remains that way, because I should hate to be obliged to discontinue the friendship (of course I speak loosely – please substitute acquaintanceship wherever I've written the other word).'

But Ken knew where his temptations lay. In still another letter to Val Orford, he referred to a mutual friend named 'Jock' who had signed a note to him, 'Your friend forever'. He wondered if it would be 'wise' for he and Jock to meet again. 'After all, a moment of weakness on both sides might result in something which we should both regret later – on the other hand, it might result in the sublimation of our friendship (or – when two people of the same sex reach that stage, can it still be called "friendship"? I wonder).'

Meanwhile, Ken was starring in a show called *Going Gay*. The current usage of the second word was unknown at the time, needless to say.

Ken was now sharing a room with Stanley Baxter, who had written the script for the show. 'He is a very likeable fellow – so vital and full of energy and ideas that his continual presence definitely tends to wear one out, but we have quite a lot in common.' They spent evenings together, huddled over a single cup of coffee in a café, laughing usually at the expense of other people they were working with. 'He has the wonderful gift of being able to imitate practically every accent in England and makes extremely funny faces whilst assuming them.'

Ken himself wasn't asking a great deal of life. He still enjoyed reading and Val Orford was sending him a great number of books – like *Mill on the Floss*, *Dr. Johnson and Company* and volumes on English literature and on poetry.

These were more than acceptable interludes from work – which he liked sometimes more than the audiences to whom he played. One day, the RAF were cheering, the next day the West Yorkshires were voting with their fleet – away from the box office. They had no desire to pay their fourpences to see the shows.

The CSE went on tour in Malaya. In some places there wasn't even a hall where they could play – so they used the local NAAFI, where there wasn't even a stage on which they could perform. 'I'm sick of putting myself out for this foul organization,' Ken said in one of those moments of temper which could be equally foul.

At this stage in his life, Ken was prepared to accept it all as part of a continuing education in life, even though he did lie in bed under a mosquito net, and there was a continuing battle with at least one rat which enjoyed scurrying around. His relationship with his officer-commanding was hardly more forthcoming. As he recalled, one morning's exchange of banter with the officer went like this – after the colonel had marched through the square ('looking like a principal boy at the Palladium'):

'Mornin' Williams'

'Mornin', Sir'

'Bloody awful headache'

'So have I'

'Ah'.

The boredom got worse – for Ken as well as his mates, whom he described as his 'fellow artistes'. Nee Soon was a 'dump', one of the other men kept singing 'The Fishermen of England' – 'a filthy number' and he himself was getting on everyone's nerves, offending many of them by being 'fearfully insulting'. It was a stance that would later be familiar to other 'fellow artistes' with whom he worked. But he was 'cheesed off with everything' – even though he had now been made a sergeant. But he wasn't a real sergeant, even if he did have three stripes to wear on his sleeve. it was what was known as a 'local, acting, unpaid' rank, but it did mean he could eat and drink in the sergeants' mess.

Val Orford had written to Ken warning him about the dangers of attending 'intimate parties', presumably involving other show people. Ken knew what he meant. 'You say you have faith in my own good sense to keep such things within reasonable limits. Well, I must be frank – I have not done so.'

He added: 'Unquestionably, I have reached a crisis in my life. I feel terribly unhappy sometimes. So worried about the future. I am becoming hopelessly in debt to various people. I am running up the most colossal bill, which I know I can never meet. In short, I am living beyond my means.'

He would concede that he was 'behaving atrociously'. He was insulted at being offered a tin of Woodbines when he asked for cigarettes in the mess. Woodbines were the cheapest 'fags' in the shops and the constant butt of wartime jokesters. When he complained to a nearby sergeant-major, the other man told him they weren't at all bad. 'Don't be ridiculous,' he replied – and stormed out.

Some people would have thought he had it made. There was a bearer who called him 'sahib' and was at his constant service. When the man came with his clean laundry, he, too, got the less civil end of the Williams tongue. He was being charged two dollars, fifty for the washing. 'I exploded – 'it's insane. I never heard anything so barmy'!'' It must have sounded like another of the Williams interruptions in *Just a Minute*, a generation later.

One of the performers in another army outfit, *Stars In Battledress* wanted to be friendly, but Ken wasn't so sure it was what he was looking for. 'He's decent looking enough – tall and averagely handsome, a blonde (*sic*), but his intellectual capacity – not much to speak of . . . He has nothing to offer me.' Worse still, the man talked about his girlfriend.

Peter Nichols, who was to immortalize this strangest of all army groups with his success, *Privates on Parade* was part of the outfit and performed with Ken and Stanley Baxter in a revue called *At Your Service*. Solders' reaction to that left little to the imagination – even their complaints about having to pay fourpence for the shows (the ENSA productions were free) were largely unprintable for the time. There were other problems – like the time their sergeant-major committed suicide and his funeral resembled a sketch in one of the CSE shows. No one wanted to volunteer to be pallbearers and the men waited for marching orders, which couldn't be given since they were normally given by the man about to be laid to rest six feet under. Ken would dine out on that day for the next forty years, always embellishing the tale with more and more detail every time.

The 'mob' went to Hong Kong, where Ken got his first broadcasting experience – on the local forces' radio station, performing a dramatization of the death of Nelson. An admiral provided the commentary – and later, drinks in the wardroom. When the august officer, in his gold braided finery, discovered that the men were mere sergeants, he arranged for the drinks to be instantly removed and his guests shunted out of the room and off the ship.

He loved Hong Kong 'the place is positively breathtaking!! Such natural beauty – such prosperity and wealth! So many lovely things in shop windows which continually tempt the eye and then the pocket book! Terribly expensive, but all very wonderful!' His room looked out on to the harbour where the China Fleet was at anchor and lit up at night. 'I remember that on board all these ships are poor tired matelots keeping horrible "watches" and things, and I thank my stars I didn't join the Navy!'

A few weeks later, Ken and the others were on another ship – bound for home. They performed on deck. As soon as they docked, they were taken by train to Aldershot. It was the last army experience for Sergeant Williams 14747886. He was demobbed.

Back home, there were tears from Louisa, mutterings from Charlie and a letter to read from Pat, who seemingly had settled well in Australia with her new husband.

Life was never to be the same again.

THREE

Ken talked to Lou and Charlie, but it was more as the dutiful son than a genuine desire to search for advice – or even for approval of what he had chosen for himself. His mind was already firmly made up. He was going to be an actor.

To Ken, it was simply formalizing a lifestyle that he had already taken for himself. There were dozens of young men of his age who would walk up and down the Charing Cross Road, with long hair, wearing loud jackets and silk cravats, discussing the theatre, as though they had the combined experience of a Laurence Olivier and the anonymous critic of *The Times*. He himself wore a large belted check overcoat and his shirts had replaceable paper collars. He alone thought he looked like a twentieth-century Beau Brummell.

Ken saw the others on his Saturday afternoon walks with Val Orford, which had now been resumed once more, and he was determined not to be of them. Every time he went to a theatre, he puffed and fumed at the ineptness he saw before him along with the rest of them, but the envy he felt was less well hidden and less secret than it was with the others. He wanted to jump out of his seat and climb on to the stage with the cast, hear the applause from the other side of the footlights.

For the moment, he was back drawing maps – with what had been Stanfords, but which in his absence had become part of George Philip, one of the biggest map-makers in the world. He was based at Acton, which was as different from the parts of the world which he had been inhabiting at the expense of His Majesty, as his job was from doing his Nellie Wallace impersonations on stage or in the barrack room.

He, himself, had changed. The boy who had revelled in office politics and the gossip he found so fascinating in the first letters from Val Orford, was now bored out of his mind by it all.

It was Stanley Baxter who convinced Ken to do something about it. He came to visit him at the Marchmont Street flat and told him he was out of his tiny mind drawing maps for a living. Fortunately for him, Charlie wasn't around to overhear the conversation – if he were, the effects could be imagined. The noise would have rebounded from one end of the street to the other. The traffic in Russell Square could have broken to a halt.

Charlie, of course, knew what was coming. He was a far more clever psychologist than his children might have believed. He still never got round to calling Ken a poofter, but seeing that belted overcoat was enough to drive him into paroxysms of contempt. Charlie was delighted that Ken did have a trade, but it was obvious enough that he was less than content with that trade. Lou, meanwhile, was just happy to have 'the boy' back home. She danced around him like a hen that had discovered a lost chick had suddenly come back.

Baxter, however, set Ken's unease into motion. He told him to buy *Spotlight*, the theatrical directory and to read *The Stage*, the closest that Britain comes to having a *Variety*, the newspaper which the Americans know as the show-biz 'Bible'. Ken did. He looked for advertisements for roles for juveniles – always something of a misnomer. The name sounds like a 'child'. In fact, it was usually a young man, frequently rather silly, encroaching on the world of his elders – and most often his betters. Ken didn't actually *want* to have to say, 'Anyone for tennis?' but if it meant the chance to take up an Equity card and begin life on the stage, he'd have grabbed the nearest racket with alacrity – if not with both hands – and put on the first available striped blazer.

The jobs weren't easy to come by. He placed his own advertisements in *The Stage*, but if he did get as far as an interview, it rarely led to an actual audition. Managements didn't care for his appearance and were not totally impressed by his qualifications.

Pat heard about his ambitions in a letter Ken sent to Australia. 'I wasn't surprised,' she told me recalling her brother's irrevocable decision to go on the stage. 'I'm a great believer in doing what you want to do – which is where I differed from Mum and Dad. Dad believed that we had to do what he told us we had to do.

'All of a sudden, he seemed to want to be an actor,' Lou told me. 'My husband, of course, didn't agree, but I told him, "Listen if he wants to do that, let him do it, Charlie. If he does anything else, he won't be happy – and if he doesn't succeed, he won't be able to blame us".'

Lou's opinion was, needless to say, more important than Charlie's – not that either of them could have talked him out of it. But he was, nevertheless, fortified by his mother's blessing.

There was, briefly, another kind of blessing he, almost secretly, was seeking now. To Val Orford, he talked about his thoughts on being a

Catholic. He was never to go through with it, but for a time he contemplated conversion. It was possibly the theatricality of the Mass that appealed to him so much, the music, the colour and the splendour of the vestments – to say nothing of the total sense of decorum among the 'audience'. But there was also the beginnings of a search for something that he didn't have at home and which Methodism, or the kind practised by the Williams family, could never provide. He would remain more religious than anyone else then living at Marchmont Street. Actually going into a church, however, demanded a degree of commitment that he was not prepared to make.

The Church, however, did seem to offer a serenity that he couldn't quite summon up the courage to grab. 'I want someone to love,' he told Val, somehow associating the two gaps in his life together, the religious membership and the close association with another human being. 'I always knew he was a homosexual,' Orford said.

For the moment, with no prospect of further advancement in the theatre in view, Ken and Val continued their friendship more or less where it left off. As far as the older man was concerned, it was *precisely* where they had left off. Ken, however, was much influenced by the years he had been away and by his ambitions – none of which Val shared. He was happy working at George Philip and wanted little more.

They still had a lot in common. They still talked about office gossip, although it had much less fascination for Ken now than it once had. They still discussed Charles I, still talked about books they had read and plays they wanted to see.

They talked politics. 'He was a Tory and I was a Tory.'

But when they talked about work, all the sparkle had gone from Ken's face. He was drawing on paper now, no longer involved in the craftsmanship of lithography which had gone over entirely to colour printing. 'The general opinion was that he was going to do well, but he found he couldn't take the life. That was why he was going into the theatre.'

Partly because he didn't share his enthusiasm for the stage being anything more than a diversion from the drudgery of the working week or a cultural outlet, Val tried to talk his friend out of this big change to his life. 'I wasn't happy about it. I thought he would start getting together with a very strange sort of theatrical people.'

Ken himself couldn't wait to do just that, but for the moment, it eluded him. He was taking a very long time indeed to become an overnight sensation. Naturally, he wanted to play Shaw and would have welcomed a chance to feature in Shakespeare. But he was anxious to begin an apprenticeship which for all its value, CSE had not been.

The first thing he did on leaving George Philip was to take out Val Orford and buy a book of poems by A. E. Housmann, one of the poets they had discussed together so often.

He sought a chance to get into a repertory company, that veritable nursery of theatrical players across the spectrum, but the opportunity eluded him along with all the others. When he couldn't even get into an audition, he secretly started to yearn to hear some producer somewhere call out from the front stalls, 'Don't call us – we'll call you.' But not even that was for him.

Strangely, he never contemplated giving up. One thing that he had inherited from Charlie was a sense of determination. Just as his father had dreamed of opening his own hairdressing salon – and once opened, making it a great success – so Ken was equally certain he had no alternative but to make a go of the stage. For the moment, he did not contemplate stardom. It wasn't the sort of pleasure he craved now. He knew he was going to make it big one day, but for the moment he just wanted to know that before long he would be able to walk into some stage-door entrance, somewhere, and make his way to a dressing room where he wouldn't be summarily evicted.

Everything about Ken's aspirations made Charlie Williams fly into a rage. He couldn't stand his son's ambitions any more than ever he could. He positively disliked the friends he was making.

Sometimes there was as much comradeship for Ken in disappointment as there would be one day in success. He wasn't the only one failing to get auditions. Neither was he the sole person to be turned away from those that he did get. Sometimes another, equally unsuccessful, budding actor would come home with him to the Marchmont Street flat. Lou was hospitality itself. Charlie was burning hatred.

One such friend was a young man who looked as though simply blowing on him would knock him over. He had a handshake that closely resembled a plaice on the counter of the fish shop down the road.

Charlie didn't keep his opinions to himself. He would look at this poor, extraordinarily harmless character and proceed to verbally bully the man. 'What's he doing here?' he'd ask scathingly. 'Bloody gutless wonder,' he'd say, 'like a bleeding mouse creeping around.'

'A very quiet sort of guy,' Lou remembers the friend. 'I never knew why Ken got interested in him. They were so very different. But they were both out of work, both going for auditions to read for something.'

Few people knew just how hard Ken was hit by his seeming failure to make the grade. Suddenly, he was more lonely than ever. Having resigned from George Philip, he was dependent on his demobilization pay – which turned out to be more than he expected. But it was not enough to keep him happy. He took to spending the time when he wasn't going out for auditions in his room, reading his books and playing his records. He was so depressed that he cried and sometimes he cried for long, long periods at a time.

If Charlie wanted to know what he was doing, he could give him the same answer he occasionally had dared to give as a child. 'Mind your own business,' he'd tell his father – who had another reason to shout loudly enough to bring the Russell Square traffic to a halt once more.

It was in April 1948 that Kenneth was first able, legitimately, to describe himself as an actor – a professional actor, that is; one who actually depends on it for his living, such as it was. He was taken on at a repertory company, which allowed him to act, but which provided barely enough cash for sustenance. It did however entitle him to his Equity card.

Repertory was still the bedrock of the British theatre. Almost every town of reasonable size had a 'rep' company of varying quality. Sometimes, the actors weren't all that polished. They would do things like putting hands through imaginary glass-covered cocktail cabinets or answering telephones that rang *after* they had been picked up. But most West End performers had their nursery training in these companies, which were based in playhouses put up at the turn of the twentieth century or in the last years of the nineteenth. By 1948, they were beginning to crumble. Few had had a coat of paint since George V's Silver Jubilee thirteen years before, and no one even contemplated the gilding and other refurbishments that would rescue just a few of these theatres in the Eighties – the ones that hadn't been pulled down, that is, or years before been turned into supermarkets or bingo halls.

Despite this lack of splendour in either buildings or casts, to the local communities they were part of life. Television, which just a handful of people could afford, presented no threats to the stage and the kind of productions offered by the 'reps' was an additional treat to those who spent at least one night a week at the cinema – which most still called 'the pictures'.

Far away from London, they were the only live theatre most people could ever expect to see. In the coastal resort towns, a night at the rep was part of people's holidays. Close to the centre of London, they were a cheap night out for people who either couldn't afford the much more expensive seats in the West End – stalls at eight shillings and sixpence

– or were simply a supplement to their theatre-going. They could see what were known as drawing room comedies, or old plays that had long since exhausted their West End shelf-life.

It was in one of those drawing rooms comedies that Kenneth Williams made his debut – like practically every other member of the company, dreaming that before long he would reach the West End. For him, it was an apprenticeship – much as a young journalist seeks employment on a local newspaper prior to storming the barricades of Fleet Street (neither the end of local theatres nor the eventual demise of Fleet Street as a geographical centre for newspapers was even contemplated in those days).

The company that took him was at Newquay, a Cornish resort town that required a theatre to show that it offered more than beaches, the sight of fishing smacks at dock and a reasonable enough supply of good weather to justify the term, the 'Cornish Riviera'.

This was his chance at playing the kind of juvenile role he had been searching for so long – playing Ninian, the young son in *The First Mrs Fraser*.

The Newquay Theatre featured plays put on by Smith and Whiley Productions, with Richard West as director of productions. He was a man who appeared to have a considerable influence on Ken. He taught him the basics of acting – like when you fluff your lines, pretend it hadn't happened; no one else will notice if you go on with what comes next.

The name Kenneth Williams appeared alongside those of Annette Kerr, Diana Vernon, Joan Dale, Pamela Stamford, James Neylin, Vere Lorrimer, Derek Good and Peter Ashby-Bailey. In the month between 27 June and 18 July 1948, they presented *It's A Boy* by Austin Melford; Somerset Maugham's *The Constant Wife*, *The Letter Box Rattles* by James Bridie and A. A. Milne's *Mr Pim Passes By*.

It was a good time for him. He had good friends in the company and for the first time, he became close to a woman. Annette Kerr was not just a very good friend, but a confidante too – the kind that not even Val Orford had represented before. 'I know he was very worried about his homosexuality at this time,' Annette Kerr told me. But she did not think he put it into practice. Also she was convinced he would never get married. He was already very fussy about the way he dressed and kept himself clean. 'Could you imagine anyone putting up with his fastidiousness?'

But he appreciated that they could talk about literature and current affairs as well as about the state of the theatre, which seemed to be just about the only subject that was guaranteed to keep the attention of the rest of the company.

'We had intelligent conversations together,' she remembered. Unlike other relationships between females and homosexuals those conversations were not at all 'womanly'.

In March 1950, both Ken and Annette were in a rep that moved from Eastbourne to Margate and back again – putting on the same play in both towns – at Devonshire Park, Eastbourne and the Winter Garden, Margate – for a fortnight each. Another section of the same company alternated both plays and theatres with them so that the show always went on at both places, all directed by Jennifer Sounes.

Ken didn't bother to recall this company in his own autobiography, although it seems to have made a distinct impression on other members of the cast. Neither does he give more than a passing reference to Annette Kerr, particularly how she vainly tried to empty an atrocious lemon curd pie into the lavatory at the digs they shared. He gives no idea of how close they were, which will become apparent very soon.

The most outstanding production at this time was Somerset Maugham's *The Letter*. Among those in the company was a very young assistant stage manager called Michael Anderson. Years later, he would be Ken's agent. In *The Letter*, Anderson also played a Chinese servant – 'with a pillow stuck up my front'. Ken was another Chinese – he made himself up to look the part; the accent was fairly unbelievable but he was always good at voices and this was apparently extraordinarily memorable – a solicitor's clerk! Charles Brodie, who says he was a 'clean-limbed British colonial policeman' told me he remembered Ken very well. 'He was very good at it. Mind you, none of us was exactly giving a National Theatre performance.

'What I remembered about Ken at this time was his knowledge of Noël Coward. He knew all the lyrics and was ready to give continuous performances of them all at the drop of a hat.' Ken's performance of *The Stately Homes of England*, in the wings after a show or in the digs in the evening, kept the rest of the company in a happier frame of mind than some of their working conditions appeared to justify. 'He was the company funny man,' Charles Brodie told me.

But Brodie never thought him happy. One evening during a spell when they were not working at either Eastbourne or Margate, they spent together at the Arts Theatre in London. On the way back to Marchmont Street, Ken told him: 'You know, I'm never going to get my personal life sorted out. Everything has to go into the theatre.' Brodie added: 'He was a very sad person – someone you could never get to know well.'

Like Annette Kerr, he saw Ken's sexual frustrations at work. 'He said his sexual life had never been a success and never could be a success.'

'He knew full well what his sexual orientation was, but he knew he could never get it to work for him. Whether that meant a kind of impotence or he couldn't satisfactorily relate to anyone, I don't know. I don't think he felt it was distasteful at all, but there must have been a great basic inner conflict.'

At the time of their rep work together – 'horrifying the people of Margate one fortnight and then those of Eastbourne the next' – Brodie watched Ken's work very carefully, almost as though he had a vested interest in his progress. In a way, he felt he had.

He had haunted the same agents' offices before the rep jobs came up – at the same time as Roger Moore and Michael Caine – and, as contemporaries do, studied his performances intently. He was impressed – even if there was nothing about what he did to give the casts of London shows apoplexy.

Ken, he remembered, 'was always very, very ambitious. He wouldn't talk about it a great deal, but one just got the idea that he was seeking every opportunity.'

Nevertheless, when success and stardom eventually came to Ken, Brodie was surprised. 'I had always known he had great ability, but because he was personally so peculiar I was a little surprised it got recognized. There was always great tension. He had considerable intellect, which somehow didn't show itself at the time. He just seemed a small, funny man with funny ways. I didn't really think he would get anywhere. He had a lack of ease.

'If I had really thought about it, I suppose he would only have worked so hard if he were trying to hide something – which I am sure he was. There was a facade there.'

Michael Anderson saw the way Ken worked and knew that he wasn't the kind of actor who just said his lines and walked off until the next ones were due to come along.

Another of the plays produced at this time was *See How They Run*. Ken's role in this – and in other productions in which they worked together – was of a 'very puckish, naughty fellow. ... He was three years older than I was and used to send me up outrageously.' Both played vicars. 'I was facing upstage, he facing downstage – and while I had my speech, he was trying – onstage – to undo my trousers. He was terribly funny.'

From Margate and Eastbourne, Ken moved to Wales and a rep company in Swansea.

The director of the company was the leading Welsh actor, Clifford Evans – later to make a national name for himself as the ruthless business-man Casell Bligh in the early TV series *The Power Game*.

In many ways it was an outstanding repertory of Wales – with Rachel Roberts playing lead roles opposite a bright young man with an extraordi-narily poetic and yet powerful voice. His name: Richard Burton. In Chekov's *The Seagull*, Burton played Konstantin. Ken was deputed to be his understudy. But since Burton was always a picture of health, Ken never bothered to learn the part. One evening, the star wasn't so well. He said he had food poisoning. He couldn't go on. The trouble was, of course, neither could Ken. He didn't know a word of the part. In the end, Burton struggled on – thanks to a concoction Ken brought in from the pub next door and the understudy's offer to give his star his entire week's salary, all of seven pounds.

In a letter to Annette Kerr – this was the start of a long correspondence which would soon become more important and longer lasting than even that with Val Orford – he described the understudy's job as 'just SHEER ballyoo! 'Cos he only wants a stand-in!!'

He wrote to Val about *The Seagull* too. It had been playing to good houses, 'but there is little doubt that the poor public are completely mysti-fied by the entire performance. However they are Welsh enough to know that *its* (at this stage in his life, Ken was plainly having trouble with apos-trophes) so profound you *arent* expected to understand a word of it, and there is quite a lot of intense acting, so they all applaud like mad at the end. Then leave the theatre feeling as though they would like to ask what the hell it was all about but *darent* in case their neighbour thinks they are foolish for not seeing it, which *doesnt* reely (*sic*. It would be years before Ken discovered how to spell the word) matter because the neighbour *didnt* see it either, and probably feels exactly the same way as they do about it. So everyone is completely frustrated in the end. The actors – because they never feel they have seen everything in the part and might have missed some amazing subtlety, the Public – because they feel faintly as if they have been swindled out of their money because there *wasnt* anything at all to laugh at. No one fell over on their bottom or anything.'

He repeated a conversation he had overheard on the bus the night before. One woman said she heard the play had been terrible. Her friend said that yes, it was 'awful boring but nice ... that's how they live out there. ... Well, Albert was home last night with the fiancée and I thought it would be a bit of a change from the pictures ... I spose it was silly reely cos he hates Tolstoy!'

His letters to Val were totally different from those to Annette. It was a plainly loving relationship on his part, if not a sexual one. His first letter was addressed to 'My darling Adored Annette'.

'CE (Clifford Evans) rehearses us every minute he's able and it's just GRUELLING,' he wrote. 'Of course, he's quite a wonderful and fascinating man, but where *does* he get all the ENERGY from – I mean !!!'

He talks about another actress who was 'terribly Grande Dame act. My dear the LOT!! Sheer NYLONS and hat veil. Gawd. Me beads!' And then he adds: '*Wish* you were here. You are the only actress who really gets LOVED in a company. You have exquisite poise – beautiful movement – and a lovely face, everything you do is tempered with good taste. So right theatrically. And you've a delicious sense of humour.'

Annette was due to join the company the following September. He thought it wise to apprise her of conditions there. 'Digs are OK. By the sea. Lav outside though. COLD and draughty for passing motions, but its an ill wind that blows nobody ... etc. etc.'

Despite his intellectual strivings, lavatory jokes – and more serious talk about lavatories and the purpose for which they were used – would always figure in Ken's conversations and writings.

In another letter (addressed to 'Honeybunch') he looks forward to Annette's coming to Swansea excitedly. 'O gay gay days in the woodwind. Well, make the most of them dear for you will soon be seeing the last of them! Already the cast has gone up for *Blithe Spirit* – and everyone is madly wondering WHAT you're going to be like!! Talk about inquisition ... Needless to say, I'm NOT in it!! No mad miscasting here. I play kids ALL the time. Just an in-between, Dear!! But terribly elevating in a sort of Peter Pan way. How can I say that so casually?'

Lou liked Annette. One can only conjecture about a secret hope that Ken's mother had that Annette and her boy might marry – today she says that she never bothered about his marrying – because the two women got on so well. They used to discuss knitting and Annette obtained some wool for Lou at a time when it was in very short supply.

There were good moments at Swansea – particularly one which would turn out to be an incredibly influential part of his life. It was here that Clifford Evans would have the inspiration to cast him as the Dauphin in Shaw's *Saint Joan*. It would be a part he would work on and hone so that for a time it virtually became his own copyright. These were, however, heady days on a shoestring and there would be better, more inventive Dauphins from Ken than this.

Towards the close of 1950, he joined a company close to London. At the New Theatre at Bromley, he played the part of a blackmailer in a popular melodrama of the day, *The Shop At Sly Corner*. Val Orford went to see it and was overwhelmed with his friend's performance. He felt very proud. He was not alone in his approval. The *Beckenham and Penge Advertiser*'s, critic 'T.H.T' – they disapproved of the personality cult in local papers in those days – headed his report, 'Promising Actor'. The critic wrote: 'Kenneth Williams (is) a young man with I'll warrant a bright future. His is an odious part, played with a sneer that seems to come from the heart, as neat a piece of acting as the company has ever given us.'

It was doubtless a cutting Ken himself would keep. In his autobiography he said that he always cut out the good reviews, the bad ones he threw into the wastepaper basket, tried to forget them and remarked to whoever would listen that today's newspapers were tomorrow's fish and chip wrappings. He plainly didn't follow the dictum of one distinguished performer who maintains that he never takes notice of bad reviews – but the corollary of that was that he mustn't savour the good ones either.

Also in *The Shop* was a very young actor named Nicholas Parsons who a generation later was to be chairman of *Just a Minute*. He was very impressed by Ken, who played it, he recalls, as a 'rather effeminate strange young boy'.

Ronnie Carr, the director at the New Theatre – now called the Churchill – who was also a teacher at RADA, the Royal Academy of Dramatic Art, brought Ken into the company for the role because he didn't have a regular in the company whom he thought could play it.

Parsons told me: 'I remember this young man arriving. He was just a very much younger edition of the Kenneth who became the star we later knew. He was eccentric, always had something to say – full of enthusiasm for theatre and show business. In one sense, he was somewhat theatrical. In another, he had a lot of potential talent.'

Ken was very intense, he said, but 'terribly involved in his work and very excited'.

In one scene, Ken had to lie on the floor while Parsons tried to strangle him. Before the killing could take place, the young Williams sat up. 'Oh isn't it exciting!' he declared. 'It's so dramatic this scene ... There's so much feeling in it.'

'I remember thinking what a marvellous extrovert quality he had. Ken wasn't shy like I was. I remember thinking what a great actor he could be.'

Ken moved to a more permanent repertory company in Guildford, doing the same kind of parts with the same kind of organization.

He was beginning to feel that his acting career which had begun in rep would end there, too – possibly with his becoming an ageing juvenile, a species not particularly admired in the profession. But at Guildford there was a turning point. A young man who was just setting up in business as a theatrical agent came to see him at work. Peter Eade criticized Ken's delivery – he didn't at all like the way he clipped his sentences – and decided to take him under his wing. Getting work would be easier after that.

Still, Ken was reluctant to join another repertory company. Annette was working in one at York and Ken was due to go there, too. Just before his starting date, he wrote asking her ('My dearest heart') to cancel the accommodation arrangements she had made on his behalf. 'It is as though I've eventually come through a long road with many turnings AND STOPPED,' he wrote. 'Curiously enough, I feel I want to stop. Stop dead and stay. Reconnoitre and find out what I have become and must go on doing. I suddenly got the feeling that I could not face rushing up to York straightway (*sic*) after finishing at Guildford over Sunday. I am physically worn out and mentally chaotic, there is a definite crisis here in my life and my mind skates round and round the issue like I perform somersaults in my mind. I am amazingly miserable, don't think I've ever been *quite* so hopeless before. There is nothing that can be done. No amount of literary clichés will help or console. It's a situation – loneliness of the soul – which MUST be resolved – in one's self. Any kind of rep following straight after Guildford would sent me up the wall.'

Work wasn't the only thing that bothered him. In the midst of a letter to his favourite woman friend ('My dear Annette') describing a visit to the Festival of Britain in May 1951 ('an unforgettable experience') he bares his soul: 'Like a skin rash, sex still breaks out with renewed emphasis – every so often – and my mental pictures become more and more elaborately perverted. Nonetheless, I remain controlled enough not to share them with anyone else in the physical sense and consequently become taut and screaming inside so that I am often quite unbearable to the nicest examples of utter mediocrity.'

A month later – the handwriting here is so different it could have been written by a different person entirely; his previous letters to Annette had big, complex characters, the writing in this is very neat and very small – he was writing to her: 'You say it's important to remember that there are others suffering from this particular loneliness and unhappy sex life. I know that you know there's no consolation in that – no point in fact, in mentioning it. Besides, I'm not concerned so much about sex life at the moment, as the point of existence into which I've been born with so much lacking. I am trying to understand the peculiar hatefulness of the universe as man has contributed to it.'

He said he was hoping to get a job 'in some theatre work UNCONNECTED with rep.' Clifford Evans was planning a pageant and he thought there might be room for him in that. 'Otherwise, I shall chuck it all together (*sic*). There is no point in living pointless when Existence has no point anyway ... I've neither fallen in love, nor indulged in any affairs – it might have been better if I had, but you know my preoccupation with "ideals".'

Despite his frustrations and his depressions, he could spare a compliment to Annette herself. He had read a review of one of her performances. 'O many sounding congratulations upon your attractive dark head ... How delightful it is to see one's friends appearing thus in print.'

His moods swung like a pendulum – in another letter to Annette he could say: 'I am certainly happiness now. In the agonizing process of turning a mental somersault and re-orientating myself philosophically – coming to accept myself AS I AM. Truly without compromising with the useless jargon or morality which the Christian faith has thrust upon me for so many years – I am coming out of the woods. Am beginning to see the sun.'

But he also said that he had been trying to compromise – 'between the thirst for ultimate and complete spiritual truth and the Christian code of ethics. It was MAD. And it nearly sent me demented with the misery of self-accusation. In truth, there was only one Christian. He died upon the Cross. How DARE we hope to cast His mantle upon others? How can you wear someone else's clothes? Surely, the very code of the real man's philosophy is individual. Whatever is good for the goose can certainly never be good for the gander.'

Ken did take part in Evans's pageant, *Land of My Fathers* for the Festival of Wales, which formed part of the bigger Festival of Britain. The production in Cardiff was in a brand new theatre and he found it very exciting.

He played a number of different parts – mainly ' a bum called Henry II' – but when it was over, he had to think again about his future, which he still hoped would exclude York.

Not going to York, he was out of work – 'again'. 'But something is going to turn up I hope – something gay, romantic and terribly, terribly exciting.' Noël Coward had really made his impact felt.

He shared poetry with Annette and his thoughts on women – 'most women do bore me, as you very well know – you being the exception that proves the rule' – but there was still something missing in his life.

It wasn't religion, although he discussed it more and more – to Pat as well as to Annette. Pat talked about the 'Japs' and about 'Krautland'. 'Don't talk like that,' he corrected her. 'It's un-Christian.'

Before long, he went to York after all. In *A Wilderness of Monkeys* there, he was seen by a casting scout for Herbert Wilcox the film producer.

Now Wilcox had already had his big moments in the cinema – particularly with the films produced for his wife Anna Neagle, like *Spring In Park Lane* and *Maytime In Mayfair*. But he was still a name to be reckoned with in the British industry. In 1951, he talked about Ken playing a small part. *Trent's Last Case*, starring Anna Neagle's long-time partner Michael Wilding and the most glamorous woman in British films, Margaret Lockwood would be Williams's first picture.

FOUR

In Australia, Pat Williams saw Ken in *Trent's Last Case* and was so excited to see her brother on the big screen, she couldn't stop telling people who he was. 'Look, that's my brother,' she shouted in the theatre. In *The Sunday Times*, Dilys Powell disliked all but Orson Welles in a character part. 'He was one of the few characters in the film I should have hesitated to murder.' She then added in parenthesis, 'I should have spared also the delightful gardener of Kenneth Williams.' That was definitely not something for the fish-and-chip wrappings.

He played the man who finds the body, the centrepiece of the action. It wouldn't be the last time he played a man closely linked to the soil.

The part was tiny, but by Williams standards, the fee was not. It was enough for him to buy a whole new wardrobe – at Hepworths, an establishment that did not have a branch in Savile Row and which specialized in hire-purchase tailoring – and a few shelves of books.

It was not his only screen début. At about the same time, he appeared on television – playing an angel in a play by H. G. Wells called *The Wonderful Visit*.

Charles Brodie went to see him while he was rehearsing the play. He was struck by the gilded wig he wore for the part.

The *Visit*, as it turned out, was not that wonderful, although to do it he had given up the chance of playing the English herald in a television version of *King John*.

It was shot live and was due for a second performance – which was cancelled because it coincided with the death of King George VI in February 1952. There was another closure at the same time. Ken was cast in the lead in a London play. Kenneth Williams was to star in *Before You Die*. However, it wasn't exactly the West End. The Chepstow at Notting Hill was what would today be called 'fringe'. So was the audience. One night, the only person present was an old lady with a bag of buns. The company decided to give her her money back and pack up – and everyone made for the nearest cinema to drown their sorrows in whatever they sipped in the back stalls.

Ken went back to rep – yet again. This time, he was at Salisbury, playing in *By Candlelight* by Siegfried Geyer and in Sheridan's *School for Scandal*. He had a row with the director Guy Verney who didn't like Ken's performance as Sir Benjamin Backbite – although he later conceded that Verney had been right all along.

But in 1952, Ken was still only twenty-six and had a lot to learn. What he did learn now was that he had made a bigger impression in his film début than he had dared hope. Herbert Wilcox liked the young man and offered him more work – this time in his new production of *The Beggar's Opera*.

The then Sir Laurence Olivier was the star – as MacHeath. Ken would play the potboy. On the set, Ken came in for more criticism. The boy born in Islington wasn't showing himself to be enough of a cockney. Before long, another actor's voice was dubbed on to the soundtrack. Ken was mortified. But the anxiety was short-lived. Not only was he pretty dreadful in the part, the film itself was undoubtedly the worst thing that Olivier himself ever did. It lasted no more than a week in the cinemas.

With that behind him, Ken was invited back on to the stage. This time, it was *really* a London theatre – although only with some stretch of the imagination could it be described as the West End.

Every year, at the Scala off the capital's Charlotte Street, was enacted a tradition called *Peter Pan*. The theatre was virtually unused all year round, but in the midst of the Christmas holidays, it came out of mothballs. J. M. Barrie's famous children's story was staged with a peculiar ritual – just as in a pantomime (which this never really was, although the children out front were always invited to shout out that they believed in fairies) the principal star was a boy played by a girl. The other two main male characters, a pirate chief and the father of the children who are made to appear to fly on stage, were always played by the same man.

In December 1952, the year the title role was performed by Brenda Bruce, Ken played in *Peter Pan* – as Slightly, one of the lost boys. He was to wish that the part if not the play had been lost, too.

He chain-smoked. He hated the play and everything to do with it. He hated the director, Cecil King – who apparently believed he had a direct line to heaven and *Peter Pan's* author. Ken always said that King – he was almost eighty at the time – claimed he held the rights of production 'direct from the dying hands of Barrie' who seems to have moaned some stuff about 'Don't let them alter all the lovely traditional Biz in the production, Cecil'. He had been stage manager in the original show.

King, in a broad cockney accent, came out of retirement every year to take charge. On her first day at rehearsal, he eyed Brenda Bruce and said, 'Look here, boy. It don't matter what you do so long as it fits the part.'

King used to stand at the back of the Scala drumming up applause that was all too difficult to get. He also kept calling Brenda Bruce, 'Miss Lockwood' – Margaret Lockwood had played the Peter Pan role the year before.

It was altogether too twee for Ken, who didn't really sit well with the boys from private schools in their neat grey flannel suits and clean caps and the girls in their Sunday-best dresses with bows in their hair.

He tried to relieve the boredom in exactly the same way as he had attempted to do back at Manchester Street school. He impersonated Cecil King – to the obvious delight of the rest of the cast, if not of King himself. The director heard the impersonation, sniffed and said in his elderly cockney voice: 'Well, one of us is terrible'. It was about the only reasonably articulate thing he did say during the play's run that year.

The troubles started early. In a letter addressed to 'My dearest Annette', Ken wrote from Marchmont Street (he now had his own notepaper, with the name 'Kenneth Williams' in blue ink over the address): 'Rehearsals for this epic are the end; chaotic to say the least. James Donald (playing Mr Darling and Captain Hook) condescending and saturnine; Brenda Bruce rather helpless and 'I am no wiser than you dear, but I insist on having the number one dressing room' and all the Conti Kids behaving like darling little bastards the whole time.' (The Conti Kids were the pupils of the Italia Conti stage school.)

Before long, Mr Donald walked out of the production, while the director, Ken claimed, 'couldn't articulate himself not for love nor money.' One eleven-year-old lost boy thought the director, only seventy years his senior, 'hasn't a clue about the geography of this scene'. The boy was 'alarmingly truthful', Ken agreed. He couldn't understand how the children could shout and scream – frequently being exceedingly rude to Mr King – without his hearing a word of it.

Ken himself had his disputes with the director. He didn't like the idea of having to wear ribbons in his hair. 'I don't feel it's in my character,' he maintained. 'My dear,' King replied, 'all the Slightlys play it with ribbons. It is the traditional biz.' As Ken noted: 'You either have hysterics or give in to utter defeat. The entire thing is DEFEAT really. That the play can still go on defeats me, that people can be so fearfully insulted by its dreadful immorality is defeating and that actors should try to bring a little reality to it is completely defeating. You just don't stand a chance.'

He was only afraid that the whole thing would get to him and before long, he would be saying things like, 'Well, it is rather charming.'

Brenda Bruce had no such inhibitions. She told me that she also greatly admired Ken. She enjoyed working with him, saw him as an accomplished actor on the threshold of bigger and better things.

The production was a bit tacky. The sets and costumes had not been changed since before World War II and the story, as Ken more than intimated, was equally antiquated.

She herself had had her problems – few Peter Pans before her had played the part totally as a boy. Usually, they had heads of curls and wore green-leaf costumes that showed curves no male Peter could possibly have had. Brenda made herself look straight and flat and wore a Tony Curtis hairstyle. One critic described her as a 'coffee-bar Peter Pan'.

Most of the early discussions for *Pan* took place in a more conventional kind of bar – at least as far as actors were concerned – in the upstairs room at the Scala. 'I thought he was terribly funny,' Ms Bruce said, recalling some of the early repertory performances of his that she had caught.

The production went on from December until April, with the last two months on tour – organized by Howard and Wyndham, the producers – to places like Manchester, Leeds, Nottingham, Newcastle, Bradford and Bristol.

They went to Hanley, one of the 'Five Towns' immortalized by Arnold Bennett in stories like *The Card*. That was an improvement on most places they visited. In another letter to Annette Kerr, Ken wrote: 'The accommodation is delightful ... pleasant house ... fresh battleship-grey paint and cream ceilings, thick carpets and big coal fires. Terribly everybody and rather me – in so far as touring goes. We are to go round the pottery works and buy export rejects madly and chatter amiably so that the world will think we all adore each other.' As for the theatre, it was 'not a little unclean. Euphemism!'

By now he had a euphemism for the play itself. He called it 'Peter Pansy'. He told Annette: 'The only woman in this company I care about at all is Violet Coleman (Mrs Darling) and we have teas and stuff together. The only reason I like her is because in many ways, she resembles you. When the resemblance fades, I begin to hate her bitterly.'

Brenda Bruce believes that she and Ken were much closer during the play's run.

It was in Bradford that the company had to find a new Captain Hook. That was when James Donald left the show after an asthma attack. He insisted on windows being left open. The management wouldn't agree

– but Ken put on his shop-steward hat once more and defended him. It was to no avail – so Donald left. No one told the rest of the cast, though, that Donald had suffered from asthma and an understudy took over.

In retrospect, it is now clear that that was when the trouble started. There were regulations about taking children away from home, particularly during term-time. So instead of the Conti kids playing the lost boys, there were, to quote Miss Bruce, 'a gang of thugs'. Ken was not like the others. He, after all, had a name part and got to wear the top hat as he flew above the stage. Ken always felt partly chastened by the fact that the part had been originated by Noël Coward.

'He was very camp,' Brenda Bruce remembered. Ken himself referred to the 'camp' dancing he did. It has to be one of the first references to that word in that context.

One of the lost boys was actually a girl – who was pregnant by the end of the April run. Ignoring her, the director was aware of the thuggish nature of this gang. 'You're a lot of little Craigs,' he kept telling them. He was referring to an infamous teenager hanged for murder at the time. Poor Mr King knew Craig's identity better than he did that of anyone else in the company.

The stage managers weren't any better – and neither were their fees. One evening, instead of sounding the bell assuring Peter that everyone in the audience believed in fairies, the stage manager turned the sprinklers on in the house, drenching the customers. Then the torch that doubled as Tinkerbell the fairy – the fairy who only appeared as a spot of light and as a tinkling bell – failed to show up. Finally, the iron safety curtain was dropped in the midst of the performance.

Ken took it upon himself to represent the rest of the company in protesting to the stage manager. 'I can't help it if it's early-closing day and I couldn't get another battery for the torch. What am I supposed to do?' 'Get the sack, I hope,' said Williams.

Ken laughed about the director and the stage manager more than anyone – King didn't know the Williams name, either. 'Ken was always great fun, never difficult.' says Brenda Bruce. 'Between Ken and I there was a very funny, great relationship.'

While the play was being performed at the Scala, they would walk each other home at night. They both lived fairly close to the theatre. They would talk about their mothers, similar women from working-class backgrounds. 'Yet I remember he would never come to my flat.'

But he would spend a lot of time in her dressing room. He saw no pleasure in being surrounded by the thugs – and once invited into the number-one dressing room, stayed. He had first gone there to try to discourage the romantic advances to her by one of the pirates in the show. Once that was out of the way, he had established his own niche in her life.

They talked books, discussed biographies both had read. 'He was very good about theatre books. He had lots of wonderful theatre stories, which he had picked up from books on Irving and Terry and, of course, Oscar Wilde and Byron.'

They did *The Times* crossword together – sitting on stage, during the interval. The stage manager did his bit there, too – bringing up the curtain while they were sitting there, wrestling with the clues. 'He was always a very private person, always a loner.'

Once the play had finished, it was as though a safety curtain had come down between them too. 'It was just sad that when it was all over, it was over. Maybe he did that with everybody, I barely saw him after that. Just in a couple of game shows on TV, which we all had to do. I remember he was very bright and sharp – and still very funny, but it was different from being in his company all the time as we were when doing *Peter Pan*.'

Ken might have blamed *Peter Pan* on Peter Eade, but then, for all he said about it, it did give him steady work at a time in his career when he needed it – and there was always the chance that he would be spotted. One or two people made notes about his appearance, particularly the parts he learned to camp up once he felt reasonably sure of himself in it.

He blamed Eade for spreading a cold to everyone around him. As he wrote to Annette Kerr, it was undoubtedly Eade who had given her the one that made her sneeze and blow.

'Of course you got it from Peter Eade, that awful charlatan! He must have given it to you! I know he was infectious. I dosed myself silly with quinine sulphate on that evening. I must have been raving but I was so frightened of catching the germs that I went much too far and took twenty five grains! When I got back home, after leaving your place, I could hardly stand! My ears were singing so loud ... that I was completely oblivious to ordinary noises and the giddiness made it well nigh impossible to stand upright. I fell into bed, and went off into the most ghastly stupor. But in the morning I knew that I had not got the Eade Germs. Thank the powers, I cried. The plague has passed me by! And it came to pass that I rose again in the morning whole and undefiled, and they cried out in wonder, saying Blessed is he that puts quinine in his lamp for he shall not be a foolish Virgin.'

With *Peter Pan* behind him, Ken went back into repertory in Birmingham.

He had been interviewed at the Arts Theatre Club in London for a part in the company's forthcoming production of *Henry VI*. The company was doing all three parts of the play – no less a rarity in Birmingham as anywhere else. Ken was to play Burgundy in Part One, the roles of Hume and Smith in the second part and of Rutland in Part Three. Ken was twenty-seven; Rutland was supposed to be a boy. To get the part – Ken thought that since he was murdered in the first act he would get away from the theatre nice and early every night – he sat on his haunches, bit his fingernails; did everything, it would appear, but pick his nose to show that he could play a youngster. The part, along with the others, was safely his.

He thought that both the play and the company – one of the most important repertory outfits in Britain – would be a prestigious episode in his career. It would not turn out to be so.

He was not happy. 'It's hell here,' he wrote. In another letter to Annette Kerr ('My darling') he discusses a performance which was not one for the memoirs. 'No, my dear the miracle didn't happen and I suppose life isn't even nearly like that. With no real characterization one becomes negative. The scene became anxiously self-conscious and ran dismally to its conclusion like an embarrassing slow puncture. I felt suicidal last night and desperately hoped that something would happen. Nothing did.'

His relationship with Annette was plainly a strong one. When she came to London and he was in Birmingham, he wanted her to take his room. He believed they had so much in common: 'It's only in outward form that we differ ... Mentally I'm compatible with a mosquitoe (*sic*): it's a sort of buzz around other people's brains.'

He only wished that she were with him. 'You would be wonderful and superb as Queen Margaret. The girl they've got is amateur and horrid. ... Big rows and factions in this company. Thank God I'm not a member of the permanent rep.'

He says nothing of this in his autobiography, although every evening he confided his thoughts to his diary. Already, the book that he had started to keep at school was blossoming with outrageous comments about people whom he either knew or saw acting.

Apart from strange happenings at rehearsal, he actually says that every-thing went according to plan. In fact, more than that. The play was so successful that the company was invited to transfer to the Old Vic in London. Ken himself was successful, too. He was offered the part of Prince Henry in the Old Vic production of *King John*. It was to star Richard Burton and Claire Bloom, but Ken wanted none of it. He didn't want to be tied to what promised to be a lengthy Old Vic production. The result was that early in 1953, Kenneth Williams was out of work, moping in his bedroom at Marchmont Street about how stupid he had been.

Ken's diary, if published, would reveal some unkind things about one of the great heroes of the British film industry in the post-war years, Jack Hawkins. He was the star of the film in which Ken appeared in 1954, called *The Seekers*, which owed precisely nothing to the folk-singing group of the following decade. This was a picture about a British sailor's family settling in New Zealand in the early nineteenth century and was fairly accurately summed up by the eminent film historian Leslie Halliwell as a 'stilted epic which never gains the viewer's sympathy or interest'.

It certainly never gained Ken's sympathy and his interest was in avoiding catching double pneumonia – since he spent one night's filming up to his waist in a water-filled trench, in what was supposed to be a rain storm.

The picture co-starred the then highly-popular Glynis Johns, but the only actor to whom he could relate was a small-part performer named Norman Mitchell, who made the few days he had to film at Pinewood seem bearable. Fortunately for Ken he himself was killed off early in the picture, so had little to do.

'I think we're both much too good for the theatre,' he wrote to Annette ('My dearest Mentor'). 'Good in the moral and artistic sense. We are better suited to the contemplative life.'

What he should have done was to start to specialize. He would have been ideal in Sheridan or Goldsmith. His rep excursion into *School for Scandal* should have been followed up by a West End or Old Vic run. *She Stoops to Conquer* was replete with potential Kenneth Williams roles, it only an enterprising manager had begun to recognize the fact from what he had produced so far. Unfortunately, he was most recognizable in the queue of the unemployment office.

In a philosophical mood, he could accept his fate without being depressed. In a February 1954 letter to Annette ('My dear Miss Kerr') he wrote: 'Of course, we're lost in many grooves. It's a long-playing record and contains one or two discordant passages. Good gracious! You don't expect the music to be sugar sweet the whole time!! It's the whole that matters.' Then he added: 'Don't forget my birthday is on the twenty-second. I don't want any cards or gifts, but thoughts and silent concentration at midday.' It was as though he regarded himself as a war memorial. In a way he did. He may only have been twenty-eight but he felt battle-scarred already.

No doubt to Val Orford's displeasure – to say nothing of Charlie Williams, who continued to mutter near-obscenities about 'poofs' in the theatre – he had no plans to go back to drawing maps. In the summer of 1954, he was once more in repertory, in Bridgwater, Somerset, playing character parts. But they were not the kind he had found in rep in his previous incarnations. This time he had greater variety in his work. He told Annette about one example 'We played a lunatic asylum (*sic*) last week and it was enchanting. Beautifully set in a delightful valley, the audience was wonderfully attentive and laughed in all the right places. It was all so civilized and sane. One felt one should have stayed there . . .'

Referring to a member of the cast, he added: 'Ashley Bumhole made a terrible patronizing curtain speech about their obvious grasp – appreciation of live entertainment etc. etc. Disgusting.'

The plays, he added, got worse every week. 'Now it is a filthy bit of excrescence (*sic*) . . . and is succeeding in driving away the little audiences they built up initially.'

He said that a young man 'with lots of handsomeness but no talent' followed him everywhere he went . . . Layers of inhibition – can't even fart without blushing . . .'

Then Ken said that life was awful for him. 'I used to be interested in people. Now, I wish I could care. All sexual desire has vanished, so I can't even moan about that old thing.' To make things worse, the landlady at his digs used to wake him every day with his morning tea – and feel his toes after putting it down.

Ken kept himself amused by reading. He had turned to American humour, but wasn't totally happy with it. He quite liked S. J. Perelman, but thought him limited, couldn't understand James Thurber at all. But when he read a novel by Mary McCarthy in a restaurant, he literally fell about laughing. He liked to think that he knew a great deal about writing – which in his way, he did – and about grammar, which he did not always do. In one letter, he complained about an author writing about 'what the data mean'. It should, he maintained, be 'what the data means'. The author and not Mr Williams was, of course, correct.

One of his closer friends was once again the Welsh actress Rachel Roberts, soon to be the wife of Rex Harrison. They went to Collin's music hall and sent up the acts. The actress was frequently depressed and he managed to cheer her up. Alas, it would be only a temporary cheer. Before very long, she would commit suicide.

Ken was good at reassuring other people, sometimes better at it than he ever could be at reassuring himself. Occasionally, there were more deep sad moods for him, as impenetrably dark as a black hole, although no one used the term in 1954.

Things got so bad for him at about this time that he satisfied himself that he was doing useful work when he helped his father do some decorating. The two men had never been as close together before. But then things began to change. He got a television role in the Shaw play *Misalliance*.

He did so well playing Bentley in that play that he was immediately – the morning after transmission – offered a part in another Shaw play. Once more, Ken was to be the Dauphin in *Saint Joan*. Only this time, it wasn't in repertory. He was playing the part in a production at the Arts Theatre. It still was not mainstream West End, but there was a degree of prestige in the production that he had not known before. Even Charlie saw that was the case, and agreed to give him a special haircut for the performance. Joan was played by Siobhan McKenna, who also got Charlie to give her a short haircut, too. It was a command performance. The senior Williams was practically for the moment almost proud that his son had gone into show business.

The magazine *Theatre World* wrote a column about him, in their series called 'Tomorrow's Lead'. 'The choice of Kenneth Williams to play the Dauphin in the revival of *Saint Joan* at the Arts Theatre, London, was an admirable one. Here, for a change, is a young actor who likes to play unusual comedy roles that have more depth and scope than the juvenile parts in most modern plays. His performance showed just how well he has mastered this style of playing, for he gave reality and meaning to a character that has so often been presented as a sickly caricature.'

The piece ended with a nice bit of Williams philosophizing. 'Unlike many other stage artists, he believes that the actor's job is purely interpretative and he is convinced that only the actor who realizes this and does not claim that his work is creative, has the necessary humility to do his work well.'

Nicholas Parsons went to see him in the play. 'He was a brilliant actor. I was convinced of it, seeing him in *Saint Joan*.'

But there was something new waiting for him that wasn't quite the sort of acting he had done before. Quite suddenly, the Kenneth Williams people would get to recognize and expect was launched. He was offered a part in what looked like being a long-running BBC radio series. It starred a young comedian called Tony Hancock. The show was *Hancock's Half Hour*.

FIVE

There are perhaps just three English-speaking personalities whose fame and legend is as strong long after their death as it was in their lifetime. One was Oscar Wilde, the second Marilyn Monroe, the third, Tony Hancock.

In Britain, you only have to say 'May Day' or 'The Blood Donor' to conjure up a mental picture of a heavy-set young man wearing a homburg hat and a heavy overcoat with its astrakhan collar. He only had to say, 'H-h-h-ancock's Half Hour' and a whole nation stopped filling in their football pools or doing their ironing to tune into the events going on at 23 Railway Cuttings, East Cheam.

That was Hancock in life, a life caught like a moth in amber by recordings that are constantly played on radio programmes today – the frightened blood donor who demands his cup of tea and packet of crisps after having his finger pricked and then solemnly responds to the announcement that a whole pint is about to be extracted from him by questioning 'A pint? That's practically an armful.' Or there's the radio ham who picks up the emergency distress signal from a ship at sea – but can't find his pencil to write down the details.

The Hancock in death has been the legend of the man on the psychiatrist's couch, the terrible inferiority complex, the infinite sadness and self-pity that led him to open a bottle of vodka and a container of pills in Australia and to commit suicide.

The blood donor and radio ham sketches were on television. Before the TV series, *Hancock's Half Hour* was the most popular programme on radio. Ken joined the cast for the second series late in 1954 – although the first four episodes had Harry Secombe in the lead. Without any explanation, Hancock disappeared just before they were about to be aired. It transpired he had taken off for Rome and not even Interpol could get him back in time for the shows. That was part of the Hancock legend, too.

If *Hancock's Half Hour* hadn't been such a huge success, chances are that he might never have taken his life. As it was, it took him to heights that this son of a Birmingham shipping office manager could never have imagined when he played Jolly Jenkins in *Red Riding Hood* – just four years earlier. It gave him feelings of an omnipotence that few ever have. He thought he knew all the answers and when he realized he didn't know them, that relying on his own sense of superiority brought a new kind of failure, he killed himself.

The imaginary house at Railway Cuttings, nevertheless, was the seed of his great triumph and Ken was part of the scene that gave it to him. The house was occupied by Anthony Aloysius St John Hancock – the name took on to such an extent, reveals his masterly biographer David Nathan, that not only did people believe it was truly his but he took to confirming the fact in newspaper interviews. The house was also occupied by his so-called friends, Sid James and Bill Kerr, with whom he had the kind of relationship one does not normally wish on anyone but worst enemies. Hattie Jacques was on hand as Miss Pugh, the secretary, and then there was Ken – always the outsider, who got funnier and funnier as the next four years wore on.

Ken was the neighbour, or the postman or the man who came to read the gas meter. He sometimes had the best lines, but none was better than the catch phrase that was for ever after to be part of him – 'stop messing about'.

He started his own messing about on radio – for this was to be the biggest break of his career to date and perhaps the most important of all the steps he ever took – thanks to *Saint Joan*.

The parallel seems strange, but then all of Ken's life was a mixture of strange parallels and paradoxes; the camp effeminate star of the *Carry On* films a decade later and the serious actor who at heart was an intellectual – or who certainly liked to think of himself as one.

Dennis Main Wilson, who was the producer of the *Half Hour*, saw *Saint Joan* at the Arts and thought that Ken would be ideal as a comedy foil who, at that time, only had some good lines – the best would come later.

It seems strange to contemplate that the Dauphin who had to recite Shaw's lines like: 'I am not such a fool as I look. I have my eyes open' could also say, 'Stop messing about'. But it was not lines that impressed Wilson. What struck him was the ease with which Ken used voices – not the voices that the girl Joan heard and which led her to the stake, but wholly appropriate for all that. In the play's epilogue, Ken played the same Dauphin as a much older man, as the now-crowned fifty-one-year-old Charles VII, Charles the Victorious. He was amazed how the pimply, gauche youth could be transformed into the middle-aged King, mainly by the change of timbre to his voice. Wilson thought he could be funny, too. If he had uttered that thought out loud it would have been a classic understatement.

Ken was not modest about his achievements. He knew he had done well and went home in the evenings to his little room at Marchmont Street with a contented look on his face. He had painted the walls stark white and had taken most of the furniture out; preparing himself for the ascetic life he felt sure would follow later on, hand-in-hand with his success.

But, as we have seen, *if* Ken was not modest about himself, what he felt – and said – about other performers was positively feline. In a letter to 'My dear Annette' he commented on his leading lady and on others who had played the role – doubtless, as he poured himself another saucer of milk. He realized that the play had been well enough received to 'put (Siobhan) on the London map. I think she is good. But not wonderful. Not very good. Not as good as Hermione. I think that Hermione is probably the Best Joan ever. Obviously better than that silly old cow Thorndike.'

The acid and the milk would be left for others in *Hancock's Half Hour*, the misanthropic Bill Kerr, who found it difficult nevertheless to put more than a couple of words together, and Sid James who made your average second-hand car salesman seem like a country parson. Ken would be there to provide the seasoning if not the scenery – the visitor to Railway Cuttings, with the nasal cockney voice.

That voice used in *Hancock's Half Hour* was by courtesy of a young man Ken had only recently met. He was shy, nervous and full of the pessimism that seemed to dominate him. He had a light, uneducated southern English accent, but he talked about the doom he felt as though he were rushing to catch a train – and in between practically every word there was a nervous laugh. That was the voice that said 'Stop messing about'. It was also the voice of the neighbour who stayed seven hours at Number 23, helping to relieve the boredom of Sunday afternoon. 'I do impressions, you know ...' 'Oh really?' asks Hancock .... 'Honk, honk, honk – that's a pig'. At the end of the seven hours of impressions, he announces he has to go. 'It's nearly twelve o'clock.' Hancock interjects: 'Is that all? I thought it was at least Tuesday.'

His first function on the programme was to play an elderly duke who lent his flat to Hancock for the weekend – and came back to say: 'Oh my goodness – there's jelly on my Rembrandt.' The old duke, Dennis Main Wilson decided, was every bit as good as the ageing king in *Saint Joan*.

As Ken was to say: 'I played a character part, a snide character who was always cheating.'

David Nathan put it like this for me: 'Kenneth Williams was able to make "Good evening"' sound snide'. In fact, it got to the point when the writers, Ray Galton and Alan Simpson, would write the word 'snide' alongside Ken's lines if that was what they wanted.

In one sketch Ken was supposed to behave like a ballet dancer, making sprinkling gestures. He was asked what he was doing. 'Sprinkling woofle dust to kill the lions,' he replies – only to be told that there weren't any lions in those parts. 'Just as well,' Ken responds. 'This isn't real woofle dust.'

If you could get a laugh from that – and Ken had them rolling, much to Hancock's evident displeasure – he was already a very good comedian indeed.

Then there was the pride of the Royal Air Force, the test pilot ordered to return to the tower because a mechanic had gone missing, and sabotage was suspected. Hancock, the pilot, hears a tapping on his windscreen as he flies at more than 2,000 miles-an-hour. The screen is opened and Ken introduces himself as the mechanic. 'Can I come in? It's cold out here'. As he tries to wiggle his way inside the cockpit he pulls first one handle, then the next – the ejector seats are operated and both end up sitting on the plane's tail.

It was all a potent mix – the writing of Galton and Simpson, the impeccable timing of Hancock and the voices of Williams (with a not imperceptible dose of timing from him too).

He would record *Hancock's Half Hour* in the mornings and play in *Saint Joan* at the Arts (and then at St Martin's Theatre) in the evenings.

Ken was beginning to show that radio was his *métier*, probably more than anything else. He was still just a character actor, but by no means a stooge, a fact that Hancock appeared to like less and less.

Yet at this stage, they seemed to be friends. Ken visited Hancock at the London Clinic, where the star was taking the 'cure' – attempting to lose weight. He had set himself a target of two stone to take off on the scales. He also had another aim – to try to discover the meaning of it all. Ken told him he had to have faith if he were to find out why there was such a thing as human existence. Hancock said it couldn't be proved. It was an argument they later carried on at Tony's flat – disputing why they were here on this earth, until the early hours arrived and all the wine in the Hyde Park Gate apartment had been drunk and all the cigarettes there smoked.

In 1956, *Hancock's Half Hour* went on television. Ken was in the first six-part series and then dropped. Both he and Hancock knew why. His character was getting too funny and Ken was getting too popular. 'It's MY show,' said Hancock over and over again. 'I don't want this to be a double-act.'

Hancock also complained that he thought some of their routines together looked 'a bit poofy'. In one scene, they quite innocently held hands.

Finally, he exploded: 'I don't want stereotypes. I don't want that in my show.' No one again would say 'Stop messing about' on a *Hancock's Half Hour* show.

Before, long, Bill Kerr and Hattie Jacques were dropped, too. The whole character of the show changed, as Tony Hancock changed writers. It was the first step to his suicide; the first time in years that critics had been harsh on him and audiences had yawned their way to the channel-changing switch.

Ken 'was deeply hurt and appalled by it all,' David Nathan told me. The degree of offence that he felt was not in the least assuaged the next – and last time – they met. It was the early Sixties and Ken was starring with Maggie Smith in the Peter Shaffer play, *The Private Ear and the Public Eye.* Hancock went along to see the play and Ken knew he was in the audience. He expected the customary dressing-room visit at the end of the performance. It didn't come. Eventually, Ken made his way to Maggie Smith's room and there, found Tony Hancock sitting in a chair chatting with Miss Smith. 'Hello,' said Hancock, 'nice to see you again.'

It was as though he had suddenly come face to face with an old neighbour whom he had never known very well and liked even less. David Nathan maintained that he had no idea of the degree to which he had caused offence. Ken was *deeply* offended. But between meetings, amazing things had happened to the career of Kenneth Williams.

SIX

Ken's singular achievement was to jump across barriers that normally had all the effect of a railway level crossing. His big failure was to stop half-way through the race, but that comes later on in the story.

Not only was he playing the Dauphin in *Saint Joan* at the same time as he was recording *Hancock's Half Hour*, but he was also rehearsing his next part − in Orson Welles's production of *Moby Dick*. The boy genius who had started at the very top with his film *Citizen Kane* and who moved so far downward that he died best known for his lager commercials, was huffing and puffing his way towards an open-stage production of Melville's play for the London theatre. No scenery. No props, just a few chairs and somewhat imaginary lighting ideas.

He saw Ken in *Saint Joan* and had heard him in *Hancock* and concluded that 'I could use some of your versatility'. Welles was already vastly over-weight and the voice that later launched a few million beer cans had already taken on its breathless timbre. When Welles approached Ken, he rightly took it as the kind of challenge he couldn't resist.

In later years, he would say that he was never bothered by ambition and was content with all that he had done. But there was no doubt that he revelled in the chance to show that he could do both comedy and serious work.

As he once said: 'They are too different gifts. There are a lot of people who can bring a degree of gravity and authority on to the stage. Another gift entirely is demanded of comedy − for they have to respond to you. It is reciprocal.' He was delighted to be able to show that he had both of those gifts.

'A straight actor can deliver his speech, the theatre can be quiet as the grave and when the curtain falls you can have a marvellous effect. But with the comedian, it must happen immediately. The laughter must be there. The reciprocity is instant. It has to be like a tennis ball. Clean.'

He was delighted to be able to show that he knew when to master those two different approaches. His relationship with Welles was taut, to say the least. It was also extraordinarily ambivalent. Ken was never a man to hide his light under anyone's bushel, but he was frequently happy to be able to shine it around that bushel or whatever else the other person happened to have. What Welles had was that almost over-powering fame, which was always so much bigger than whatever it was that he was currently producing. Ken would talk about his relationship with Welles at the press of a microphone button.

What he didn't like about Welles was the fluctuations of moods. He would go from what he called 'thunderous denunciation to a humorous chuckle'. Welles was a great one for anecdotes and looking back to past triumphs and disasters, just as Ken would himself be a generation later.

There was fascination for Ken in that. But it didn't mean he had to toady to him in the process. As self-assured outwardly as he was insecure inside, he found it easy to argue with the both mentally and physically enormous Orson. In his autobiography, Ken recalls a discussion he and Welles had about the English language – and Orson's determination that only Americans – with their 'generosity,' as he put it – could master the English language and pronounce it properly. That was enough to send Kenneth Williams into a rage that took a lot to bring out – at least most of the time. Ken asked him what he thought about John Gielgud, almost sticking out his tongue and saying 'So there' in the course of his diatribe. Welles had to back down on that point. Ken had raised the one example that he had to accept.

But he would not accept that Williams was the kind of man with whom he could easily lose an argument. 'Not since Ruth Chatterton,' Ken was to recall him saying, 'not since Ruth Chatterton left high-society drama has anyone in the theatre been so damned difficult as you!' That little altercation ended, Ken remembered, in he himself collapsing laughing, along with everyone else around them.

At least, it was better than being called 'boring' which was precisely what Orson called Ken's acting earlier, at the rehearsal stage. That was the reason, he said, he had cut a number of the Williams lines.

They were recited in the course of the various roles he was meant to play – from Elijah the carpenter, a New England old salt, who was his main character, through any number of other assorted characters, including the sailor who kept having to say, 'Thar' she blows' or words to that effect.

It was not totally stimulating. There were reasons, however, for Ken to think about it affectionately. *Moby Dick* provided Ken with an oppor-tunity to meet Gordon Jackson, an actor who had already appeared in a score or more motion pictures but who was not to reach the zenith of his success and fame until he played Hudson, the Scottish butler in the immensely successful TV series about manners in a London stately home, *Upstairs Downstairs*.

They became instant friends, and the friendship would last until Ken's death much as that with Stanley Baxter lasted, too. Jackson played the part of Ishmael. Jackson was to say that Ken approached him soon after their meeting, saying, 'I'm Kenneth Williams, the only one in the cast worth knowing, let's go and have a coffee together.' Ken said that he couldn't remember saying anything of the kind. He did not disagree that those were his sentiments.

Indeed, there were other impressive figures, like Joan Plowright, for instance, who played Pip the cabin boy.

The play ran for less than a month at the Duke of York's Theatre and nobody was really surprised. Ken was very much concerned with the Art of Theatre or, as he told Annette Kerr in another letter, 'the core of what we consider theatre to be'. But by the time the play had finished its run, Welles had another Orsonian idea: he was going to film *Moby Dick*.

Ken was called back to duty and told to report to the Hackney Empire, a music hall more used in its heyday to the sound of Marie Lloyd than Melville. There was Welles on both sides of the camera and with Ken and Gordon Jackson in their original roles and Christopher Lee on hand, too. But the whole thing was disastrous. Not only did Welles film it all precisely as he had directed it on stage, but he made no concessions at all to the needs of film. He didn't even want to change the lighting, with predictably dire results.

The film was never released and remained for years on Orson's own shelves, gathering dust before turning into dust itself. Just as well. Simultaneous with his own efforts, John Huston was shooting an altogether more ambitious and spectacular version of the *Moby Dick* story, starring Gregory Peck, who at the time could do no wrong in the cinema-going public's eyes. This picture changed that situation. Huston's movie, too, was pretty awful – and succeeded in almost losing its star clinging to a huge rubber whale in the midst of a heavy fog over the English Channel. Peck was eventually rescued. The whale supposedly is still sailing somewhere, like some big rubber Marie Celeste. Ken and the rest of the Welles cast were lucky to be out of it, too.

Nevertheless, Orson Welles remained optimistic – as he always would, sure that one day he would recreate *Citizen Kane* and the Mercury Theatre and all that went with it. He tried to persuade Ken to go back to New

York with him. He said he had three plays for him.

Ken replied that he wasn't interested. He had a new musical show to go into – one that would require him to wear short trousers. Welles looked shocked. 'Why do you do such rubbish?' he asked – a question that would haunt Kenneth Williams for years to come. 'You should aim for quality.'

Ken tried to avoid answering the question with a simple statement of logic. He was being paid a lot of money for actually starring in a show. All of forty pounds a week, which to most people in 1955 was a virtual fortune. 'You will tread the road to oblivion,' Welles countered – without, presumably, even dreaming of those lager commercials in what, if he had thought about it, must have seemed like a life to come.

But, as far as Ken was concerned, there were other things to do – even if he did occasionally wax nostalgically about his lost chance to visit New York, a city he was never to see.

The new show was called *The Buccaneer*. It was a musical – in which Ken played a boy editor. Yes, a *boy* editor. He was close to thirty when the show opened in Brighton, went on to Southsea and then to the Lyric, Hammersmith, perhaps an actor's favourite try-out theatre – it was almost in central London, was very easy to travel to, particularly for Ken who hadn't learned to drive and depended on the Tube. The critics found it an easy place to get to as well. On the whole, they seemed to like it.

Ken was worried about the part. How could he play a boy? At thirty? He put the problem to Gordon Jackson – who told him to forget about the age and just play it naturally. Ken decided to sing the songs in what used to be described on the labels of old seventy-eight records as a 'light baritone'.

There he was on stage, a pile of magazines on a table in front of him, a pair of large glasses on his nose (and a number of young ladies dressed scantily around him), singing: 'I'm not craving to start off shaving every morning at eight. That's for adults only and I can wait . . .'

The public, on the other hand, could not wait. Five months after the opening at the Lyric, on 22 February 1956, Ken's thirtieth birthday, the show opened at the Apollo Theatre in the West End. Less than three weeks later, it closed. In the meantime, however, Ken was to glory in a moment of stardom.

The play was by Sandy Wilson, who three years earlier had had his sensational success with *The Boyfriend*. That he didn't repeat that success was not altogether expected. The anonymous reviewer in *The Tatler* noted that *The Buccaneer* 'confirmed his status as a leading musical hope of the British stage.'

Even so, David Lewin in the *Daily Express* wrote: '*The Buccaneer* is no *Boyfriend*. It is smarter, wittier and the music is more consistently melodious ...' Then he added in a line that immediately got itself engraved on Ken's innermost soul: 'The real star is the boy editor played by twenty-nine-year-old Kenneth Williams in a pair of short trousers. He has a wicked wit.'

Even Charlie Williams thought so. He was the proudest man in Shaftesbury Avenue, the night the show opened. Suddenly the very one who had thought his son was turning into a poof was cock of the walk. Customers at Marchmont Street were left in no doubt who the star of the family was. The hairdresser whose interests were restricted to the dogs and the pub suddenly started thinking about the theatre.

When he and Ken spoke – and now they were speaking to each other more than ever before – the older man had no doubt where his son was headed: 'You'll make your name in comedy,' he told him. 'Although,' as Pat recalled, 'we all thought he was going to be a fairly serious actor, perhaps the kind that Ian Holm became later on. Even a classical actor, despite his lack of stature.'

Charlie, who Pat remembers as a 'dogmatic Victorian bastard', no longer spoke of Ken 'wasting his time' in the theatre.

However, Lou recalls: 'I wouldn't say that even then their relationship was good. They really still had nothing in common.'

Pat admits that she never actually liked her father and is sure that Ken felt the same.

In *The Buccaneer* Ken had had his name in lights. It happened again in his next play, *Hotel Paradiso* in which he shared billing with Sir Alec Guinness. 'The only time Charlie was proud of me,' said Pat, 'was when he saw me in uniform, but when he saw Ken's name up there all lit up, he was *very* proud.'

Not too proud, however, to change his lifestyle. On every first night from now on there was a virtually unalterable routine. Pat would call out, 'I'll get the taxi, Dad.'

'What for?' Charlie answered.

'To take us to the theatre.'

'What do I need a taxi for? A 14 bus stops outside. I'll get the bus.'

And he did. Lou and Pat went by taxi to the theatre, dressed in what served as their finery and feeling very grand. Charlie took the 14 bus, wearing his Sunday-best suit, but never a dinner jacket, which at the time was *de rigueur* on opening nights. Charlie would never have countenanced wearing one of those. He certainly didn't own one.

'As long as he had his own way,' said Lou, remembering her husband, 'he was all right. But why should he have his own way?' The memory still rankles with her.

But the arguments over taxis and the implied criticism that both Ken and Pat extended for his lack of dressing up changed neither his personality nor the pride he felt for his son. When he got off his 14 bus and with a few minutes to spare before the curtain went up, he started wandering through the crowds milling outside the theatre. He tried to eavesdrop on their conversations hoping to hear them mention Ken's name. After the show, he repeated the same routine, this time wanting to hear favourable reactions to his son's performance. He usually did hear them. It wasn't easy to talk about the shows Ken was in now without coupling it all with the Williams name. If he didn't hear what he wanted, he prompted the discussion. 'Young Kenneth Williams was good, wasn't he?' he'd ask a total stranger, struggling to get out into the rain-soaked street and either hail a taxi or make his way to the Underground or a bus stop. Usually, he got the answer he wanted to hear.

'We were all excited by the atmosphere of the first night, watching people come in,' said Pat. 'The old man was outside looking up at the lights and talking to the other people.'

All Charlie would have really wanted was for Ken to come home with a girl. But he had given that up by now and drew his main satisfaction from his success on stage.

Hotel Paradiso was notable more than anything for the link between Ken and Alec Guinness, the newcomer who was being noted by the critics and the man who was already established as one of Britain's leading actors. His first screen role in *Great Expectations* was only ten years earlier but it had swiftly led to a succession of parts in which Guinness leapt from one triumph to another.

Oliver Twist was quickly followed by *Kind Hearts and Coronets, The Lavender Hill Mob, The Lady Killers* – all great successes.

By 1956, he was ready to go back to the stage. *Hotel Paradiso* was a farce in the typical Feydeau mould. It didn't totally thrill Ken, but it gave him a chance to see one of the masters of the stage at work – Guinness was only forty-six but had achieved so much more than Ken himself thought he could ever do, although the ambition was there in abundance. It also provided Ken with the opportunity to work with the youngest member of the cast – Billie Whitelaw – who played the French maid, as saucy as her bulging breasts and black-stockinged legs could make her.

But Miss Whitelaw was no more happy with the show than Ken was himself and they confided their doubts to each other in rehearsals and then on tour in places like Birmingham, Newcastle and Glasgow – spots on the map which Ken had got to know almost intimately from his days in rep.

Eventually, *Hotel Paradiso* came to London and opened at the Winter Garden. Alec Guinness sent Ken a bottle of champagne. He also gave him some advice. Later on during a performance, Ken noticed that the big star was jostling him – as far out of the public view as possible, and frequently behind a potted palm.

Ken couldn't understand why. When the curtain went down, he explained: the Williams flies were undone. 'Always watch your flies and blow your nose before you come out,' he advised. Ken was to say that never again, would he go out on stage without checking this essential part of his dress first – even though he always undid his trousers in his dressing room. It prevented them getting creased and made him feel a lot more comfortable.

But it was a lesson to be learned.

He was not just learning about the theatre now, he was teaching, too – in an unofficial way, writing to Annette, but teaching nevertheless. As frequently before in his correspondence, he was concerned with homosexuality on the stage.

All contemporary writing on homosexuality was basically the same. The main character just had to come to a sticky end – in the play they had seen, by committing suicide. Ken tried to analyse why this was – possibly because 'the man decides that his position is abnormal, is incompatible with his position in society'; or because he wishes to show that 'the frustration involved with abnormality is so great that the human spirit cannot bear the strain; or because the man 'believes his desires to be wicked and decides to kill his own wicked self'; or the author 'wishes to show that the homosexual, believing his desires would horrify those he loves, sacrifices himself in order to spare their feelings'.

Was Ken merely explaining the play, or was he also going into the despair felt by homosexuals? His letter referred exclusively to the play, but they were ideas he brought up in conversation with other people in the course of his life.

Indeed, in this same letter he extended the thought by going into the reasons for homosexual suicides in general – and, by the way, saying that he believed that writers constantly killed off their homosexual characters to make them seem 'heroic'.

Ken wrote in his letter, 'So we are forced to examine the position of the homosexual in society. Forced to try to understand why homosexual writing has such a self-pitying masochistic flavour. All the worst of the Oscar Wildean – Each man kills the thing he loves – philosophy so adolescent and fatuous in itself.'

The reasons, he suggested, were not hard to find. 'We have created a situation in society where more and more homosexuals are encouraged to regard themselves as persecuted. They band together and become gregarious as a result and create freemasonries of their own, in countless industries and organizations.'

Thus, Ken was demonstrating – for Annette's attention at least – his own dissociation from homosexual society. He was saying that he might be camp in his stage appearances and in conversation, but he was not interested in being part of that freemasonry himself.

Significantly, he added: 'Of course, the creative homosexual sees the trap and tries to avoid it. If he succeeds, he often only becomes a lonely bitter person pouring his frustration into his writing. Seeing himself as the proud tortured soul, who is unable to declare his love for the beautiful, but alas, normal young man and killing himself as the result.'

As far as plays in general were concerned, 'if we believe in the best, if we believe in art and the poetic vision of life, as an ennobling and enriching element in humanity, then we have our values. They are not reach-me-down and shoddy, they increase our perception, they make an eye more sharp, more intelligent, less able to be satisfied with the half truths (however cleverly expressed) and progress every day toward the ideal. That ideal of course is the unfathomable.'

He was in one of his philosophical states of mind. In another letter to 'My dearest Annette', he wrote: 'Now and again my whole life wobbles uncertainly on the tightrope of belief which I have stretched for myself over the yawning abyss that represents my particular vaccuum (*sic*).' Somewhat touchingly, he added: 'It's not always a good thing to let others see you wobbling – and then there is my terrible pride to be placated.' Ken's letters now had a new address. For the first time in his life he had a flat of his own – at Endsleigh Court in Woburn Place, much more Bloomsbury than Marchmont Street, a comparatively wide open space within easy reach of buses and a script's throw from Euston Station.

It was furnished in the same spartan fashion as his single room in Marchmont Street, no decorations, no pictures. He had to pay £800 'key money' to cover furniture and fittings which were practically non-existent. All was made a little brighter by some curtains made by his Auntie Daisy, his favourite aunt and Lou's younger sister. He would always say he liked his flat because it was nice and simple. Yet when he visited Pat's new home at Bickley, Kent, he eyed it most enviously. 'You have the knack of finding the right place.' he said. 'It's not right that you should be living like this and not me. After all, I'm the star.'

For the moment, he wasn't quite that. But there were signs that it could be happening sooner than he might have thought possible just months before.

At a *Night of a Hundred Stars* ('O! meretricious title!') benefit at the London Palladium, Ken did a double act with Zsa Zsa Gabor. He played what he called a 'Goony reporter'. Sir Laurence Olivier, who appeared with John Mills and Danny Kaye in a Teddy Boy routine, congratulated Ken on his act. 'I feel I've met you before somewhere ...' he told him. Ken reminded him of *The Beggars' Opera*. 'O God! Yes!' said Sir Larry, looking, Kenneth thought, as though he were remembering every penny he had lost on the venture.

About this time, Ken was also keeping busy with a radio play with Tony Hancock – a comparatively serious one at that by H. G. Wells, *The Man Who Could Work Miracles*.

He was also given a new West End role, in a play called *The Wit To Woo*, – no great success – but it was seen by the right people, always the best of all yardsticks in the theatre.

Ken played Kite, a somewhat less than respectful servant working in a big house. In his own book, Ken wrote that Peter Wood, the director, described him as very talented, and was, therefore, the most discerning director he had ever met. The play at the Arts Theatre didn't set any critics on fire when it opened in March 1957 and by August that year, he was ready for something new. The something new was called *Share My Lettuce*. And this time when Charlie Williams haunted the streets close to the Lyric, Hammersmith, he was hearing a buzz that stayed with him all the way back to Marchmont Street – and seemed to drown all the hairdryers and clippers he would hear for days afterwards.

SEVEN

It was one of those shows that *deserves* a cliché – a landmark. And the reason it was a landmark was because nothing in the show itself was a cliché. What it was, though, was a series of firsts.

It was the first show to confirm Kenneth Williams as a star. There was no doubt about it. Acting and clowning around and singing and laughing in *Share My Lettuce*, Kenneth Williams was a British star. For once, however, let's not dwell totally on Ken.

There was also a bespectacled Cambridge undergraduate, aged twenty-two called Bamber Gascoigne – later to be best known for his TV quiz show success *University Challenge*. He wrote *Lettuce* and had put the show on in Cambridge before it had come to London.

There was also another young man with theatrical ambitions who wondered if they would ever be satisfied, even though he had produced *The Wit To Woo*. His name, Michael Codron. He produced the show.

But then there was also the *ingénue*, a young girl with all the sparkle of a Guy Fawkes night fireworks display, who appeared in one scene in a straw boater and what looked very like a parson's dog collar and had everyone in the audience drooling – just as they had on Broadway where in *New Faces* she had had her break a few months before. Her name, Maggie Smith. She co-starred in *Share My Lettuce* with Ken.

Audiences were thrilled, box office cash registers jingled and careers were made. Even so, not everything about the show appealed to everyone. John Lambert wrote in the *Daily Express* that Maggie Smith was a 'rare commodity – a very funny girl whom most men would like to get serious with. But it's a pity she did not have a better showcase for her talents. A nibble is quite enough of this lettuce.' Mr Lambert then pointed out that there were thirty-two items in the show. 'I laughed out loud at three, smiled at four and felt sour at the rest.' Then there was this final paragraph: 'The one other consolation is a waspish young man called Kenneth Williams. He is funny and would be funnier if he were less affected.'

On the other hand, the *Sunday Express* was less equivocal. 'Maggie Smith and Kenneth Williams are two good reasons why you should take a look at a small brittle show called *Share My Lettuce* ... Kenneth Williams, the main prop of the show is a young man with a face which twists into grimaces of anguish and leers of terrible delight at the minutest provocation. He is one of the few comedians who, when someone truthfully observes, "I say, you're sitting in a dustbin", can make the classic reply, "Oh, so I am' sound like an hilarious joke."

By this time, *Share My Lettuce* had moved to the West End and the Comedy Theatre. The show, said the *Sunday Express*, 'is no food for ponderous thought. It is young, bright, light, a thin thread of turns strung together in the manner – but not with the mastery – of *Cranks*.' *Cranks* was another revue that had become a sort of watchword for the kind of show this was.

Share My Lettuce was much more of a commercial success than it was a critical triumph. The audiences didn't appear to have the reservations of the critics. For Michael Codron, it marked the start of an outstanding production career – which had seemed to bode so ill for him during the run of *The Wit To Woo*, a play that had no happier associations for him than it had for Ken.

The *Cranks* comparison was constantly being made. In *The Times*, an anonymous critic wrote: 'Resourcefully fey and lyrically frivolous, the new "diversion with music" at the Lyric, Hammersmith – *Share My Lettuce* – erratically follows in more familiar (and more varied) idioms the new directions in revue signposted by *Cranks* ... *Share My Lettuce* boasts an original if rather undernourished droll in Kenneth Williams (remember him as the alarming brat in *The Buccaneer*? His face-pulling, sidling humour has a family relationship with the hands-on-hip simpering beloved of pseudo comedians who, when in doubt, "camp it up", but Mr Williams assumes a stage personality which is elegant, faintly macabre and immensely funny, a curious blend of music hall fairy and the awful child.'

The show was very much about young people and their attitudes to life. There were sketches about parties, about dating, about jilting, and what youngsters told to their tape recorders, a novelty indeed in 1957. Ken had one of these new toys himself – and invited Annette Kerr to come and 'perform into it'.

The *News Chronicle*'s Alan Dent was convinced that Ken was the show's 'mainstay' (the *Sunday Express* said he was the 'main prop') 'an impish sprite who does many unaccountable, inscrutable and impish things'.

Ken may have been well into his thirties now, but he still saw things very much as he did as a youngster, as though the editor he had played in *The Buccaneer* had been reincarnated into the Kenneth Williams starring

– and now there was no other word for it; that was precisely what he was doing – in *Share My Lettuce*. In another letter to Annette, he wrote about love and its problems. He recalled the movie *Member of the Wedding* which he described as 'the ONLY adult film I have ever seen which made a serious attempt to analyse the idea of adolescent loneliness being the prelude to alone-ness.' In that, he was really laying on line precisely what he felt and what he enjoyed. Ken wasn't lonely, but he was a loner. That was how he liked life – chatting with people at work, going home to see mother (and, of necessity, father, but he tried to avoid that when possible now) and confining social contact to those he really wanted to be with, when he wanted to be with them. He was usually satisfied with writing his longish philosophical letters to people like Annette and only occasionally now, Val Orford.

He told Annette that he understood Chekhov's philosophy – 'That in the loving is the escape from loneliness. That nobody can really stand being loved in the ultimate sense. That it is never reciprocal in that sense. That the lover knows this and understands that love is a solitary thing, the value and quality of any love is determined solely by the lover himself or herself.'

The value and quality of Ken's performance was no secret. Bamber Gascoigne, who had never seen him at work before his show, told me: 'He was absolutely wonderful in it. He brought to it a very quirky individual.' He also enjoyed him off-stage. As he added: 'I had never been with anyone who was always so very, very funny.'

Ken was as always a perfect raconteur during his off-stage moments while in *Lettuce*. About this time, there was a family funeral – with all the mock solemnity and grandeur of a cockney day out. One of Ken's aunts had come up in the world and arrived at the cemetery wearing a fur coat which was donned purely and simply to impress the other members of the family. Ken's clan didn't take kindly to that and rounded on the woman, who sought some kind of defence. She found it in her wreath. 'What are you grumbling about?' she demanded. 'I gave the Gates of Heaven Ajar, didn't I?' Where she came from, the Gates of Heaven Ajar were the finest tribute, floral or otherwise, that she could offer. Ken told the story as though it had been scripted for him for *Hancock's Half Hour*. If Hancock himself had been around, he would have doubtless squirmed as the audience laughed their heads off.

At one stage in the show's run, he wouldn't have been alone in the squirming department. Michael Codron would have joined him. That was the day in October 1957 that Ken spent the afternoon rehearsing a new routine. When he finished he went home for a rest. 'Just 40 winks,' he told himself. The problem was that the 40 turned into something more like 400.

The audience were in their seats for the first of the two evening performances. Five minutes went by. Then seven. Then ten – and the manager came on stage to say that the star, Kenneth Williams, had been taken ill. Since the understudy was off with flu, there could be no show. People could either have their money back or tickets for another evening. Ken, of course, wasn't ill, but the management had no way of knowing. They tried phoning, but there was no reply. He had been so tired that he couldn't hear either the telephone or his alarm clock. Ultimately, he dashed out of bed and caught a cab to the theatre – where he arrived thirty minutes after what should have been curtain time, to see his erstwhile audience walking away, dejected looks on most of the faces. Fortunately, Charlie wasn't in the audience that day. Had he been, he would have made Michael Codron's chastisement seem like a love paean.

The second show of the evening went ahead as though there had been no problems. At the end of the performance, Ken was presented with a whole batch of new alarm clocks – on stage by his fellow performers. A watch and clock manufacturer had seen the PR value in Ken's predicament and cashed in – as indeed did the Comedy Theatre's box office. Ken was even invited on to television news to talk about it. What Ken, as technically-minded as ever, didn't notice was that all the clocks had been set to go off in the middle of the night – which, needless to say, they all did.

Part of the success of the show was, in its way, Ken's own success. He showed his ability to adapt his performance as either the whim took him or as he was taken by circumstances. A first-night mishap had turned into one of the funniest sketches in the whole show. This was the 'Wallflower Waltz' number – in which the girls in the show, led by Maggie Smith who sang wistfully about none of them having a dancing partner, while the men on stage waltzed with sheets of chiffon floating down from the flies. Ken was one of the men – but that night, his chiffon failed to appear. He spent the rest of the number trying to latch on to the 'partners' of all the other male dancers. None of the people on stage knew what was happening, the girls continued to sing their plaintive song and the other men danced on with their own pieces of chiffon, hoping that Ken would go away and disappear for ever. But he wasn't in the disappearing business. As he tried to grab hold of the beautifully-lit see-through material held by the other men in the show, he called out, 'Give me a bit! I ain't got a bit! Give us a bit! You've got my bit!' The girls continued to sing, 'Wallflower waltz, where we sit around the walls ...' Meanwhile, the audience were all but collapsing in their seats, as Kenneth danced around like, as he put it, 'a demented fairy, asking for a bit'. After the show, Michael Codron ordered the number to be performed exactly the same way for every performance thereafter.

Codron felt the same way about Ken as Bamber Gascoigne had felt – and knew he had cast the right man in the right sort of roles. 'He just made one laugh so much,' he told me.

'There was something about him that made me know he was the best revue star we had.'

He was more than that by now. *Hancock's Half Hour* may have finished for him, but there was another big radio show on the way. He had just made a pilot for what was hoped to be a series called *Beyond Our Ken* – although the Ken in the title was not he but one of the most respected performers on radio, Kenneth Horne. Simultaneously, he was working on a TV series, *Dick and the Duchess* and in *Share My Lettuce* at night. There was no suggestion, however, that anyone would be allowed to think they were sharing their Williams. For him at that moment, the show was not just the thing, it was the priority. Michael Codron had reason to be grateful that it was, especially when in January 1958 it transferred for a third time – or even a fifth, if the pre-West End runs at the Theatre Royal Brighton, and the original Cambridge version, were taken into account – to the Garrick Theatre. Business was so good a new home had to be found when the Comedy had to go on to other previously arranged bookings.

Ken and Codron had got together professionally in the first place because of what he called their 'Grill and Cheese relationship'. The Grill and Cheese was the first-floor restaurant in Lyons Corner House at Coventry Street, in between Piccadilly Circus and Leicester Square. The Corner Houses were London institutions. They were huge baroque establishments set up by J. Lyons and Co., as a sort of poor-man's Café Royal – several different kinds of restaurants and cafeterias under one roof. One entered the building – and there were other Corner Houses at Marble Arch and the Strand – via a large marble hall where the overpowering, but pleasant, smell of the delicatessen on sale there mingled with the warmth of Lyons tea being brewed all around.

Downstairs was the brasserie where a palm-court orchestra would play selections from the shows of the day. Up on the first floor, in the Grill and Cheese, Ken would hold court for his various theatrical acquaintances – although few of them were really close friends.

It was the talk of the trade that Ken would be outrageous there on certain afternoons of the week, telling about his great aunt and the Gates of Heaven Ajar or pulling one of his fellow actors down to his own idea of size. Michael Codron had been going there as part of the Kenneth Williams set since the time he worked for the Jack Hylton organization.

Codron had gone up to Cambridge to see the show and knew then that it would be worth bringing to London. He also judged that Ken would be excellent as that 'main prop' the critic was to write about. 'I thought he showed great courage in agreeing to be in what was after all an undergraduate revue.' What he should also have realized was that, although the play had been a flop, *The Wit To Woo* demonstrated to Ken that the producer was a man to be trusted.

For Codron it was very much a turning point. 'Had it not gone, I was about to give up the idea of being a producer in my own right.' As it was, the show had 'gone' very well indeed. 'I had done two shows with spectacular unsuccess. I was looking for something in my own hand-writing. Knowing Bamber Gascoigne, I went to see the show and knew that it really was my cup of tea.'

It established one other thing, Ken was now one of the producer's best friends, in fact, the only actor friend whom he had.

But Ken had friends a-plenty, even if he didn't always recognize them as such.

One night two men very big in British film comedy came to see the show. Their names were Gerald Thomas and Peter Rogers. They had a movie idea they wanted to try out and there was a part in it for Ken if he wanted it. If he wanted it? One short discussion with Peter Eade convinced him that want it he did. The film was going to be called *Carry On Sergeant*. No one could have any idea to where that was going to lead.

EIGHT

Nobody thought that much of *Carry on Sergeant*. It was a very low-budget British picture, shot at Pinewood studios in black and white and sought to do little more than provide an entertaining hour and a half or so, with a topic to which a great many people could relate – National Service.

It was the dying days of the citizen Army, the young men who were reluctantly called up to serve their Queen and country – to learn how to fire a gun, to march in step and to use contraceptives when they took out the girl from the NAAFI on Saturday nights.

There were all sorts of jokes about National Service and this was going to be one of them – the barracks filled with misfits who no more wanted to wear a khaki uniform than they felt like taking poison (which some of them thought was what they were given three times a day in the cook-house).

The real success formula became evident from the very begining – a mixture of good humour, innuendo, cliché, double-entendre all mixed together in a cauldron of what was plainly goodwill and a desire for a good time.

All the ingredients would be there in *Carry on Sergeant* and although most of the stock characters would come later, the basic idea was evident from the first ever laughs for a 'Carry On' film in 1958. Already, the lavatory jokes and the sickroom banter were there – well, of course they were. Going to see the doctor meant taking your clothes off. Hattie Jacques was the army doctor. Sex appeal? In a way, the fat lady doctor turned sex on to its head and in those prepermissive days when no woman appeared on screen showing more than a couple of inches of cleavage, it was enough.

There was also Kenneth Connor, another mainstay of the team. He played a part that was made to measure, a scarf-wearing, nose-blowing hypochondriac who Dr Jacques was to put firmly in his place. Of course, there had to be the barrack weakling. Charles Hawtrey played him and repeated the part in almost every 'Carry On' film that followed.

And then there was Ken as James Bailey, the egghead who knew more about everything than anyone else and never stopped saying so. It was all beneath his dignity, this business of charging around with rifles in your hand and going on parade.

Terry Scott played a sergeant (and then disappeared until quite a bit later in the series).

There were also all the stock characters in an army unit who stayed on when the Pinewood machine swept into the sequel business. Bob Monkhouse – already established as a leading comedy writer and just moving into performing – playing the poor wretch called up on his wedding day and Shirley Eaton as the NAAFI girl who would come back for just one more 'Carry On'.

The plot in any 'Carry On' film was never terribly important, not when there were the opportunities to give words double meanings that even the scripwriters sometimes hadn't thought of. In *Carry on Sergeant*, the story was probably more important than in most of the other components of the series. Here we had a poor suffering sergeant – he suffered a very great deal every time a new 'shower' like this lot came his way – just on the verge of retirement. He dreamed of going out in glory, winning the best-platoon prize – a dream that appeared to be shattered when he saw Ken and his barrack mates arrive.

The Sergeant was played by William Hartnell, best known as the first of TV's *Dr Who*. Even he got a few of the good lines, none better than when a malingerer produced a succession of 'chits' excusing him one arduous duty after the other. Looking at the man, he says, 'You're nothing but a pile of chits.' That went down very well indeed among the squaddies of 1958.

Hovering in the background to it all was the commanding officer (played by Eric Barker, also to be seen in a few of the other early 'Carry On' films) and his instruction that was so familiar to every 'sprog' who ever put on a uniform, 'Carry on Sergeant'.

No one, least of all Peter Rogers and Gerald Thomas, had any intention of its forming the foundation stone for one of the most successful series that the British film industry ever spawned.

'You don't go out of your way to make a series,' said Peter Rogers, who produced the entire batch. 'It was a piece of luck really – and quite an accident. You only make a series by public demand.'

Carry on Sergeant may have been made on something of a shoestring (or maybe it should have been an army bootstring) with Ken making no more than £800 for his work, but efforts *were* made to get it all remarkably accurate. Part of the location work was shot at the Queen's Barracks in the heart of the Surrey countryside at Stoughton. It became a rule of the 'Carry On' outfit that everything had to be filmed within spitting distance of Pinewood – and there were real sergeants to carry on the business of teaching them what life in the Army was like. To Ken, it was all too reminiscent of his own life in the Army, but he enjoyed the filming. It made a nice change from *Share My Lettuce* to which he switched every evening. But in May 1958 even that show came to an end – a London bus strike was killing business, which also gives some idea of how long ago that was. Today so few threatregoers travel by bus that it would take more than a strike of the red giants to kill anything on stage.

Nothing, however, seemed to kill *Carry on Sergeant*. The two men behind the project, Gerald Thomas who directed and Peter Rogers, were as surprised as the audiences. They were also as pleased as the audiences.

As Gerald Thomas told me: 'Our success appeared to be based on the demise of the British music hall, the slightly lavatorial humour that appealed to father and son alike – and to the fact that people knew what they were getting, like Heinz baked beans or Lux toilet soap.'

Pat Williams told me she thought they were ' a load of tripe', but it was tripe that brought people into the cinemas for more than two decades and Ken became the staple part of a diet for which at one time the public seemed to have an insatiable appetite

Because both Rogers and Thomas had seen *Share My Lettuce* they knew he would be good for the part of the supercilious National Serviceman. 'But he came to us through normal casting,' said Rogers. 'We wanted a certain type and Betty White, our casting director, said there was this young man in revue we ought to have a look at.' They did have a 'look at' Ken in *Share My Lettuce* and concluded that she was right.

What appealed to both partners was that by doing so well in the revue, Ken had become an established comedy actor – not comedian, but comedy actor – and that was the kind they were looking for. They didn't want to have to break in a newcomer.

In 1958 Ken's star was rising faster than anyone who had known him could have thought possible. But by joining the 'Carry On' team he was not necessarily doing himself a great favour. In Peter Rogers's words, 'He lost the ambition to go outside.'

He certainly had it in the early days of *Carry On Sergeant*. Ken himself would have gone along with Michael Codron's judgement of being the finest revue actor of the day – not realizing that revue was about to go the way of music hall. He did have the ambition to do more serious work, as he had in *Saint Joan* and he had done in those early days in rep, but suddenly, he had got sucked into a formula that became a very comfortable rut indeed and, surprisingly for those who thought they knew him well, he didn't want to find a way out.

'Kenny wasn't an ugly bugger but he was no romantic lead,' said Gerald Thomas. 'He was a good actor limited to the parts he could play, but he wasn't an attractive man. So comedy was his forte.'

He was also, as Peter Rogers put it, 'a bit of a show off', discussing art and the world scene in an off-screen moment that was as different from a 'Carry On' routine as *Moby Dick* had been from *Peter Pan*. He also played cards with other members of the crew as they sat in their canvas-backed chairs waiting for the cameras to roll.

The success of *Carry on Sergeant* did dictate that there would be another 'Carry On' as soon as the finance and the equipment and the cast could be assembled. After the first success, that could never be in doubt.

There was also another stage show planned. Meanwhile, the pilot of *Beyond Our Ken* was listened to by the BBC mandarins, who decided they liked a great deal about it and decreed it would definitely become a radio series. Ken was a veritable factory of show business activity. His own brand of performing was taking on a very definite shape. Suddenly, he became synonymous with that new word 'camp' and he revelled in it.

It couldn't have come at a better time. The *Hancock Half Hours* seemed to be finally at an end and both Ken and his public were ready for something in which 'Stop messing about' would mean something more than an admonition to an actor to concentrate on his script.

The strange thing – and the rewarding thing – about these events was that they coincided. At the same time as a new, totally devoted audience had been found for a different kind of comedy film, an equally devoted public was on hand for his radio show.

It is in a way, of course, unfair to call it Ken's radio show, Kenneth Williams's, that is. It belonged almost in its entirety to Kenneth Horne, around whom the show was built, but there was enough left over for the supporting players, Betty Marsden, Hugh Paddick, Bill Pertwee and Ken, all of whom built up their won individual following.

It was a vastly different audience from that for the *Carry On* films, a more sophisticated group who followed Ken from *Hancock* and wanted more of the voices he had introduced, much to Hancock's growing distaste. Ken himself always said that it was a modernized version of the kind of radio entertainment that Tommy Handley had brought with his famous wartime comedy series, ITMA ('It's That Man Again'). That was an oversimplification and did neither of the shows full justice.

Ken produced some of his standard characters that were to become as closely identified with him as was 'Stop messing about' – which didn't disappear totally from the airways. Much to his evident surprise, he was invited back to do another Hancock series, but by then the show was in its death throes and Ken no more wanted to be a part of it than Hancock wanted to have him. He was reduced to saying one or two lines, then disappearing. Ken, never the most modest man about his talents, finally declared himself mortally offended and after four episodes was out for ever.

He was proud of the fact that he could switch from serious drama to the comedy of radio and the 'Carry On' film.

Beyond Our Ken was a different situation entirely from *Hancock's Half Hour*, partly due to the fact that its leading character was a totally different sort of personality. Kenneth Horne was a professional entertainer who neither looked nor sounded the part. He was also a highly successful businessman, the extremely active chairman of two public limited companies, so he didn't need the money that radio brought him. One could therefore have been forgiven for wondering if he took it all totally seriously. He did, which accounts for the show's huge success.

His demeanour however, was closer to the big businessman than the professional comedian, so there was always the lingering suspicion that he was really the benevolent boss who made the directors laugh at board meetings and probably did conjuring tricks at the weekend. The fact that he appeared for every show wearing an immaculate double-breasted blue suit with a carnation in his lapel only served to further that reputation. You had to be in on the script meetings and the rehearsals to realize that underneath that company executive exterior lurked a funny man who took it all very seriously indeed.

Horne had first made his name on radio in the days when most people still called it the wireless – on another wartime show which supposedly told everything you ever wanted to know about an RAF station. This was *Much Binding In The Marsh*. Horne and his aide Richard Murdoch were both RAF officers when the show had its debut. It was so hugely successful that it was still being broadcast long after they were both demobilized.

Kenneth Williams was a marvellous prop for Kenneth Horne and like all good props, sometimes it seemed as if the whole thing would collapse without him. When he played the old rustic Arthur Fallowfield, radio audiences all over Britain – to say nothing of those listening to the BBC's various overseas services – sat up waiting for the virtually immortal words, 'the answer lies in the soil'. And that answer fitted every question he was asked, as did his response to any poser that could be put to him, 'thirty-five years'.

Then there was the traffic jam. Ken in a car, joining the taxi driver and the lady motorist and the cockney labourer stuck behind faulty traffic lights. 'You've been listening,' announced Ken in a pointed BBC accent, 'to an excerpt from *Forever Amber.*'

In one episode of the show he played a cloakroom attendant marrying a ladies' lavatory superintendent. 'You might call it' he said, 'a marriage of convenience.'

And there was the pair, Rodney and Charles. Ken playing Rodney, Hugh Paddick as Charles, two frightfully, frightfully Mayfair types, doing ridiculous things together like dressing up as red Indians when they took a canoeing holiday.

Ken enjoyed the show. He also greatly enjoyed Kenneth Horne, although his memory of the show in his autobiography was somewhat limited. He recalled, however, enjoying Ken's warm-up to the audience before a show's recording – 'For those of you who are not familiar with the studios, remember the Ladies is on the right and the Gents is on the left – no I'm sorry, the Gents is on the right and the ladies is ... oh, what does it matter? You'll make a lot of new friends.'

Ken also gratefully remembered Horne's kindness. Once when Williams was ill, Horne called at his flat and dropped through his letter box details of a holiday plan which he though might do him some good. He didn't stay for Ken's thanks. Things like that were not forgotten in a hurry.

A great deal of the success for the show was due to its writers. Barry Took, who wrote the first forty shows of the series with Bernard Merriman, remembers it all with an affection that is certainly not confined to the money it bought him.

They had appeared together, Ken and he, in an early BBC TV show hosted by Gilbert Harding, but the first time they really worked together was on *Beyond Our Ken*, a show that he remembers somewhat less affectionately than the later *Round The Horne*. 'It was rather cliché-ridden,' he told me. It didn't prevent it being a huge public success.

Part of that was undoubtedly due to Ken. 'He was easy to work with; wonderfully professional. He was a Stradivarius among performers; a perfect instrument on which you could play anything. He wasn't a composer as such but a great translator, not just a violin but also a violinist, an Itzhak Perlman of actors.'

He was conscious that this loner of a man lived only for his work.

But he was aware of Ken's sexual problems, just as he had confessed then in those letters to Val Orford and Annette Kerr. 'He had a tremendously guilty conscience about his desires.' Ken once told him that he greatly envied his 'Carry On' mate Charles Hawtrey. 'He can sit in a bar and pick up sailors and have a wonderful time. I couldn't do it.' He was aware of his fastidiousness in his living habits and his health concerns which only got worse and worse.

Meanwhile, the Kenneth Williams show business operation went rolling ahead like a steam locomotive. Peter Eade had never been so busy in his life, answering telephone calls, personal visitors and piles of letters that came with scripts for Ken's attention. If success is measured by the thickness of the pile of scripts on offer – and to many people it is – then Ken was very successful indeed.

He took part in a television series starring Billie Whitelaw called *Time Out For Peggy*, playing a verse writer for a greetings card manufacturer, and in a Margaret Rutherford TV play, *The Noble Spaniard*. He also had two more demanding projects – pantomime and a second *Carry On* film.

Like Kenneth Horne, he had to take his work as seriously as though he were about to play Macbeth – and he did, every trouser-dropping, each double-entendre reciting, any nasal-sounding 'stop messing about' moment.

Meanwhile, Ken was back on the London stage once more – with the role of one of the ugly sisters in the London Coliseum's production of *Cinderella* – which, despite his and other interpretations was not quite a pantomime. For one thing, the score was by Rodgers and Hammerstein who had never seen a pantomime in their lives – such things were totally unknown on the other side of the Atlantic – and wrote music and lyrics for the show which fitted very well indeed in their repertoire that began with *Oklahoma*! and went on, via such epics as *South Pacific* and *The King And I*, all the way to *The Sound of Music*. The other difference was that Prince Charming was not, as convention dictated, played by the principal boy who, of course, was always a girl, but by the singer Bruce Trent. So there was much about it that was like a Broadway musical. On the other hand, there was Cinderella herself played by Yana, an enticingly beautiful singer of the day whose hit, 'Climb Up The Garden Wall' made many a man feel like doing precisely that. Buttons was played by a young Tommy Steele and Ken was Portia, a sister so ugly that he almost frightened himself every time he looked in the mirror. His face was rouged and he wore voluminous skirts covered in electric light bulbs – powered by a huge battery strapped to a leg.

Reaction to the show was encouraging and word of mouth most rewarding of all. People were constantly coming to see Ken in his dressing room. One night, Noël Coward beat the familiar trail. Ken remembers part of the story of that visit in his autobiography – but only part. He recalls with pride. 'The Master's' praise for his 'dreadfully vulgar' walk and his assessment of Ken's 'wonderful' performance. He also remembers telling the older man that a lot of his best lines were cut – (Coward's injunction – put them back in again, if only gradually, which, he said, he knew that he would do anyway).

What Ken did not tell was that he was sitting on a chamber pot when Sir Noel walked into the dressing room. He always had a deep mistrust of other people's lavatories and, indeed, would never allow a visitor to his own flat to use his. When he moved into a theatre, his own toilet went with him.

He was at this time already suffering from an ailment from which he and his friends would suffer until the end of his life – piles. The affliction was a subject for after-dinner conversation whenever he felt like talking about it, which was almost every time he ever had a conversation.

There is nothing on record to show that he and Coward discussed the affliction at the time of their Coliseum meeting, but they probably did. They also no doubt discussed the album of songs by Sir Noël that Ken had just recorded for HMV. Ken was nervous of cutting a disc. He said that he didn't sound like 'The Master' and was frightened of upsetting him, but the label checked with the composer and the approval was granted. It wasn't easy for him. As he said, he not only had to learn the very complicated lines but also how to copy Coward's abdominal breathing techniques. In the end, he achieved 'Mad Dogs and Englishmen' and 'Don't Put Your Daughter On The Stage, Mrs Worthington'. At times – but only at times – he sounded more like Coward than Coward did. He even had the temerity to do an ad-lib at the end of the 'Mrs Worthington' number. To the injunction against the daughter going on the stage, he added ... 'or your son'. 'The Master' did not complain.

Nor did most people who heard the record – some of them were tempted to buy it after seeing Ken in *Cinderella*.

The newspapers confined themselves to the show itself. 'Whatever money can buy this show has set out to buy,' wrote John Thompson in the *Daily Express*. As a pay-off to his review of a production that relied 'too much on spectacular effects', he wrote: 'Kenneth Williams makes a most malicious Ugly Sister; a nice professional performance this. But all that money has not bought enough magic.'

Magic, however, seemed to precisely describe the success of the 'Carry On' formula after the *Sergeant* film.

Carry On Nurse was the first sequel, the first picture to demonstrate that the *Carry On Sergeant* formula could be transferred. Moving it from the training camp ground to the hospital ward was the most commercial – and seemingly the most obvious – course to be taken. There was always such a lot of scope in hospitals, certainly far more than in the Army sick room. There were bed-baths and nurses – nurses who if they didn't yet seem to be bursting out of their brassières, were certainly stretching their blouses to danger point. Hattie Jacques was the matron, a part so suited to her size and manner that the very occupation of hospital head nurse might have been created for her, let alone the role in 'Carry On' films. Ken played a role very similar to his *Sergeant* part, the snooty intellectual thrust into a society not of his choosing – this time the ward he shared with the likes of Kenneth Connor and Leslie Phillips. Shirley Eaton looked fetching in her nurse's uniform and a young probationer nurse was laying the tracks for a totally new profession for herself as the overemotional wallflower among the blossoming beauties of the hospital. She was a youngster called Joan Sims.

This was officially based on a play called *Ring For Catty*, about life in a TB sanatorium, although once the 'Carry On' formula was applied any resemblance between the two was almost purely coincidental. The amazing thing about this second 'Carry On' was not so much that it succeeded at all, but that it outgrossed the first in the series. Even more surprisingly, this little black and white indictment of the National Health Service did almost as well in the United States as it did in Britain.

Peter Rogers knew he had hit a gold mine, even if it didn't always seem to the performers that he was totally on their side. Like the time he told an actor who demanded funnier lines because he was a comedian – 'your secret is safe with me'.

Rogers always seemed as unlike a comedy film producer as Kenneth Horne differed from the conventional idea of comedian. He speaks with a public school accent and looks every inch the business executive he, of course, is. His ingredients for success were the same as those of practically everyone connected with the series. While the films were being made, they represented the most important work any of them could ever have done.

Audiences felt much the same way. To them, the Kenneth Williams voices and the Kenneth Williams faces, the flared nostrils and that snide look that had become as much a trademark as the 'stop messing about' sounds on radio were instantly recognizable. People seeing 'Carry On' films found it all as natural as those who a generation earlier had greeted the squeal of bobby soxers for Frank Sinatra or, before that earlier the sight of Al Jolson in blackface.

That was stardom and Kenneth Williams was a star, even if his appeal was mostly on home territory. The success of *Carry On Nurse* in America didn't alter the fact that the fans were mostly in Britain and the Commonwealth, but the mail poured in from places as far apart as Kenya and Hong Kong.

Perhaps the audiences realized that in that film, Ken was stretching even his normal acting powers. It was the first acting venture in which he was called upon to perform a love scene. He worried about that, but even if it had succeeded simply because it was just another of the ridiculous and unbelievable antics in a 'Carry On' film, succeed it did. Certainly, he never looked for one moment as though there were a dose of castor oil beneath his nose. His partner was the curvaceous Jill Ireland, who made it all seem no less exciting to her than would have been an embrace from Gregory Peck. It was, of course, long before her marriage to Charles Bronson and her ultimately unsuccessful battle against cancer. Ken was undoubtedly happy with himself. He left the set that day looking for all the world like a nine-stone weakling who had just thrown sand in the face of the beach bully.

Surprisingly perhaps, Jill, the extraordinarily feminine beauty, and Ken, who spent so much of his life these days camping himself, became great friends. 'They got on so well together, it was amazing,' Gerald Thomas told me. Thomas was by now the delight of his cast who appreciated his avuncular style, so different from the more urbane Peter Rogers.

This was not the only 'Carry On' film that year. *Carry On Teacher* was the second in 1959 and the third in the series. In this, Ken played a drama instructor caught up in the then current controversy over corporal punishment. The script had him deliver a line that was in sharp contrast to most of the seemingly right-wing reactionary statements he was making whenever a camera wasn't turning or when a curtain was not up: 'Extraordinary theory – you bend a child double in order to give him an upright character.'

Most of the other characters in the film were upright to their now expected formulae; Joan Sims, Charles Hawtrey and Kenneth Connor were members of the staff room – led by the formidable-as-ever Hattie Jacques, as the maths mistress who wore her gown and mortar board as much in this film as she had worn her matron's uniform in the previous one. Leslie Phillips played a psychiatrist and the part of the headmaster was played by the popular radio comedian Ted Ray – making his only 'Carry On' picture (he would have made more, but Associated British who had him under contract but had never used him, refused to allow him to make them).

Ken now was ready to go back to stage revue, as though he wanted to translate some of the craziness of 'Carry On' to that more sophisticated theatre public. The answer was the most successful of all his shows of that kind, *Pieces of Eight*.

NINE

Pieces of Eight marked a new self-confident Kenneth Williams who had only occasionally revealed himself until then. The star was also the boss. Not in the employer-employee sense, but as the man who was able to walk on stage, argue with the director and get his own way without having to have Noël Coward behind him before he would reinstate lines that someone else had cut.

Revue was on its way out. There could be no doubt about that, the public taste was already showing signs of wanting something else on stage. The intimacy of television meant that this strange animal that liked to subtitle itself 'intimate revue' had to be breathing its last. That did not mean that it wouldn't go out in style. It was still bright, highly professional and while it still had a very little life, Kenneth Williams was its king. 'He was the best revue star we ever had,' said Michael Codron. 'And it's a great pity that revue died – and virtually died with us.'

It opened at the Apollo Theatre in September 1959 and was widely acclaimed. Charlie Williams took his number 14 bus to Shaftesbury Avenue, looked at Ken's name in lights and had he heard anyone say anything against 'the boy' would have had no difficulty in punching him one. Not that Ken appreciated it. Lou was still the goddess of Marchmont Street, his confidante, his regular companion. Charlie was an embarrassment who was safely left ignored in a corner of his life that he didn't really have to reveal if he didn't choose to do so.

He was much more concerned with what the critics would think of it all. They gave Ken the best reviews he had had to date – and the best he could possibly wish for.

Bernard Levin praised Ken's 'malicious brilliance', which was praise indeed.

The *Evening Standard* wrote of 'the genius of Kenneth Williams', so more could not possibly have been said. 'It is Kenneth Williams's evening. A good deal of expendable material is saved by this small urchin actor who can deafen the upper circle with a single sniff of disapproval and apparently rearrange his features at will.'

And if that were not enough, the paper's critic went on: 'His performance is continually kept from affectation by underlying cockney savagery;
he releases in us all the longing to put out tongues, chalk on walls and
pull faces behind the back of authority.'

Patrick Gibbs of the *Daily Telegraph* liked him almost as much. Gibbs
described the show as a 'bright, lively little entertainment, especially clever
in the way it picks a middle path between the demands of sophisticated
and popular taste.'

It was one of the only revues to take music seriously. The producers
cared about the songs as much as about the sketches. As much care was
taken getting the tunes right as getting the set for the cricket scene
organized.

Ken, as that star, received star treatment from this reviewer of the
revue – which incidentally got its title from being a company of eight
performing at eight o'clock each evening. 'The specialist in nonsense,'
he wrote, 'was Kenneth Williams. As an insistent talker in a railway carriage
who was carrying a viper in a cardboard box or as a thin man bewailing
his bad luck at being unable to apply for the job of fat man at the fair,
he provided great amusement largely by the assumption of odd accents
and the pulling of extraordinary faces.' Perhaps the best part of the show
was the 'If only ...' sketch in which he reflected on what might have
been.

Ken also played a man selling luminous leprechauns and a newspaper
seller talking inconsequential nonsense to the proprietor of a coffee stall.
That sketch was written by Harold Pinter and he played it straight –
the way Pinter wrote it, with the nuances that Pinter intended, the pauses
in the right place.

They were all things to which the audience could relate and the more
they related the more they laughed – which gave instant satisfaction not
just to Charlie Williams and Lou (who, of course, thought that everything
her Ken did was wonderful) but to Michael Codron, the producer and
the young man who wrote it all – Peter Cook.

Actually, it was Cook who killed off the revue form. His *Beyond The
Fringe* was so innovative that nothing could follow it.

Codron told me that one of the most potent memories he had of *Pieces
of Eight* was the 'violent love-hate relationship' Ken had with his co-star
Fenella Fielding. She was in some ways, a female Kenneth Williams, an
eccentric who could emote facially and vocally in a way in which Ken
had established himself the master.

Ken's equally eccentric behaviour towards her became evident early on in the out-of-town try-outs in Brighton, Liverpool and Oxford. 'He was very ruthless,' Fenella told me. 'When we were out of town, he terrified me, absolutely put the fear of God into me.'

Sometimes it seemed that the fear of God or of some other supernatural force was well inside of Ken, too. As Michael Codron recalled: 'You could never say that Kenneth was ever happy. But I never saw him depressed. He got very angry quite often– when actors were not doing what he thought was professionally required of them.'

In a more relaxed moment – and there were not many of these – Ken told Fenella that he always felt 'obliged to go much more out on a limb than most people.' It was as though he were making up for inadequacies of which he was aware but which he tried to pretend were not there.

But they were obvious to most people, even though they were magnified by those who didn't know him well. This became clear to Fenella during the Liverpool run.

They walked together across a cobbled square. Ken was in his usual attire of raincoat over flannel trousers. Fenella was dressed entirely in black, a black sweater over a black skirt, black stockings and on top of the outfit a black hat covering all her hair. She looked like a refugee from one of those films that at the time constantly glamourized the Paris left bank – like Audrey Hepburn in *Funny Face* or Juliet Greco in so many roles.

She admits she was outlandish in her appearance, a walking exaggeration. But she was also beautiful and had a marvellously expressive voice. She was also totally heterosexual.

That was, of course, not what people automatically thought of Ken. As they walked across the square, the cobbles echoing the sound of their feet, someone threw a stone – then two, then three. A gang of boys were using Kenneth Williams as a mobile target.

'I don't remember what he did,' she told me, 'so I suppose he didn't do anything.' And charitably she added: 'To this day, I don't know if it was because of what he looked like or because of what I looked like.' As she says, the way she dressed wasn't exactly usual for Liverpool in those days.

Fenella was an old Kenneth Williams fan. She used to regularly get tickets for *Hancock's Half Hour* radio shows simply for the chance to see Ken at work – 'Men used to fight to escort me to the broadcasts.' It was the popularity of the show rather than herself she had in mind, although her own extraordinarily sexy form in those days *could* just have had something to do with it.

She told me she worried about working with him in the show. 'He had a very low boredom threshold.'

One evening, he took her into a side room at the theatre to emphasize just how bad and terrible and boring he thought it all was. He particularly disliked a sketch by Pinter and Cook which Fenella describes as 'beautifully written' – but Ken thought it was rubbish. 'We've got to revitalize and ad-lib it,' he told her. She admits that she trusted him totally and went along with his judgement – a fact, she tends today to regret somewhat. 'But he was very single-minded then and the fact that something was very good already did not mean he could not improvise.'

And because people knew he was going to do so, they came back night after night to see how things were changed. 'It became a kind of cult,' she remembered. 'Sometimes the whole show was a mass of ad-libs. But if he were tired, we'd go back to the original which was terrific.'

The love-hate relationship was obvious to her as well as to Codron and the others around them. 'He wanted me to be good,' she explained, 'but not too good. So it became a tussle between us. He either wouldn't give me a line or would say my line himself.' Such behaviour is not guaranteed to foster good relations between two self-respecting performers and neither did it between them. The tennis game to which Ken had likened comedy was now a ping-pong match between two equally determined performers, neither of whom wanted to allow their ball to fall to the floor.

'Sometimes, though,' she confessed, 'it was wonderful – bliss because he was so good. He, however, always called the shots.'

Simultaneously with doing the evening performances – two on Saturday, at five and eight – he was recording episodes of *Beyond Our Ken* and making the latest 'Carry On' film – *Carry On Constable* – and it began to show with the way *Pieces of Eight* proceeded. The cult followers who came every night started getting a little disappointed – Ken was following the script which the tougher the regimen became more and more rigid.

'If he were tired,' said Miss Fielding, 'he would put me in the driving seat – except that my part wasn't written for that to happen. It seemed to me he was trying to turn an apple into an orange or an aeroplane into a horse.' As she added: 'He was a genius and geniuses tend to be kind of childlike. But he was pleased when I did take off at his command. Like a baby, he did what he wanted to do.'

At those times, they got on well together. She kept on his wavelength by talking about the subjects that pleased him most – and these frequently concentrated on the state of his behind. 'I used to initiate talk about his bum by my own behaviour,' she admitted to me. 'I was taken to squeezing people's behinds. I used to stand in the wings and feel his bum.'

Sometimes, he complained about his front, too. Ken arrived on stage in a flying scene – an entrance which Fenella Feilding remembers as 'stunning'. He flew on to the stage on wires attached to a harness which, she said, 'is terribly painful for chaps. He always used to complain about it.'

There were times when he was just plain outrageous. I remember myself calling at his dressing room during the run of *Pieces of Eight*. He was by now active in Actors Equity, a member of the council, and there was a running sore in the profession – about the state of theatre green rooms. 'Things are *terrible*,' he told me. 'Come on, have a look.' Instead of going into the green room, we went to the girls' dressing room. 'Come on have a good look while you can. They've all got nothing on.' Not that ladies in the theatre bothered very much about that.

Fenella's complaints continued to be mostly about the way he treated her on stage. 'He would make up chunks of speech for me. Then he'd pinch my lines which, of course, I couldn't repeat, so I'd be left speechless.' Even today, she doesn't think he was being cruel in doing that. 'I think he was more self-centred than evil.'

The real crunch came, however, in the sketch that regularly brought the roof down at the Apollo. They both played spies – 'spies who meet up in that ludicrous wonderland of revue'. She herself was dressed in sequins from head to toe. He wore a black suit and a black hat. 'Each of us was complaining about the spies' equipment with which we had both been issued. He was saying that I had a better disguise than he did. We both had death pills. I would die first – leaving him to die on stage while I went off into the wings.'

One night, he refused to allow her to die. He wouldn't feed her the line that would enable her to end her days peacefully in public view. That was the night the love turned into all hate.

'Instead of trying to outdo him, I stopped still – and said, "Last one dead is a Cissy." I died – and walked off in the dark.'

To Ken that remark was like a public statement impugning behaviour on his part that was still completely illegal. 'It wasn't long before I wished I had never said that. He was shaking. He was like a piece of jelly, like someone who had no bones.'

He wasn't just mortally offended. He was embarrassed more than he had ever felt in public before. It was one thing behaving in his limp way whenever he himself felt like doing so. It was quite another having someone else call those kind of shots. 'You called me a homosexual in front of the audience,' he proclaimed, those nostrils now flared in genuine anger. 'Why?'

She replied that she had no such intention. It was the kind of thing that children at the time said constantly in the playground. He was not to be mollified.

'He didn't speak to me for months. I asked the management to release me from my contract.' They begged her not to take it so much to heart and pleaded with Ken to regard it all as a joke not to be treated seriously.

Plainly, she had said something that was too close to his real personality for comfort. It was something that he took very much to heart, but to this day, she doesn't see it that way. 'It had nothing to do with his homosexuality,' she maintains. 'It was an excuse. He didn't like to be bested.' They talked sex, the way he talked about it to many people with whom he grew close in a working relationship. He told her he didn't have sex of any kind. 'Because it allows me to be single-minded in my work.' Before long, he agreed that it suited his single-minded purpose to make peace with his co-star. They didn't discuss the matter again.

Needless to say, what Ken wanted mattered. Without him in this show there would quite frankly have been no show. He was having an increasingly similar role to play in his other work, even though in the 'Carry On' pictures he was just one of a team and in *Beyond Our Ken* was playing second fiddle to the other Kenneth.

There was a great deal of respect for what he did. As Hugh Paddick told me: 'We respected each other's work. I liked him enormously. I knew him very well. I think I knew him better than he thought I did.'

After a while, there was almost a telepathy between them. 'I think the success of our "Hello Rodney, Hello Charles" routine was that it never sounded rehearsed – which I suppose it wasn't. It was like the old-time variety acts who just came in with their music, performed and went away again.'

They never read the scripts until they walked into the narration room for what was supposed to be the rehearsal. Ken would start off telling us about his week and then go into the same – what I would call – bumhole jokes, always the same about the problems he had with his bum. But even though week after week the jokes were the same, we always laughed. We read our lines together for the first time – but never as we would do them on the actual recording.

'Ken was such a brilliant bloke that if he had an idea of how to deliver a line, he'd try to find a way to block it. Not in an evil way at all, but if you gave him half a chance he'd hammer you into the ground and stamp on you. But he could be pricked like a balloon.'

Answer him back, recalls Paddick, 'and he would crumple. He would be so apologetic!'

Ken tried to make friends if he thought he'd upset a colleague whom he did respect or value. On one occasion he asked Paddick out for dinner. 'I thought he meant at his place, but, of course, he never invited anyone to his home for dinner. So we went to a restaurant in the King's Road.'

That evening revealed a petulance Hugh Paddick had not known before, but which would become quite familiar to the few Williams intimates. They arrived at the restaurant, were shown to a table, handed menus and started a reasonably convivial conversation either about Ken's rear-end, the radio show or about *Pieces of Eight* which finally closed in the autumn of 1960.

Suddenly, a fact struck Ken that did not please him at all. He had become aware that nobody recognized him. For a star that was like notice that he was totally washed up.

Ken's method on such occasions was to raise his voice – on the theory that if nobody recognized his face, they wouldn't fail to relate to the sounds he was making, the variety of Kenneth Williams voices, alternately cockney, Oxford and the sing-song that went with most of his radio characters. He did all but say, 'Stop messing about.'

It worked – but too well. As Hugh Paddick remembers: 'People then came up to him and asked for his autograph. After a few minutes, he had had enough of this – and we had to get up and leave.'

Even that didn't alter the respect they had for each other. Hugh Paddick recalled an event during the *Beyond Our Ken* period when this became very apparent.

In this sketch, Ken was supposed to be shot dead. The script called for a pistol shot, the thump of Williams falling to the ground and Paddick left with the last line.

When it came to the actual recording, there was the sound of the pistol shot – followed not by the thump but by Ken wailing as only Kenneth Williams could wail. 'Oh ... ooohohooo-o-o.'

Those familiar with the Williams repertoire will recognize the notes that his voice produced.

As Hugh Paddick recalls, he waited for every possible noise that Ken could produce – and it went on and on – and then there was silence. 'I couldn't talk over him. I couldn't top it.' What he did was wait ...

and then say, "Was that it?" The 'oos' and 'aahs' went out on air – and so did Paddick's riposte, 'Was that it?'

Following that episode, Kenneth Horne used to scribble on his script before any similar sketch, 'You're not going to do one of your dying bits, are you?'

But Ken's opinion was valued – even if the advice he gave was not always accepted. When it was suggested that Bill Pertwee might be a useful addition to the cast, Ken was consulted and took part in the audition, such as it was. At that time, Pertwee – later to be most famous as the air-raid warden in *Dad's Army* – was by far the most successful ingredient of a summer show at Eastbourne. Kenneth Horne and the producer Jacques Brown, went with Williams to the South Coast to see the show, *The Foll De Rolls* – the whole purpose of which was to view Pertwee at work.

By this time, there had been six *Beyond Our Kens*, but Horne and his producer thought another comic input was necessary. Ken was not at all happy. But he went along for the ride, hoping he could put his spoke in and cancel the idea. He felt like a little boy suddenly told by his mother to share an afternoon at the cinema with another child.

'What do you want him for?' he asked, using his mock-Cockney voice – was this the real Williams sound? No one ever knew – in a very serious bit of comedy indeed. After sitting in the stalls and watching the summer show, the other two were convinced that they had good reason enough to want him. Despite Ken's protests, Pertwee was appointed as a 'utility man', an actor who could do anything when it was required, a couple of lines here, a longer speech there.

He stayed for the life of the series.

'But Ken was making it very clear to me from the very beginning that I was not going to get away with anything,' Pertwee told me. 'It didn't bother me really. Despite what he was saying, I liked him anyway. I also liked his work very much indeed.'

Not even the Williams petulance – and when it was there, Ken was very petulant indeed – could stop him seeming very, very funny.

The show was recorded at the Paris theatre in Piccadilly. Rehearsals were held every Wednesday morning. 'All I can say about them is that they were a real joy,' Bill Pertwee remembers.

Ken's mother remembers them equally affectionately. Lou went along with him for every show, with a place always reserved for her in the front row. She laughed with everyone else in the audience and the cast frequently laughed at her, too. Sometimes she was so funny that it seemed she ought to be given a show of her own.

But Ken would have outpaced her. He wouldn't have allowed her to grab his spotlight, even on radio. But he could be generous, even to potential rivals. When Pertwee's act, after six or seven weeks, started expanding, Ken watched him anxiously. He did well at it – and Ken was the first to congratulate him. The Cockney voice came out again. 'Ooh,' he said, smiling and flaring those nostrils once more, 'very nice ... very nice. Yes. Very nice, wasn't it?' But there was always a reserve about him. 'I don't think you could ever call Ken a friend. I don't think he was anyone's really close friend.' It was true. It was difficult to be part of the life of a man who was as much of a loner as at any time. The only person he would allow into his innermost secrets – and then only occasionally – was Lou.

But Pertwee was allowed one privilege that was reserved for very, very few. He went to Ken's flat – with Kenneth Horne; neither of whom would be allowed to use the lavatory.

Ken was about to move by then. He hated the noise of Endsleigh Court and for a time shared the flat of a friend – mistaking his haemorrhoid cream for toothpaste. But, as he was to say, it gave him a chance to hear about a convenient 'bum doctor' in Harley Street. The specialist gave him a series of injections which didn't exactly help him feel happy. Nevertheless, on the whole audiences didn't get to notice. In fact, he was very much the resident funny man in what was already a very amusing show indeed.

It was Ken who did the warm-ups for the audience, telling jokes he wouldn't dare come out with on the air. He had by now developed a routine that would never vary – a peculiar Kenneth Williams walk, prancing up and down stage with his bottom sticking out. That, naturally enough, was quite appropriate. Most of his jokes turned on his posterior and the various crises for which he was having to see whatever proctologist he was currently consulting.

Cinemagoers meanwhile got to see more of the 'bum' than he intended. There was one scene in *Carry on Constable* when virtually the whole male cast – Ken, Leslie Phillips, Kenneth Connor included – had to show their behinds and to have make-up applied.

The scene was in a shower room being used simultaneously by the policemen in the film – at the very moment that Woman Constable Joan Sims entered by mistake. They were all supposed to grab towels and run for their lives. But as Kenneth Connor told me, 'What she actually saw was the first full frontals ever on view during the making of a British film. In the first take we all ran totally naked off the set – Ken, nostrils flaring as camp as ever – into a whole group of girls who had heard it was going to happen. There we were, stark naked, and there was every girl working at the place, gathering around like pigeons at St Martin-in-the-Fields.'

Connor told Ken that looking at him was like 'seeing a mouse in a bag of oats'.

Most people on the set thought the incident was funnier than anything seen in a 'Carry On' film before. Gerald Thomas allowed himself to add: 'I don't know what all the fuss is about.'

Leslie Phillips speaks affectionately of Ken at this time. 'It is not difficult to have vivid memories of him,' he told me. He had worked with him before during one of Ken's repertory experiences, this time at Salisbury. At Pinewood, he was a different man altogether. 'He never stopped being funny. He was an extraordinary person, quite extraordinary. Unlike most entertainers, he had a great many facets.'

What Ken hated most of all when working was being alone – in total contrast to the facet of the man who wanted no company at all when he wasn't fully employed. Leslie Phillips remembers him, sitting on the canvas chair bearing his name, waiting to be called before the cameras. 'He would sit and look around until he had an audience – then he'd start.'

They were filming in the street, on Ealing Broadway when Ken jumped on to the back of a van. He started to tell stories, to sing. People gathered around him like a Pied Piper.

That was one of the sides of Ken that Leslie Phillips saw. Another was his ripostes to people whom he found less than entertaining – or important. 'He had a strong tongue,' Phillips remembers. 'He chose his friends very carefully. He didn't suffer fools gladly. But if he ever thought he'd upset you he was quick to apologize. Once he thought he had upset me, he ran after me. He couldn't bear to think that he had.'

Ken would go on upsetting people and then apologizing for his actions. One of those who saw it all happen was a young actress called Sheila Hancock.

TEN

Ken was as busy as ever now. Radio. Another 'Carry On' film – *Carry on Regardless*, which seemed to offer nothing new and might have died a death at the box office had it not had those magic first two words in the title which by now assured a box office hit. And after the huge success of *Pieces of Eight*, there was a sequel to that, too – *One Over The Eight*, which opened at the Duke of York's Theatre in April 1961.

Ken wasn't as happy with this one as he had been with its predecessor. On the whole, neither were the critics. Clive Barnes – later to become one of the 'Butchers of Broadway', as critic for the *New York Times* wrote: 'Although *One Over The Eight* is described as a "new revue" do not for a moment be fooled. This gay, trivial and frequently tedious little extravaganza seemed as old and dated as last year's calendar.' And he went on: 'The wit was without barbs, the humour without sting and even worse, often without point.'

But there was a redeeming feature. As he said: 'Except for one thing nothing more need be said. That thing is the performance of the show's star Kenneth Williams, who triumphantly rose above his material in a positive feat of levitation. Whether as an ever optimistic bird-watcher, or a gentlemanly hairdresser, Mr Williams with his ice-cold face and tortured vowels, was a delight. Yet for all his diabolical skill, he can no more make this revue than one swallow can make a summer.'

The cliché at the end of that piece could not diminish the success Ken had achieved. And he let the others in the cast know it, including that young actress, Sheila Hancock, who was soon to become the major star she now is.

They had met socially before the show went into rehearsal, seemingly all over Britain. The first run was at Stratford-upon-Avon, a place that was used to a different kind of theatre entirely, and ended at what was regarded as the graveyard of intimate revue, Blackpool. He made her laugh at those dinner parties and other gatherings where they had been together. On stage, and in the rehearsal room, he was something very different.

'He was pretty terrifying. I was just a novice and he was fairly frightening, not giving an inch until he had sounded you out. He was particularly difficult with women. He would try to break you.'

That was how he behaved day after day in rehearsal and night after night on stage. 'The break came,' she recalled, 'one night when I answered him back in an ad-lib. I took him on and we did a massive improvization on the spot and he began to respect me.'

The sketch was one where he played a man contemplating how different life might have been had there not been a world war. Ken said that the war clouds were looming. Except that he made it 'loo-oo-oo-ming'. Sheila picked it up. 'Yes, the gloo-oo-my war clouds were loo-oo-oo-ming.' As she said, 'The audience didn't know what the f— we were on about and it went on for simply ages, but Ken could be very indulgent with that sort of manic streak.'

That was the point that she knew that the barrier had been broken. 'He liked you to stand up to him and give as good as he got. He could come on very strong. 'He didn't suffer fools gladly. But when he loved you, he gave his love completely. But he couldn't tolerate incompetence.'

He suspected everyone around him of that incompetence until he had a contrary situation proved to him. 'It was a difficult show for him,' Sheila Hancock recalls. 'It wasn't an easy show for him and he was very conscious of carrying it all the way. I was cast opposite him but I was nothing like the draw he was and we had had a dodgy time on tour. But then, it was wonderful.'

Their relationship continued on that sort of basis outside the theatre too. Both served on the Equity Council. 'He veered to the right, I veered strongly to the left and we had many a set to.'

Ken's answer when he knew he had met his match was to say: 'I'm going to put you in my diary.'

One of the many rows between them at Equity meetings was over actor's pay. Ken said that many performers ought to pay managements for the privilege of working on the stage. That was a red rag to a bull, especially one called Sheila Hancock. 'How bloody ridiculous,' she countered.

'He didn't really mean it,' she now recalls. 'That was the thing about Ken. He could row one way one minute and if he found you agreeing with him, he would take the opposite argument on principle.'

It was difficult to get through to him. 'But he was touched by the love people showed him. I used to give him the odd cuddle and I used to give him lifts home on my bike. I had a Lambretta at the time.'

Home for Ken was now the Park West block of flats off the Edgware Road, a far more posh environment than any he had been used to up to then. But he kept it as spartan as all his previous homes. He padded his bedroom – literally like a padded cell – so that he wouldn't hear the noise of traffic outside. His living room had just a couple of chairs and a radio set and some books. No pictures on the wall. No television – that box killed conversation.

'I've got all the comforts I need,' he told his sister Pat. 'I've got chairs to sit on. If guests come, I've got chairs for them. I've got a comfortable bed to sleep on, a desk and a comfortable chair. What more do I need?'

'I thought he was bloody mad,' Pat says. He was rarely home, even Pat only went to his flat three or four times. 'He would say if you want to get me, you would have to get me at eight o'clock in the morning.'

'I was occasionally admitted to the inner sanctum,' Sheila Hancock now remembers. I just sympathized with him. I always thought he was a lonely little chap. He liked people who had a family, which was why he enjoyed being with Gordon Jackson so much. He liked hearing about their families, although he never was part of that.'

He also liked to be around children. 'He was always wonderful with my kids. He was rude to them, but great fun.'

Sometimes, he would tell the Hancock children, 'You're very spotty today.' or, 'You're mother's a total failure. I trust you'll do better. She was early promise never fulfilled.'

As she recalls: 'Most children would be very hurt to hear that. But mine just thought he was terribly funny.'

Another performer in *One Over The Eight* who took to Kenneth with the greatest of affection was Lance Percival, soon to make a national name for himself with the top TV satire show of the Sixties, *That Was The Week That Was*.

Ken had been at the auditions that Michael Codron organized, when he was looking for a feed for Williams. He didn't know Ken was there until he heard a cackle coming from the back of the stalls. People who knew the Williams cackle, from the NAAFI in Singapore, through repertory in Birmingham to Shaftesbury Avenue, could identify it anywhere.

The job was his. It was the beginning of a good relationship which survived the tour – and if *that* tour could be survived, it bode well for their friendship. 'He was absolutely fine. He was very straightforward and kind. I had no trouble at all. But I know that he made it very hard for Sheila. She was the female lead and therefore a rival. I was no rival at all.

'I learned my lines and did all right.' What was more, he coped with Ken's ad-libs. 'I got to know after a time that he ad-libbed because he got bored with his lines. In the end, you just couldn't recognize the script. It·wasn't that he was bored with the show, he was bored with his lines. He just got inventive. But he would come back to the right cues, so I could cope.'

Ken appeared to need very little to cope with his life. He laughed with other actors, was outrageous in restaurants, shouting orders to waiters who could never be sure if he was being serious or playing another part. Away from what most other people would regard as glamour, he retreated to that padded cell off the Edgware Road.

By this time, Lou and Charlie had moved too – the business had been running down for a long period and there was no point in staying in a flat over a shop that didn't exist any more. The mental torture of that for Charlie would have been tremendous. They moved to a flat in Kensington that Ken financed for them – to the point that he made *Carry On Regardless* solely to recoup some of his losses. Lou wasn't at all happy there, but she was in good health and that was the only thing that Ken bothered about.

He seemed to have resolved his sexual hang-ups for the time being and was content with his lonely existence. When the *Daily Telegraph* thundered on to his front doormat, he could get up and do the crossword over the pot of tea that served as his breakfast.

With all these things going well, Ken seemed as happy as possible – although Michael Codron could find no reason to amend his belief that Ken could never be happy.

But he rejoiced in his success. When Roy Plomley invited him to be his guest on *Desert Island Discs*, he thought that his cup runneth over. But he was no more comfortable on the radio programme than he would have been on the real desert island. He found the whole conversation stilted and turgid. He wasn't even let off the hook when it was all over. Stanley Baxter wondered whether choosing Michelangelo's famous male nude, 'The Boy David' as his luxury item was quite the choice a man with Kenneth's reputation should have made.

But he survived it. Plomley didn't regard the show as one of his greatest successes and no one else seemed to remember it. Something more to put down to experience, and his friends were kind.

It wasn't easy for him to make *new* friends, particularly outside of whatever cast list he was currently a part, but occasionally it happened – as during the run of *One Over The Eight*.

An American came to see the show one night and was practically addicted to it. As a result he became addicted to Ken. The man was a visiting Texan who was in Britain as manager of a fellow countryman, a concert pianist. He had been recommended to see Ken's show, took a box for the evening and couldn't stop laughing. In fact, he laughed so loud and so often that *One Over The Eight* practically came to a halt.

'This was the only time I ever saw Ken himself break up and get stuck,' remembers Lance Percival. It was during the sketch in which Ken played a hairdresser. He laughed so much that his laughter became the centre of attraction in the theatre. Even Ken couldn't keep his mind on the action. 'This guy laughed so much that everything came to a stop.' As a result, Ken and the Texan became firm friends.

Meanwhile, Ken was happy to do good turns to anyone who wasn't a threat. He invited Gerald Thomas and Peter Rogers to come and see the show – mainly so that they could watch Lance Percival at work. As a result they offered him small parts in the next two films in which Ken would star.

They were not strictly speaking, 'Carry Ons' but you could have fooled the audiences. Only the title was missing from this story about life in a music academy – perhaps that was the reason; 'Carry On Student' or even 'Carry On Musician' wasn't guaranteed to have the customers rolling in. But it was produced by Peter Rogers, directed by Gerald Thomas and in addition to Ken and Lance Percival, there was also Leslie Phillips and Eric Barker (returning to the team after *Carry On Sergeant*), Sid James and Liz Frazer, who had been introduced to the series in *Carry on Regardless* and would be as much part of the set-up as Ken himself. There was also James Robertson Justice who had starred in the 'Carry Ons' direct ancestors, the *Doctor In The House* series.

Twice Round The Daffodils was ostensibly a more serious subject – about life in a TB sanitorium and caused a modicum of controversy among people who thought that tuberculosis was not a matter for 'Carry On' style laughs. As the *Daily Express* noted: 'Much as I disliked this film and its cheap exploitation of suffering and illness, I must concede that it has been made with the dead-on professionalism that is characteristic of the other "Carry Ons."'

Nevertheless, somehow Rogers and Thomas got the message across that TB was hardly the scourge it once had been and there was really no reason not to laugh at those who were generally prepared to laugh at themselves, although there were serious moments too.

'I just thought that Ken was right for the part,' said Gerald Thomas.

'I knew he would get the humour and the pathos just right and I was proved correct. I was very happy with him in that part. I have never not been happy with him in anything he has done.'

Sheila Hancock was in that film too, as was Nanette Newman, both of whom told me how Ken would while away his time discussing the medical advances of which apparently the medical staff in the picture were not aware. Ken's reading always was advanced. Jill Ireland renewed her cuddling relationship with Williams and Donald Sinden, Donald Houston and Andrew Ray were among those who spent a great deal of their time wearing bathrobes and dressing gowns, hopping in and out of bed – for strictly medical reasons, of course. Ken, however, was more than once seen to go into his bed and fall fast asleep – undoubtedly the pressure of working in the theatre at night and recording *Beyond Our Ken* on other mornings proved too much and was reminiscent of another time when he fell asleep.

Ken's friendships and the way he established them continued to surprise those who were on the periphery of his activities. What, for instance, would Ken have in common with Andrew Ray, who was then just twenty-three years old (Ken was now forty) and who made known and very clear the attraction he felt for a pretty girl?

'I do, though, think he found me attractive,' Andrew told me. 'There was a scene in the showers and when it was over, Kenneth came up to me and said, "Oh you ought to have seen all the people gathering around you". We all had swimsuits on, we weren't stripped naked. I do think that Ken fancied me, and he actually said he thought I was beautiful. But I was never aghast at it. It never came out in any really sexual way.'

That may be difficult to comprehend, but Andrew Ray thinks he understands it. 'Maybe Kenneth fancied quite a few of his friends in some ways, but it never came out physically. I think Kenneth had a strong sexual imagination and I am sure that a lot went through his mind, but I don't think it went further than that.'

'I never thought there was anything strange in it at all,' he told me. 'We both spent most of our time working on the film, walking or sitting about in our dressing gowns and we had a great time together.'

The great time was continued outside of Pinewood, too. For years, they would meet at Lyons Corner House, have lunch and then spend the afternoon at the cinema. 'We'd buy the *Evening Standard*, look in the amusement pages and he'd say, "What do you fancy? Oh look – that's all right for time." Afterwards, we'd go to the Quality Inn for a poached egg.'

Sometimes, they went to the National Gallery together. Ken's favourite

Ken when he was evacuated at Bicester, 1941. He was fifteen

By 1945, Ken, a soldier, had a trade – as a draughtsman

Ken was now in the Army. Pat was a qualified wireless operator, 1944

Above The young actor thought this was the debonair look, 1949

Right At the beginning of Ken's repertory career in *Little Lambs Eat Ivy*. He said of this picture 'The pose that failed.'

His father would have been proud. Ken, in 1944 (on the right of the army drill instructor, second row) for once not afraid to show his chest.

Kenneth Williams's contribution to the age of chivalry. With Glynis
Johns in *The Seekers*, 1954

Quite a carry on – except that *The Seekers* was almost a decade before the
series for which he became famous. In this film he is surrounded by Jack
Hawkins and apparently some refugees from the Black and White Minstrels

The first sign of real talent. As
the Dauphin in *Saint Joan*, 1954

Ken in *Raising The Wind*,
1961

Pat Williams, 1951

Charlie and Lou Williams, 1962

With his friend, actor Richard Pearson and his sons Patrick and Simon at their home in Beckenham, about 1960

Ken in *Raising the Wind*, 1961. Pat liked the picture so much that she used to have it on her office desk

Photographs from
Barbara Windsor's
honeymoon. The
Williams clan join the
honeymoon couple in
Lisbon, 1964

Foto Perestrellos

Ken and Lou having a day out at Richard Pearson's (centre) home in
Beckenham in 1964

Ken and Pat in 1971

The Ken Pat likes to remember, 1970

Flexing his muscles in *Carry On Emmannuelle*, 1978

Second childhood in *Carry On Regardless*, 1960

picture was 'The Incredulity of Thomas' – which showed St Thomas sticking his finger into the wound of Jesus.

'It is an amusing portrait as Ken pointed it out to me, discussing the intricacies of the brushwork as well as the subject matter and its religious significance.'

They would talk politics. 'Ken, of course, was fairly right-wing and I was of the opposite persuasion.'

He would go to Ray's house for dinner. He liked the way Andrew cooked. 'I don't think he liked my daughter Madeleine very much. I think it was simply because she was a little girl and he couldn't get on with her. He wasn't openly hostile towards her, but I think he had a natural reaction against the sex. But he adored little boys and when my son Mark was born, he became his godfather.'

On the other hand he was kindness itself to Andrew's mother-in-law. Ken took her around London, with Andrew, and they walked arm-in-arm through the Strand, saying 'Come on girl.' It was better than when Andrew took his then girlfriend, now his wife, to the cinema with them. 'He was so furious, he hardly spoke to me at all.'

On another occasion, the two were walking through a West End street when a voice behind called out: 'Hi, Andrew!' It was one of his friends, an Italian singer named Tony Dalli. Ken froze. 'Don't answer, don't turn round,' he instructed. Andrew did as he was told – and regretted it. 'I just had to accept that was him. He had so many wonderful sides to him I had to accept that this was just another one. It was a pity that he could be so hurtful.'

Once, Andrew Ray told Gordon Jackson about the hurt. 'That's just Kenneth,' Jackson told him. 'We all know Kenneth. Just ring him up and have lunch with him the next day and it'll be all right.'

And,' said Ray, 'it always was. He was right.'

Actually, the relationship between Ken and Gordon Jackson was a very strong one indeed. 'I think,' said Andrew Ray, 'he saw the kind of man he would like to have been had he been straight. He admired his responsible attitude towards his own family. A good responsible, straight man. Time and again he would talk about Gordon, but only respectfully.'

The relationship with Stanly Baxter, Ray believes, was different. 'I think there was much more of a sense of rivalry between them,' he told me. 'I even detected a love-hate relationship. He loved Stanley, and thought that he dared do things he wouldn't dare do himself.'

Sometimes, Andrew's hurt brought on by Ken was deep indeed. 'I remember being in a mood once when he told me, "You'll go mad some day". That was very brutal and hurtful when I felt down. But that was a small side of the personal relationship. Most of it was helpful and extremely kind.'

And they had one particularly favourite occupation. 'We'd go to the public gallery at the Old Bailey and listen to the trials. Ken particularly used to enjoy the murder trials – not for any morbid curiosity, but for the drama unfolding. We would then discuss them and the barristers, as if we were criticizing a play. We used to say that the counsel gave some very tacky performances that wouldn't stand up to cross-examination from Michael Denison (star of the 1948 law courts drama, *The Blind Goddess*).

'For some cases, we'd come back day after day, and chat to people in the queue. I remember a big insurance scandal in which someone was bumped off and another case where a dustman was having sex with his two daughters. Ken loved them. He'd read books about murders and we talked about them for years. I remember he was fascinated about the Nilson murders, the man who cut up bodies and melted them down in his garden.' But it was the show business aspect of the trials that appealed to him.

After the hearings, they would walk through Fleet Street and its environs. 'It was then that I got to realize Ken's great knowledge of London and of history. He really should have been an Oxford don or something. I had always been interested in history, but Ken with his great command of English was able to explain it and put life into it, particularly when talking about his hero, Charles I.'

After the walking tour, they would go and have tea together. Sometimes, they would meet for lunch at the Grill and Cheese at the Corner House, where Ken regularly gave a private performance for the other people waiting to be seated. 'What yer gonna have today?' Ken would ask in his best Marchmont Street tones, 'Gonna have the fillet?' Ken would see Andrew to his bus to Victoria where he'd catch his train to Brighton.

On the way, men working in a gang on the building site they passed would call out to him, 'Hello, Ken,' they would call. 'How yer doin' mate?' He would reply in their own language. 'All right, mate' he'd call. 'You all right.'

But the real matiness of Ken came a short while later. Andrew also saw the other side of Kenneth Williams, Williams the depressive. He was down and sometimes it seemed as if nothing was going to shake him out of it, apart from a laugh at someone else's expense or a shared moment of despair.

'I had had those moments myself, so I could appreciate them,' says

Ray. In fact, Andrew attempted suicide not long after the film was completed. Ken was among the first to rush to his bedside in the psychiatric ward of the Middlesex Hospital. 'He came to see me several times and even brought Gordon [Jackson] along too. 'He was always very supportive and helpful. Depending on how I was, on my own mood, he could be very funny.'

In the end the Middlesex authorities asked Andrew to leave – so many show people like Ken and Diana Dors came to see him that the noise along the corridors was unbearable. 'It was constantly party time,' he recalls. 'I got hauled up before the chief psychiatrist because of the champagne that was flowing.'

Andrew was particularly concerned about work and about going into new things. Ken encouraged him to do Shaw and ran over the lines with him until he felt he had got it.

For about nine years, they saw each other constantly. 'I would ring him and he'd answer the phone almost immediately. It seemed as if he would answer it before it rang and we'd arrange to go out.'

But then the time came for the friendship to end. Ken himself was seeing a psychiatrist because of his own depressions. 'He told me,' said Ray, 'that I wasn't doing him any good, two depressives together. He wrote me a letter. 'My doctor,'' he said, ''has told me that because we are both very depressive types of people, perhaps because we know what life is about that I shouldn't meet people who were the same way as I am and get depressed about things.'' I was very, very sorry, but I just left the letter around and didn't see him for about three years. It was just the way he was at that particular time. I wasn't hurt. I just understood Ken. We both knew only too well because of the business we were in and the sort of people we were what could happen.'

Whatever was wrong with Ken at that time, Andrew Ray is convinced it wasn't sex. 'I don't think it was a problem for him. He never had any long-term physical relationships as far as I know. I think it was all in Kenneth's mind and I think Kenneth's hang-up about his backside and his obsession with cleanliness would have made physical love very difficult for him.'

But there *was* evidence that Ken did attempt it, even if he never went through with any serious kind of sexual activity.

'I believe he did have an occasional Guardsman home,' said Ray. 'They would always be pick-ups. I think he might have tried, thinking that he must fulfill this sexual desire that he had in some way. But I don't think anything happened.'

There was a story he told about the man who came to his flat and said in a gruff voice, 'Come on then – let's get on with it then.' Ken was so put off that this potential sexual-encounter never went any further.

Andrew Ray recalled: 'There were various things about Guardsmen that came up in conversation. He once told me, 'You can't trust them you know. They'll always steal something, you know. You'll usually find that the toothpaste's gone or something.'

Andrew is fairly convinced about the Guardsman theory. 'I know that if Ken had had any kind of sexual relationship it wouldn't have been with anyone he knew well. It would have been a casual thing and not with anyone who was camp, like him. It would have been with someone butch, a Guardsman or a man on a building site. A real man. I think that appealed.'

He would make comments about them 'in the same way you or I would comment on a pretty girl and a wonderful pair of knockers'.

Ken's more serious side was, as far as his fellow performers were concerned, more obvious in the books he read. 'I remember during *One Over The Eight*,' said Lance Percival, 'he was reading about the French Revolution and that's all he would talk about.'

In fact, it got quite unnerving. Other actors were trying to think of a way to get a laugh while Ken was more concerned with the fate of Robespierre. 'He came out with bits of information that were never of any use to anyone. But Ken could turn any conversation into an erudite discussion – and also make jokes about them.'

Ken was constantly outrageous – 'but outrageous for the sake of being so, rather than deliberately trying to upset anyone.'

He was, though, still unwilling to put up with people who he felt were beneath his intellectual level. He could also be terribly rude. That was clearly illustrated during the run of *One Over The Eight*. A stage-hand upset him and he replied with a withering flow of invective, the kind for which he was not generally known.

As Lance Percival tells the story, it was not a pleasant occasion. A new stage-hand stood watching Ken's routine as a bank robber armed with sticks. He had to say, 'Stick up your sticks' – from behind a flat. Ken was disturbed to know that he was being watched during a live performance, even by a man who was providing an audience out of sheer admiration. Ken broke off the routine in mid-flow and went back behind the flat. He glared at the stage-hand. 'Why don't you fuck off you cunt,' he told him – and went back to work. The stage-hand was destroyed.

But memories of Ken at this time still tend to revolve more around the fun. He could also still imitate anyone with whom he came into contact, although his days of giving his impressions of Winston Churchill or Nellie Wallace (nobody would know who Nellie Wallace was in 1962) were by now over.

In fact, Lance Percival came to a conclusion as long ago as when the *One Over The Eight* show was still running that Ken wouldn't have minded if his comedy days had been over, too. But there was a living to be made in comedy which he still did so well and he got on with it.

In fact, it was a correct judgement and one that would remain valid for the rest of Williams's life. Always at the back of his mind was a serious actor trying to break out of the 'Carry On' mould, but while he was wanted for nothing more, says Percival, he was ready to go on showing that he was better than anyone else.

'He was actually a very quiet, introspective person.'

Carry On Cruising followed at the not inappropriate speed of knots. Lance Percival was in that, too. 'I remember we had a preview on a ship in Southampton. I think that was the nearest we ever got to going to far-away places. Peter Rogers's idea of location was behind a tree, two and a half miles away from Pinewood.'

Wherever the film was being shot, Ken was ready to take the lead – and not give it away. 'If you could film all Ken's words and actions when no cameraman was supposed to be looking, you'd have another "Carry On" film. He was outrageous between takes and everyone else there was his willing audience.'

As he also said: Peter Rogers and Gerald Thomas were delighted to pour champagne down people's throats between takes – they weren't paying anyone very much – to listen to Ken's routines. Whether he had prepared them in advance, of course, we'll never know.'

What Lance Percival also says is that he will never know the depth of Ken's sexual feelings, although others have produced stronger evidence. 'He was the most neutral man I ever knew. I was with him constantly for a whole year and in that time I never saw him with anyone, man or woman. I would defy anyone to be able to define Kenneth perfectly. Everyone has a different angle, but I don't think anyone knew him properly. He made an absolute mastery of hiding himself behind the personalities he created.'

ELEVEN

Nobody will ever know for sure how much Ken tried to rid himself of the camp, 'Carry On' image. What is much more certain is that it was a huge release for him, a safety valve by which the loner could open up, expand and express himself. But at the age of forty he was at last beginning to wonder whether the image he created for himself in his twenties could stay with him for ever.

After a year of *One Over The Eight*, ('Kenneth Williams is the best of the genre,' wrote Robert Muller in the *Daily Mail*) Ken left the cast and his part was taken over by Kenneth Connor. It would last for another six months, but by the time it ended, intimate revue was finally dead. There would be no more shows of the kind. He himself had other plans, although for the moment he was keeping them fairly close to his chest.

Lou continued to be the nearest he had to a first and real love and she still went to all the broadcasts and visited Pinewood for every film, sitting on her own canvas chair, sometimes by herself, frequently with her sister Daisy, of whom Ken himself was still very fond. Charlie was taking a lot of the pressure off her now. Pat, divorced, but living her own distinct life, was an executive with a computer company in London, a new feature on the industrial scene but already well established. She found her father a job – as the internal postman. The fact that Charlie managed to run a book on the side only contributed to his contentment and stability.

Ken, meanwhile, believed he had found a play that suited his temperament and talents better than most of the things on which he had been working to date. In fact, he was so happy with the idea that had come to him from the writer, Peter Shaffer, he began the serious rethink of his career which friends like Lance Percival had been thinking for some time was overdue. For one thing, he was not going to make the seventh 'Carry On' film, *Carry On Cabbie*.

Peter Shaffer had written a two-part play called *The Private Ear and the Public Eye*. The role he proposed for Ken was too good for him to pass up. Ken agreed to play Julian Christaforou, the Anglo-Greek detective, the public eye in the second of the two plays after a dinner. Ken had chosen the restaurant, but was frightened of being pestered by fans, so asked the head waiter to produce the screens. That way, he would be left alone without worrying why no one was asking him for an autograph. The schizophrenia of Kenneth Williams was thus complete. 'He was two people,' recalls Shaffer today. 'The public and the private literally.'

Maggie Smith would be the female lead in both halves, but Ken didn't come on until after the interval. He worried about that, at first, until Shaffer persuaded him that he could make enough of the dialogue at his disposal, through the sheer weight of the quality of his performance.

He had wanted the part of the young boy who couldn't make it with his date in the first play, but he was a juvenile no more and Peter Shaffer had to convince him that it wouldn't work.

He was enthralled at playing with Maggie Smith again. She was no longer the ingénue who had wowed audiences on Broadway with *New Faces*. Her part in *Share My Lettuce* had done as much for her own theatrical career as the show had done for Ken, and she was embarking on a series of films that would make her an international reputation. She and Ken were a pair, soul brother and sister.

In a way, she brought him down to earth. But, like Ken, she had a devastating wit and the repartee between them was a joy to listen to.

They talked about the director Peter Wood. 'In a way,' recalls Richard Pearson, who played Maggie's husband, a dull businessman, 'he kept the director in his place'.

Maggie's then boyfriend – and later husband – Beverley Cross, became a close friend of Ken's at the time, too.

'I thought he was a very amusing and extraordinary person, unique, extremely amusing.'

With the change from revue complete and the rest from 'Carry On' beginning, Cross took it upon himself to 'bully him'. He kept telling him to go back to being a serious actor. 'I kept saying that he ought to be in Shakespeare and not waste his time.' Cross took him to Stratford to see the Bard's work, 'but he wanted the comfort of the BBC and the "Carry Ons"'. Cross now admits that he thought Ken was 'probably too eccentric for Shakespeare'. But he also noted the occasional whiff of nostalgia as he contemplated the 'what-might-have-been' as far as classical theatre was concerned. He did talk about his time as the Dauphin in a way that made people fairly sure that if the Stratford management had come to him with an offer, he would have grabbed it.

On the other hand, there were friends who thought that the Shaffer play was just the sort of thing that Kenneth Williams needed to do.

Andrew Ray told me: 'I often saw Kenneth and some of the things he did and thought to myself, "What a waste!" I realized what a marvellous actor he was when I saw him in this and only wished that he hadn't relied so much on the funny voices and hidden behind the easier way out of doing the characters that he could do so easily – and it was easy for him. It was much harder to show a side of your nature and your soul as an actor as he did in *The Private Ear and the Public Eye*.'

But he did also want to put his all into this new play with Maggie Smith that seemed to offer so much.

They conspired with each other. When they both protested, seemingly in vain, at having lines cut, they came up with their own solutions – they would accept the cuts, but make do with them badly. In fact, they were so bad in the one matinée performance in which they were tried out, that the original speeches were reinstated by the time the curtain went up at the Globe Theatre that evening.

Maggie Smith once said about him: 'Kenneth taught me how to recognize the one word in a sentence which would turn it from a commonplace statement into something wildly funny.'

Then, they had the perfect solution to the problem of audience laughter. Should they stop because the people out front were drowning everything coming from the stage? They decided between them that that would make the apparent spontaneity of their performances artificial. They talked nonsense until there was sufficient calm in the stalls and circle to allow them to continue with the lines as written in the script.

Richard Pearson played Maggie Smith's husband in the play, the dull businessman. He was eight years older than Ken. 'But, strange as it may be to say about someone who was younger, I learnt a great deal from him.'

Ken was, he said, a 'fine technician'. He discovered just how good during the three weeks that elapsed between the signing of contracts and the opening. Most of the rehearsal time was reserved for the first play and Ken and Pearson would do much of their own rehearsing together.

At first, there were slight disagreements between them. The main one was that Kenneth wanted no time between speeches. He wanted to give Pearson the cue and hear him respond absolutely instantly, sharply.

'That wasn't the way I was used to playing a part. I liked to think before saying my lines. But the director was all for it, too, and as Kenneth pointed out, we didn't wait between talking naturally in our private conversations. I had to accept that was right, although at first it seemed rather artificial to me. But he was very experienced in that.'

Once or twice, Ken argued with him and said: 'There was a pause there. You weren't in on time. In our regular conversation, we talk over each other.'

Towards the end of the play's run, he got more indulgent with Pearson. 'You can pause all you like,' he told him. 'I'm not going to spoil a friendship over a pause.' It was as if, the actor now thinks, he hadn't wanted to complain all along, but his professionalism wouldn't allow him not to say it.

The one-act play began in Pearson's office, with Ken – a funny little gnome-like figure – up a library ladder looking at a book, while Pearson walks in holding his briefcase and bowler hat, humming Ravel's Bolero. He had to do a double take, bumping into a filing cabinet.

Pearson protested about that. 'I don't do double-takes,' he insisted, but Ken said, 'I'll teach you.'

Both audiences and critics seemed to like what they saw and heard. Ken and Maggie were in for a long run.

Beverley Cross said that it was an admiration of one performer for another 'and also he had such a soft spot for her after that year in *Share My Lettuce*. He was immensely encouraging to her. He admired her enormously and she did what he wanted to do – went into the really serious theatre while he stayed the same.'

Sheila Hancock told me she remembered Ken being very proud of the play. Her memory did not let her down. Everyone connected with the play felt much the same way.

Peter Shaffer has only the fondest memories of a performer who appears to have been a playwright's delight. He was convinced from the beginning that Ken was perfect for the role of the slightly dotty but romantic detective in the white raincoat, a man who existed on a diet of macaroons he produced from out of a black Gladstone bag. Peter Wood, the director, and H.M. Tennent, the producers, were of the same mind.

'We all thought that if he would do it, it would be a wonderful idea,' said Shaffer. He knew he wasn't going to regret the move from the moment they all assembled for the first rehearsal.

'He was a marvellous rehearser and a marvellous *precisian*. He was a man who wanted to speak the text exactly as written. No improvizations.' Which was not the way he had usually behaved.

Just occasionally, he would allow himself an ad-lib. In one scene he had to take a handkerchief out of his pocket, and in the process shower Maggie Smith with nuts. Sometimes, he would add lines like: 'You've got to pick them up from the carpet, or they'll tread in. They'll tread in-n-n-n.' In contrast with *One Over The Eight* in which he constantly said his 'gloo – oo-oo-m' words or would take a word like 'now' and repeat it excessively, he behaved with total seriousness in this; a different character entirely. But then, as Shaffer remembers, 'he was a very paradoxical figure, Kenneth'. The solitary figure in private life contrasted with the man he describes as giving a 'firework display' in public.

'There was this public person, acting that part – sometimes the hysterical story teller and raconteur plunging into that great bath of imitation, nostrils flaring and eyes sparkling, and putting on those extremely funny lofty voices. The other person was a man who could actually speak for hours about his reading, which was extensive. His views on religion and philosophy – some of his views were very contorted.'

Ken was also a good listener. He did hear what other people said to him – 'although with somewhat less relish than when he spoke himself. But he did listen. He was a good listener – and he was egged on to be a performer by his listeners.'

'I think in some ways he was a very despairing man.' He knew of Ken's depressions. He saw them, although the ones he witnessed were different from the black clouds he had heard about. 'I found him sometimes in a sort of energized depression', said Shaffer.

'He would verbalize his sadnesses, throw his arms about as he told elaborate stories concerning people who had upset him at the time, even when going into sad tales about people who were important to him. But as Shaffer remembers: 'He could be talking about a death and get himself very worked up about what he was saying, very passionate about whatever made him worried or angry. But what was coming out was pure comic monologue.'

'Part of him would be very pleased that you were laughing at him. The other part would not be pleased because really he meant what he was saying.'

The principal frustration at the time was with Charlie and Lou – mainly with Charlie, however, as was predictable. Ken had mortgaged himself to the hilt with the flat in Brunswick Gardens, Kensington and after one interminable row following another, he told his parents to leave the flat. They did – and then came back again. The row became a one-man show for Shaffer and the others assembled instantly as an audience for Kenneth Williams.

As Shaffer added: 'What distinguished him was the energy he always demonstrated. At his best, he was one of the funniest storytellers you ever heard. At his less than best he was like a child showing off. Because he was so vastly entertaining, you took those times with the others.'

Not everyone was always quite so generous. Kenneth Williams resorted to so many different voices which sometimes gave the impression that he wasn't always sure himself which one was going to come out. Just occasionally, one could be forgiven for thinking that the dummy had overtaken the ventriloquist.

But Peter Shaffer himself was delighted with the public Williams – the public voice as well as the Public Eye. 'He was unique and startling with this inexhaustible energy and the most violent precision of timing. People adored him. They were mesmerized by him and he drove the comedic tension forward at a great rate.'

The last few minutes of the play were, Shaffer told me 'simply an object lesson in comic timing. When he assumed the role of the accountant and conducted the whole conversation with someone at the other end who was trying to make an appointment, he was brilliant.' The brilliance of that moment was underlined by the fact that Williams, playing a man with a particularly sweet tooth, was eating a sour grapefruit without sugar at the time. Having made the appointment with the stranger, he asks casually: 'And do you think you could bring a canister of demerara sugar with you?'

'One is always grateful for that kind of comic genius who takes your script and plays it for everything that's in it,' as Shaffer told me. He and Shaffer got on well together and became firm friends. 'What he liked about the play was that he enjoyed speaking it. He liked the elaboration of the language. He was very funny in it. Very exact. He didn't like any kind of sloppiness on stage. He liked to be exact. He was always so tidy.'

The play had an out-of-town try-out in Oxford. Shaffer drove him there from the Park West flat. 'I only entered the flat for a brief moment. I may even have just called for him and stood at the door. But I could see there was something monk-like about the space there. I could see a sort of Army bed. It was so austere. There was such a paradox between the baroque personality of Mr Williams and this extremely Carthusian background against which he lived.'

His taste in furniture was in some ways mirrored by his choice of restaurants. He still favoured Lyons Corner House, although by now he had graduated from the Grill and Cheese to the Seven Stars. Now these were perfectly fine eating establishments that served wholesome food on crisp white table cloths, but were not the usual sort of house favoured by top stars. Ken, though, liked it enormously and it was very close to the Globe.

On matinée days, Ken would take other members of the cast to the Kardoma restaurant in Piccadilly for a poached egg. 'He'd say let's go and have a poached,' Richard Pearson told me. 'Or he'd have minced meat on toast. He had very plebian taste – although he'd say he didn't.' They would go for walks in the area. 'We'd go to Wellington Place. Ken knew all the statues and who they were of.'

After the play, he and Maggie Smith and Peter Shaffer would assemble at the Seven Stars for a late dinner. 'He hated people staring at him,' Shaffer told me. 'So we ate several meals there behind screens.'

Like other people, Richard Pearson recalled the attraction that simple, conventional family life held for Ken – the bachelor who was so very confirmed in his status was most of the time frightened of anything else.

' I don't think he would have trusted himself to be married,' the actor remembered for me. But he used to go down to Pearson's house in Beckenham, Kent and spend time with his children, Simon and Patrick. 'He was attracted to me because I and my life were so very ordinary.'

They talked religion. Ken was a great fan of the then Archbishop of Canterbury, Dr Ramsey, and talked about him a great deal. 'He wasn't a church-goer, but very religious. He was, funnily enough, a marvellous impersonator of bishops.'

On one of his visits to Beckenham, Pearson told him about a little girl neighbour, a Downs Syndrome child, who loved seeing Kenneth Williams in films or on television. Ken wrote her a letter – and then several others followed, although he never met her.

He and Pearson had first met in 1960 at the BBC Television Centre. 'He was very generous about Harold Pinter's *The Birthday Party* in which I played. He could be very kind to another performer. On the other hand, he could be very acerbic.'

He would visit his home, making faces at the Pearson children as they hung out their bedroom windows looking for him. 'He came in a hired car in those days. Very grand. In later years, I'd take him to the station and he'd get a train home.' Then he'd write long letters to Richard, telling precisely how long the train journey took and describing colourfully the other people with whom he shared the carriage.

It was easier going to the house – he and Richard's wife Pat used to swap wartime evacuation stories with each other and then they would play verbal tennis, making conversation out of the spoken lyrics of Forties' songs – than going to the theatre to see other actors, as they sometimes did together after the run of *Public Eye*.

'He wasn't much good as an audience. He would shuffle around in his seat and then be highly critical, but he always knew what was going on. On the other hand, talk to him about a book – like one that Gordon Jackson lent him – and he would go overboard about it.' With a good book, Ken could be alone. In a theatre he frequently took refuge in a lavatory – not to solve his omnipresent bowel problems necessarily but to escape from autograph-hunters. On the other hand, had he not thought they would be there, he wouldn't have gone into the building at all. But while he was in the Shaffer play, there was no time to see other actors at work.

Ken was in *The Private Ear and the Public Eye* for a year – Maggie left slightly earlier to play in *Mary, Mary*. Afterwards, he and Peter Shaffer lost touch. 'I had the sense he was rather sad,' the writer now remembers. 'I loved him. Within the limits of his absolutely individual personality he was genuinely and truly extraordinary.'

The only people who did keep in touch with Ken for more than a block of years in which they were extremely close, only for it all to fade away, were Stanley Baxter and Gordon Jackson. There was, though, always Lou, to whom Ken had introduced the delights of a theatre that she had hardly known existed. 'He was everything to her,' Richard Pearson, like so many others, noted. 'But he could be sharp with her too – boss her around. But she loved it. She was a wonderful foil for him.'

Andrew Ray also experienced that sharpness between them. 'I think that the relationship wasn't entirely healthy. He loved and worshipped Louisa. But there were times when he was very hard on her.'

He himself was very much aware of the differences in the relationships between Ken and his mother and that with his father Charlie. On one occasion he went with Ken to visit Charlie and Lou in their basement flat in Kensington.

'He treated his father with such disdain, it was almost as though he weren't there. He was almost ignoring his very presence. I had the feeling that he thought that his father didn't look after Lou well enough.'

By this time, there was concern as to whether Charlie was capable of looking after himself. His bookmaking activities in the computer company were even reasonably harmless signs of his eccentricities.

He had never got over having to give up the shop, caused as much by growing bronchial problems as by falling business.

By now there were more serious difficulties affecting Charlie's behaviour that became considerably more alarming.

It hadn't been an easy decision for him in any regard. Pat had come to him and asked to be able to buy the shop – not with any money she had available at that time, but on a never-never basis, letting him have a share in the takings until the value of the business had been reached. 'Go and sod yourself,' he told her.

Moving to Kensington unnerved him. As the years went by, things got worse and worse.

'He got under Mum's feet,' said Pat. But that was also just a minor problem. So he got the job as the postman, yet even that didn't stop him behaving strangely.

He would take off for days and no one would see him. Even his mother, Grandma Williams – who was ending her days boasting to people in the pub about her famous grandson, telling distant relatives who suddenly appeared out of the woodwork about him and regaling the family with stories about her strange neighbours – became scared of him. When he hired a taxi to take her to Eastbourne for the day (the same man who took a bus to the theatre, rather than pay for a cab) she jumped out at the lights near Oval cricket ground because she was so disturbed by his erratic behaviour.

Once he came into Ken's dressing room, asking for ten pounds to buy dinner at a nearby restaurant – this, from a man who never ate out in his life.

Pat told me of her father' schemes for making money which, of course, never came to anything. 'I'll make your fortune for you, girl,' he kept telling her.

'He used to go into the bathroom and lock himself in there for hours. Then he'd come up with one mad scheme after another, like buying a sack of pigeon food and selling it to people in Trafalgar Square. When I used to say, "Oh yeah", he'd reply, "Don't be cheeky, you're not too old to get a clip round the ear." She was in her thirties at this time. 'He would go into the most terrible tantrums, all of this totally out of character.' He also designed a bed that could be raised up and down and told Pat to go to the patent office with the plan which would make them both a fortune. She tried to tell him that hospitals had been using such beds for years, but he just went into another tantrum. Later, when he was lying ill at the Brompton Hospital, Pat went to visit him. She was greeted from one end of the ward to the other by a stream of swearing and other abuse.

The bronchial attacks got worse. In the middle of a Saturday night in October 1962, he woke up and was unable to get back to sleep. He rolled himself a cigarette and started coughing. He coughed so badly that he found his way to the bathroom and took some Liquafruta cough syrup.

The problem was that it was NOT cough syrup, but a hefty dose of Thawpit cleansing spirit that had been put into the medicine bottle, probably because it was the left-overs from a bigger can.

He took the dose and immediately collapsed, rolling around on the floor in a kind of agony that most people could not contemplate. Lou heard him in the throes of his pain. 'He could hardly walk,' she said as she remembered trying to pick him up. Immediately, she sent for an ambulance and he was taken to the Mary Abbots Hospital in Kensington, where he died soon afterwards. He was sixty-two.

The family persuaded Ken not to attend the inquest at Hammersmith Coroner's Court, in the hope that the name Charlie Williams wouldn't mean anything to the Press. Seeing Ken there would automatically bring attention from the National Press.

The coroner heard it revealed for the first time – none of the family knew it – that Charlie had had a stroke a few months before, which explained the strange behaviour. A verdict of death by misadventure was recorded. Peter Eade escorted Lou and Pat to the court.

Ken was momentarily saddened by his father's death. Grandma Williams was hit most seriously of all by it; the death of her first-born was a crushing blow and she died herself soon afterwards. But he couldn't invent a love that had never been there and he felt that Lou would be better off without him.

After the cremation, Ken instructed his mother and sister: 'No tears now. Come on.' They obeyed the order.

The funeral was held in the morning of 23 October, so that Ken could appear on stage in *The Private Ear and the Public Eye* for a matinée that day. 'How that boy could go and do a comedy show that afternoon, I'll never know. Neither of us really liked Charlie,' Pat told me, 'but we were upset.'

'To tell the truth, it was not a happy marriage.' Lou says.

After the funeral at Golders Green Crematorium, the entire Williams clan – including cousins neither Pat nor Ken had seen for a quarter of a century – assembled for drinks, 'a real old Cockney wake,' as Pat put it.

The final tribute was, in fact, worthy of a 'Carry On Funeral' film. Ken had brought in an old army chum who was now in the catering business, to handle the more convivial aspects of the occasion. This man transported his gear in an old ambulance.

Ken tried to rid himself of the guests, so that he could get away to the theatre, by telling Pat to call him to an imaginary telephone call.

Before anyone had a drink, Ken called out his apologies and the guests left, leaving behind just the immediate family and Lou's sister, Alice, and her husband, who ran a pub in Hornsey. After Ken went, they drove off to Hornsey in the ambulance and stopped first for a Chinese meal – much against Lou's wishes; she doesn't like Chinese – followed by a session at the pub. After that, the day of the funeral ended with a jolly old knees-up. Ken, meanwhile, was living a more abstemious existence on stage. They left at two o'clock in the morning, with Lou repeating constantly, 'Oh, you'd never guess I've buried my Charlie this morning.'

Ken himself would never have participated in such carrying-ons. The only drinking in which he took part was to have the occasional gin and tonic to which he kept adding more and more tonic. He was also a snob, as Pat readily admits.

Snobbery does not, however, seem to have influenced his friendships. While working in *Public Eye* Ken cemented his already strong relationship with Maggie Smith and Beverley Cross. When he finally left the cast in 1963, that friendship seemed as strong as ever.

'He adored Maggie,' Pat told me. 'And we all went to their house in Kensington for Christmas a couple of times.'

He would go to Maggie's home but wouldn't spend the night, although frequently invited to do so. He didn't like the country and used to say that the birds kept him awake. When Beverley, who had written the hits *Boeing Boeing* and *Half A Sixpence*, suggested that what Ken really needed was a good holiday, the two of them took off together for Greece. It was not perhaps the easiest of vacations that Beverley now recalls.

'I was there more as a minder than anything else,' he explained. The first of two holidays they spent together was on a cruise ship, the *SS Romantica* which took them to the Greek Islands.

There were the predictable problems with sanitary arrangements. Ken complained about the state of the ship's lavatories. 'I just told him to shut up and make do,' Cross told me.

'My job was really to keep a distance between Kenneth and other passengers,' he said. 'Of course, if no one recognized him, he got rather upset.' Others *had* noticed that before.

'But he was a good companion even if we had trouble with the bowels.' The following year, they went on to Turkey and Venice. 'He was very interested in going to Constantinople, for instance. But three weeks was about it. My patience was getting totally exhausted. I never got cross, but he wanted an audience and I was prepared to be one. But three weeks was just about it. It went a long way.'

He was aware of one thing about Ken on these trips: his concern about a lack of education which he made up for with his voracious reading.

Cross didn't experience any of the Williams depressions. 'He got a bit upset when the bowels didn't work and let me know it,' he recalls. 'But I suppose it was a very superficial friendship really. I do remember affectionately those little jaunts that we did together.'

Later Ken stayed in France, near where Beverley Cross had a home. Again, he was in an hotel, although not the kind he would normally care to frequent. When he got back, Pat asked him if he had had a good holiday.

'Holiday! Holiday!,' he stormed. 'That was no fucking holiday. I didn't get a wink of sleep.' It turned out to be the main dropping off point for the Tour de France and was at its noisiest when most civilized people were asleep. But the friendship with Beverley Cross continued unabated.

I asked him if he thought that perhaps he was a steadying influence on Ken. 'I would like to think so,' he said, 'I would like to think that was so.'

Ken liked cruises and frequently took Lou on them, too. He would also go to Tangier to be close to his friend, the Hon George Borwick, who was married to a South African diamond multi-millionairess and was a member of the baking powder business.

'But he wouldn't even stay with George Borwick. He didn't like staying in anyone else's home. At Tangier, he would stay at an hotel nearby.' He used to say that staying with friends was the best way to kill a friendship.

TWELVE

The name Kenneth Williams undoubtedly represented box office in the mid-sixties. If it also represented self-confidence, Ken would have been a happy man. As it was, the arrogance that he showed others in his business was mirrored by the doubts that he felt about himself. When Ken was in a bad mood or turned on people who regarded themselves as close friends, it was mostly a reaction to the way he saw himself – a failure to be what he wanted to be most.

All the bravado about earning his living, enjoying comedy and making the faces cut little ice with those who knew his capabilities. He lacked the self-confidence to do more. When an offer came in 1963 for a play that was as different from a 'Carry On' as a lunch at the Grill and Cheese was from one at Le Caprice, he hesitated – and went on holiday.

Robert Bolt, the eminent playwright who had produced *A Man For All Seasons* and had just seen his screenplay for *Lawrence of Arabia* completed, wanted Ken for a Puck-like part for his forthcoming play, *Gentle Jack*.

Ken would be starring in the play opposite Dame Edith Evans, who was admittedly close to the end of her remarkable career and hadn't yet lived down that famous interpretation of hers in the film of *The Importance of Being Earnest*. Of all the roles she had played in the theatre, of all the great works that had come her way, she was fated to be remembered mostly for how she pronounced the rhetorical question, 'A *hand*-bag?'

There would be other eminent actors in the play, people like Michael Bryant and Timothy West. Instead of feeling encouraged Ken hedged.

In his autobiography, he explains that this was a play 'more concerned with philosophy than drama'. Jack was a 'wood god'. He wasn't sure that a god of any kind would make asides to the audience, let along speak in Middle English and quote Wordsworth.

His doubts only increased when he performed another job, midway to finally making up his mind about the Bolt play. He agreed to narrate Gogol's *Diary of A Madman* for the film animator Richard Williams.

He found the whole thing depressing, to the point that he says in *Just Williams* that he wrote 'The madness screamed up inside me. So many awful thoughts – this terrible sense of doom hanging over me. I wonder if anyone will ever know about the emptiness of my life.

His problems were complicated by the fact that the director was constantly demanding more than Ken felt able to deliver. He, of course, did deliver and was able to record in his diary finally that he felt in such a buoyant mood that he could fly.

Things were helped by the fact that he was moving home again – this time to a flat in Farley Court over Baker Street station, close to the London Planetarium near Baker Street. The other home was still too noisy. Even worse, his fans had got to know where he lived and were pestering him.

His next-door neighbour was Sir Adrian Boult, the conductor, but there is no evidence of their being neighbourly in any accepted sense of the word. The flat looked down on the dome of the Planetarium. Ken meanwhile was beginning to look down on a great deal of what he had been asked to do professionally. He wanted to expand his opportunities.

Maybe the successful completion of the recording sessions, coupled with the move, persuaded Ken finally to agree to do *Gentle Jack* – if only for three months. The play opened at the Queen's Theatre at the end of November 1963 to less than rapturous applause.

The company had already anticipated that. The try-out in Brighton had been something less than brilliant and Michael Bryant was not impressed by Ken. 'He wasn't my sort of actor,' he told me, 'I don't want to say more.'

Timothy West, on the other hand, is more forthcoming. West, who played the village idiot in the play, experienced many of Ken's doubts and those of the audiences.

'We became quite friendly,' he recalled. 'I liked him for that. I thought it was very nice of him to have made friends with me. After all, I was a very junior actor at the time.'

Totally divorced from that friendship is his assessment of Ken as an actor. 'He was very, very good in it,' he told me. 'At times, very chilling.'

There was the speech he made asking people to listen to his point of view. Ken was brilliant in it, especially the parts where he moved from medieval English to Anglo-Saxon and then to just some noises. The trouble was that very few members of the audience at the Theatre Royal, Brighton, understood either what he was saying or why they had spent the money on going to see him in the first place.

The cast actually thought that thanks to Kenneth Williams they had achieved something significant. That illusion was quickly dispersed, however – largely as a result of a walk down one of the crooked alleys that mark Brighton from most other seaside towns.

As Timothy West tells it, this was a moment as chilling as any Ken was able to conjure up in the theatre.

Two elderly women approached him. Ken was in one of his usual moods trying to get his mental computer working – does he ignore them brusquely or does he make one of his faces and willingly sign an autograph?

It didn't come to that. One of the ladies pointed her umbrella at him. 'Mr Williams,' she said, 'I think you owe us some money. We came to see your play last night and we were absolutely disgusted. We were not expecting anything like that.'

It was clear, notes Timothy West now, precisely what it was that they were expecting – as he says, 'a combination of "Carry On" and "Beyond Our Ken".'

But that was no reason not to accept these women's judgements. As Timothy told me, 'Whereas I was happy to laugh the whole thing off, Ken took these two old ladies very seriously.' He had to think about what they said if not their demand for a refund. It measured up to precisely what he felt himself and he decided to put it to a higher power. Ken asked to see Robert Bolt and demanded the speech to be cut.

As a result it was cut down. 'But,' says West, 'it lost its magic and disturbing quality – and from that time on, he began to respond much more to what the audience expected him to be – and much less to all the original feeling he had shown for it.'

Lance Percival was in the audience the night that Ken descended on the stage from a rope, curled up his lips, flared his nostrils and in the snide voice he had used a hundred times in the Hancock shows slipped in a 'Hello' that had the Williams fans rolling. Percival said that he was aware of Dame Edith's not being too pleased about that. In fact she called him to her dressing room after the performance and all but ordered him to leave his normal persona behind. After all, *she* didn't say anything about a *hand*-bag.

There are, even today, all sorts of varying views on Ken's theatrical performances and how seriously he took his opportunities to rid himself of the cliché Kenneth Williams image. His sister Pat is convinced that he thoroughly enjoyed *Gentle Jack* despite all the things said about it and about his own performance. 'He liked it because it was a limited run and he was able to expand his performance,' she told me.

Timothy West believes that he didn't take the opportunities that were offered to him far enough.

Quite intuitively, he told me: 'Had he stuck to what he originally put into the part, he would probably have had a totally different career over the next twenty years or so. I thought that was very tragic. I was struck by the fact that he was a person of very little confidence.

'He crumbled over those two little old ladies he met in Brighton, and didn't being to take the chance that had been offered to him. A great shame.'

Ken had another function while in Brighton. It wasn't enough for him to have to learn a series of speeches that no one else was expected to begin to comprehend, but he was also deputed to be Dame Edith's guardian angel.

Their rooms at the Royal Albion Hotel were just a few doors from each other and it was Ken's job to see that she always had her mug of cocoa before going to bed – and indeed that she was warmly tucked up at the right time for a lady of her years and responsibilities.

She, too, was unhappy about the play – to say nothing about the fact that all too few people came to see her in her dressing room, a circumstance that was startling to her, even though she didn't react in the way that Ken himself would have done. There were no depressions from her or tears that her days were over. She just thought that people were remarkably ill-advised in not coming to offer her love and devotion, especially in a town that had residents as diverse as Lord Olivier and Dame Flora Robson – and Dora Bryan.

So Ken's function was also to show her how admired and loved she still was. She believed him, as well she might. One evening, Ken told Timothy West, she assured him: 'You're a very nice boy to stay up with me and chat about things every night – and I wouldn't be surprised if the right little lady doesn't come along soon.'

There were times when Ken was enjoying himself – with Dame Edith and with the part. He dreamed up mad little schemes that both gave him a great deal of pleasure and helped him to avoid some of the inevitable boredom of an out-of-town tour production.

It was the time of the mods-and-rockers' invasion of the seaside towns. Ken would invent scenarios for himself that those with him thought funnier than anything he did on screen or on the radio. 'Look,' he would say as they sat in one of those cafés with the plate glass windows looking out on to the beach and the sea, 'there's a rocker over there. If I go and tell that mod over there that he's insulted his tie and then I go and tell the rocker that the mod's been rude about him, we'll get them burning down the pier.' His mouth watered at the prospect.

He talked to West about his sex life and his inclinations. 'He talked quite freely at a time when very few people did. Actually, I think he did quite a lot for gay understanding, to not wrap up those characters he played at all. I suppose he did a great service by making people laugh with those outrageous characters rather than at them.'

That, however, was also part of the paradox of Kenneth Williams. Nothing about him was straightforward. While at the same time as not merely coming out of the closet about his sexuality – in fact, by hardly admitting there was a closet there at all – he was also locking so many of his innermost thoughts away.

'There was,' said Timothy West, a 'dark quality about him that he didn't let people see very much of. He could have developed that and it would have been tremendously useful to him. I am sure that the talent was there. It seemed to me that various things he did could have gone into other directions, but some kind of self-protective mechanism of his just pulled him back and he did what he knew.'

It was not a good time for him in many ways. Timothy West saw some of those dark Williams depressions descend from over the horizon. These were mainly after the move from Brighton to London.

The notices were poor and Ken cocooned himself in one of those invisible cloaks that he believed protected him from any contact with the outside world. The ostrich dug his head in and believed that there was nobody out there who could notice – and if they did, what did it matter? Suddenly the ebullient performer was no more. Until the two old ladies with their umbrellas shattered his dream, he had walked through the streets of Brighton as if it were his own kingdom, doffing his flat cap to passers-by who couldn't help hearing him coming from two blocks away. After that experience, he slinked from the hotel to the theatre.

In London, he was no more able to show himself. His fellow performers saw him only in the wings. He left at the end of the evening and that was it.

'He sort of closed himself off,' said Timothy West. 'people who knew him very well must have had quite a hard time with him, he was so depressed. But to people like me, well we just couldn't talk to him any more.'

Herbert Kretzmer wrote in the *Daily Express* that he heard a voice call out, 'Rubbish' – to which he himself responded: 'Though I find this kind of boorishness both repulsive and depressing I am bound to state that the solitary heckler was probably articulating a mood felt by many.

The applause was tepid.'

Ken saw the reactions to the play as reactions to himself – reactions that he didn't like. The fact that nobody wrote and said that he was brilliant and was a genius convinced him that it wasn't Robert Bolt who was at fault or the director Noel Willman, but himself as an actor. He wasn't helped by the fact that Stanley Baxter told him he thought he was inhibited in the part.

Timothy West has his own feelings on the subject. 'The play suffered not from wrong direction, but from wrong production,' he maintains and firmly lays the fault at the door of the H. M. Tennent organization.

'Tennents did it in the wrong way. In the first place, they shouldn't have cast Dame Edith, who played the lady in the house where the whole thing takes place. It should have been played by some very good supporting character actress.'

Instead, she was allowed to dominate the play, instead of Ken, or instead of Michael Bryant, around whom the action took place, the character who was being pulled in all directions. One day at rehearsal, to cheer up Dame Edith, the producers gave her £1,000 to go to Hardy Amies so that he could design a new wardrobe for her.

That sort of expenditure, instead of encouraging the rest of the cast to believe that the management had faith in the production, only served to dispirit them, thinks West.

The sets were lavish, the lighting very romantic. 'But it was a hard, argumentative, dark play, ahead of its time. It didn't get its chance. It didn't get a go. It was an attempt to produce a play of classical dimensions in a modern idiom, which in 1963 was a brave thing to do. It should have been something that the Royal Shakespeare did and not Tennents trying to turn it into a West End night out.'

Binkie Beaumont, the head of Tennents, was fond of Ken and wanted to give him a star vehicle – his part was bigger than those of Dame Edith and Michael Bryant put together. But they were all swamped by the fripperies of the play and by Dame Edith who, as Timothy West says, 'didn't have the faintest idea whether she was coming or going'. She was also very deaf. Whenever Ken had to speak to her he had to shout. 'If that's my cue you're giving me dear,' she told him in rehearsal, 'you'll really have to speak much louder.'

Unfortunately, as we have seen, the people who spoke loudest were the critics. Ken waited for the reviews anxiously, as he always did. He booked the second floor of the Ivy restaurant near the theatre and there Lou and Pat, and his closest friends of the moment, would drink endless cups of coffee until the first editions of the paper came out.

On the first night of *Gentle Jack*, Ken knew what they would be like. His sister knew, too. She went back to the dressing room immediately after the final curtain came down, to pour a few trays of drinks ready for those who would come back to congratulate as they would commiserate. There were dry gingers and tonics prepared for the whiskies and gins which everyone hoped would drown the star's sorrows.

That night, there was little to mitigate his depression. 'He came back to the dressing room in tears,' Pat remembered for me. 'What do you think?' he blubbed. 'How did it go?'

'I always told him,' she said, 'that he was fabulous – because I genuinely thought he was. I said, it would run for years.'

Ken cried as he washed the make-up off his legs, hauling them into the sink and then washing them in basins he had on the floor. 'You don't wash your feet and put them on the dirty floor, do you?' he asked as he got ready for the guests who would sooth the painful passage towards the critics.

But he couldn't quite wash away the concerns he felt. And he didn't feel any happier as the weeks went by. All he could feel was that he was out of his depth. The play ended in January 1964, just a couple of months after the opening.

When an offer came for another 'Carry On' film, he grabbed it.

THIRTEEN

Most people involved with the 'Carry On' films regarded Ken's participation in them as totally professional. They were glad to have him in the gang and he was delighted to be among them.

He regaled them with his philosophies on life and on all the things he had read the night before. If Pinewood studios had been in need of a resident historian – and the days of historical dramas emanating from that studio seemed themselves to have been consigned to history – Kenneth Williams would have fulfilled that role.

He was a happy and contented member of a new kind of club, and since the last thing Ken wanted to do was join a club, it was a measure of his new triumph that he became part of this one.

He was liked, not to say loved, by members of the team. He made friendships that were lasting. And although none of the critics called him a genius for playing in them, none argued about the extent of his talent either.

He knew he was worthy of better. His friends knew he was capable of more. His sister Pat still called them 'a load of tripe'. When she asked him why he 'wasted' his time doing the pictures, he replied simply: 'It pays the income tax.' As Pat told me: 'One film a year and he paid all his tax. Two and he had jam with it, too.'

Tax was always a concern with him. He paid it in the same spirit that he washed himself – obsessively. His father had kept two sets of books – following the advice of an accountant who was a friend of a friend. In the end, Charlie had had to find £300 to keep the Inland Revenue happy. Ken was determined not to get involved in that sort of thing. He could have waited a year before he paid the tax but he always paid it immediately. In fact, usually, he never saw the cheques he got for the 'Carry On' films. They would go straight to his agent, who would deduct his commission and the rest went to pay the tax man.

Peter Rogers, who produced all the movies, told me that he said that as long as he had enough money to keep himself and his mother he was happy.

Pat always had tremendous faith in her brother's business acumen. 'He was an extremely good businessman. He always had an agent and an accountant. He didn't worry about money,' she told me. 'In fact, I never knew he had any – at least during the "Carry On" years. We never discussed it.'

To him, the 'Carry On' films represented a kind of rest cure. He told Pat, she remembers, 'I'm not going to break my back eight times a week in the theatre.'

But she worried about the image the films made for him. 'I know the words he came out with were those of other people, the writers, but they were written with him in mind. Why did he always go for those parts, those *double entendres*? I wish he hadn't.' Val Orford told me he felt much the same way. 'I didn't like the way he camped everything up. He was so different in real life,' he maintained.

To Gerald Thomas, who experienced a lot of Ken's problems – mainly his sexual difficulties, the director remembered for me; his dissatisfaction with a part of his life which was neither fulfilled nor which he even wanted fulfilled – Ken was 'a child, a child who was always showing off'.

Certainly, there is not the slightest suggestion that he was unhappy about the choice he made. The 'Carry Ons' allowed him to go home to read in the evenings, to sit playing his classical piano records in the still sparsely-fitted flat at Farley Court, an apartment even more spartan than his previous homes, complete with whitewashed walls. He also had time to record his radio shows and to think about the scripts that still mounted up in Peter Eade's office.

If he had regrets, they were unconnected with his work. 'I've never learned to play the piano,' he said in the early Sixties. 'I've always wanted to. I've never seen the fabulous city of New York and I've never finished reading *The Rise of the Dutch Republic*.'

By the time the eighth 'Carry On' film went before the cameras when *Gentle Jack* was drawing to its conclusion, he was established as the honorary patron of the club.

And it was one that was admired far outside the sort of people who were generally believed to be 'Carry On' fans. The critics were noticing the films. One wrote: (The pictures) 'do not and cannot surpass themselves.'

There was a round table always set aside for the 'Carry On' team in the baronial hall that served as the Pinewood restaurant. Ken always had a plate of mackerel served for him. If it was hot and fresh, Ken was a happy man. If he were not, there are stories still told of the Williams temperament. But on the whole, the table was the centre of a convivial spirit not totally common in the film business. 'Not everybody chose to go there,' Joan Sims recalled, 'but it was wonderful for us all to be there.'

Carry on Jack had nothing whatsoever to do with the Jack he had played on stage. It was also fairly remarkable because, apart from Ken and Charles Hawtrey, the only links with the previous pictures in the series were the producer Peter Rogers and the director, Gerald Thomas, of course. Replacing either of them – and they ran the series as a sort of family business, the Marks and Spencer of movie comedy – would have been professional suicide.

Ken's roles were not to change. No one was allowed to think that his origins were less than upper middle class, to say nothing of aristocratic. It would have been impossible to consider that the captain in his white tights and blue tunic with all the gold braid in this story of piracy at sea had spent his infancy so close to the Caledonian Road.

The black and white *Carry On Spying* (A notice in the entertainments programme for the British Embassy in Moscow read: '13 Aug 8 pm. Club opens. 8.30 Film, *Carry On Spying*. Espionage comedy.') was even more true to form, with Bernard Cribbins cementing the début he made in *Carry On Jack*, but with the addition of Eric Barker, Charles Hawtrey and Jim Dale (who was to appear in a number of the series). Most significant of all, this 1964 picture starred the woman with the most notable breasts in British movie history, yet who always managed – if only just and with the aid of her equally pretty hands – to keep them to herself, Barbara Windsor. Miss Windsor was always much more intelligent than the all-bust-and-bum dumb blonde image she had created for herself. Ken appreciated it and for almost a quarter of a century afterwards they would be close friends.

In fact, the friendship was very quick in cementing itself. Soon after their first meeting, Barbara met her husband-to-be Ronnie Knight and announced that she was going to Madeira for her honeymoon. 'That's funny,' said Ken, 'I was thinking of going there for my holiday.' He did, together with Lou and Pat, staying at the same hotel as the newlyweds. No one appears to have recognized any difficulties with that.

As she told me: 'I had no question about saying straight away after our first picture together that Kenneth Williams was the one I would choose to spend time with on a desert island.' She took no account of the problems with his bowels or of other difficulties in the anal region or of his depressions. It would have been enough simply to hear his stories.

She was to say that she always knew his moods. When he arrived on the set all hunched up with his head down to his waist, she knew there were going to be problems on the way. When they went out to a restaurant together, he would always complain – very loudly so that the proprietor would know who he was and so there would be people around about whom he could fuss were pestering him for his autograph. When the meal was over, however, he would usually lick his lips and say, 'Mmm, quite nice here, isn't it?'

Most people on the 'Carry Ons' seemed to think that it was quite nice having Ken around, which assuredly had a lot to do with his love of the series. It was a typical loner's situation – the depressive who, though wanting to be alone, worried about having no one around and was so grateful to feel wanted.

'We were all so close,' Peter Rogers told me, 'that it was like talking about members of our own family, especially Ken. He was a very earnest, very intelligent gentleman – and very much a gentleman, whom I never thought of as particularly ambitious. He didn't want to go into any other kind of films. He was just a happy member of the team.' For that, Rogers will be eternally grateful to Betty White, the casting director who first suggested him.

While other members of the cast were betting on horses, doing their football pools or playing cards, Ken would be the centre of a small circle that also included Hattie Jacques, Joan Sims and Kenneth Connor, doing the *Times* crossword.

In fact, according to Gerald Thomas, it was always a toss-up as to who was the most popular character on the 'Carry On' lot at any one time, Ken or Sidney James. Sid James hadn't made a picture since the one that was without the Williams credit, *Cabby*, but he was soon to be almost a fixture on the set, playing parts as stereotyped as Ken's.

Peter Rogers, however, is adamant that neither of then could be called the real star of the 'Carry Ons'. 'We always said, no one is going above the title. The title is the star of the series. For that reason, there was no single star.'

There were more difficulties with *Carry on Spying*. Harry Saltzman, the producer of the James Bond pictures, objected to both Charlies Hawtrey's being called Agent 001½ and to the name Charlie Bind. Peter Rogers gave way on the first count but was unmoved by the second.

Later in 1964, there was yet another picture for the team, the third that year. *Carry On Cleo*, in colour, seemed more adventurous than the others. Even the togas in this spoof on the Julius Caesar-and-Cleopatra story –. 'The eunuchs are on strike. They are complaining about loss of assets' – looked as though they hadn't come out of the

Bermans and Nathans mothballs.

Ken played Julius Caesar in a picture that, with no apologies, was intended to cash in on the fame of the Elizabeth Taylor–Richard Burton fiasco of the previous year. More apologies *were* needed, however, to the board of Marks and Spencer – the slave market was called 'Marcus et Spencius'. In the end, no one took it too seriously and no apology was officially made.

The company did have some copyright problems with the *Cleo* story, however. A judge decided that the poster advertising the film was much too close to the one used for the original *Cleopatra*. One, showing Sid James looking like a sphinx, was substituted instead.

In all, it was good, respectable 'Carry On' material. Sid James, Joan Sims, Kenneth Connor, Charles Hawtrey, Jim Dale and Ken linking up for once with Sheila Hancock in this epic which seemed to satisfy everybody.

'Ken loved to shock,' Sheila Hancock recalls. Once at this time, she shocked him. They did a charity concert together and Ken, caring as little as at any time in his career, started ad-libbing. He went on and on about his mother. Finally, Sheila, standing on the stage, wondering when she was going to regain her part of what served as a script, said, 'Silly old cow!'

It was more than Ken could take. 'He was *outraged*,' she recalled for me. 'How dare you talk about my mother like that!'

He took it seriously at first, affronted that anyone could say anything about anyone so close to him, but before very long, he saw the funny side.

But, as she remembered, he would tell that story time after time, particularly to the 'Carry On' lot 'and with glee'.

'He was a sort of out-front version of me and I identified with what he did a lot. You get very fed up with people being sycophantic, toadying to you, as a symptom of success. When someone comes along and gives you a mouthful, not maliciously but to put you right, boy do you like it!'

She saw some of his problems and how he was affected by them. She used to go to him and say, 'Are you all right? Do you want to talk about it?'

He was never very forthcoming, she said. At the same time, he needed to have someone to 'come along and set up a boundary. In a way, Kenneth was retarded. He needed still to have Mummy come along and say, "No! That's enough."'

A few months after that, the 'Carry On' factory produced *Carry On Cowboy* from its assembly line, with Ken playing Judge Burke and the busty Joan Sims as Belle – 'My intimates call me Ding Dong'.

She defied much of the casting formulae employed with the 'Carry On' concept. Sometimes, Joan was the dowdy, make-up-less wallflower with curves that looked more like sacks. At other times, she was stunningly beautiful. Looking back on the almost thirty-year-long era of the series, one does not automatically think of these essential mammerial features of the femme fatale when talking about Miss Sims. Think of breasts and it's always Miss Windsor and her efforts to keep everything hidden. Yet in *Carry On Cowboy* and, later on *Carry On Henry*, Joan Sims's cleavage was imposing indeed. In *Carry On – Follow That Camel*, her shape under a crisp white satin blouse was guaranteed to send even Kenneth Williams, as the German commandant of the French Foreign Legion battalion, crying for his Mütter.

He normally didn't like wearing uniforms in films, but wore them with aplomb. Ken did, however, fight against playing in drag. 'He was too embarrassed by it', says Gerald Thomas.

Ken didn't have to put on drag in *Carry On Screaming*, the first of three 1966 releases, but in *Carry On – Don't Lose Your Head*, he did get to wear a woman's frilly corset which didn't go all that badly with the curled wig he wore as Citizen Camembert, the 'big cheese' of the French Revolutionary secret police.

By the time *Follow That Camel* went before the cameras as the third 'Carry On' picture that year – filmed 'on location' with Camber Sands on the then almost freezing Sussex coast, doubling somewhat unconvincingly for the North African desert – the distribution company for the 'Carry Ons' had changed from Anglo-Amalgamated to the Rank Organization. It took a little bit of deft footwork to satisfy themselves that the first firm would not object to Rank using 'Carry On' in the title. By the time the news came through, the preliminary advertising had already gone into production, but before long, it had become *Carry On – Follow That Camel*.

Rank wanted to be sure of an international market for their newly-acquired product. Their answer – to bring in an American star. The choice was not altogether fortuitous. Phil Silvers had made an institution for himself out of the rank of an army sergeant. But Nocker, the part he played in *Camel* was no Bilko, even though he threw his weight around just as though he were head of the transport squad at Fort Baxter.

He succeeded in getting up everyone's nose, particularly the flared nostrils of Kenneth Williams who saw a foreigner – in the Foreign Legion

– usurping his position as the mentor of the team.

But there was the required amount of glamour in the movie, largely through the introduction of Anita Harris, who had been both hit pop singer and dancer before moving on to the 'Carry On' lot.

Her first day there confirmed the differences between the regulars and the outsiders. The team were sitting round in a semi-circle when she was introduced to them – although no one gave *her* a chair, or at least one with her name on it.

'The loudest voice of all was that of Mr Williams – followed by Phil Silvers.'

She was conscious of one undoubted fact: 'He was directing all his conversations to Joan Sims at this time, so I felt as though I were being talked at, rather than talked to.'

By now, Joan Sims and Ken seemed birds of a feather. 'I admired Kenneth for his tremendous wit,' says Joan today. 'He had a fantastic brain and could keep you amused for hours – and not just amused. He was very erudite. In fact, I don't think I knew what the word 'erudite' meant until I met Kenneth. I often thought I should like to have been taught by someone like him.'

Despite the joy she had out of being with him on the 'Carry On' set, she for one thought that he was wasting a great deal of his time. 'He wasn't wasted on the series. He was one of the people who actually made the series, but I have to say that I never thought his career was channelled in the right direction. Kenneth deserved so much better. He was such a very, very talented man.'

'It's a terrible thing. If people associate you with the 'Carry On' films, they don't think of you as anything else. I would like to think of him as something else.'

That was not to say that she herself thought of the films as being an easy option. 'They were very hard work,' she told me. 'I think it is true that much of the time we spent together we were going over our lines early in the morning in the make-up room.'

Most of the pictures were made in something like six or eight weeks.

She remembered him as a very private person. 'I wouldn't have liked to have known more about him, even though Hattie Jacques and I had the deepest philosophical discussions with him.'

There was, she recalls, 'a sort of madness that overtook him. He was a very religious person. He could be demonic – like the time someone fresh came to the "Carry On" team, who wasn't quite as professional as he would have liked.'

The matter reached its peak at the round table over lunch. Ken saw the newcomer and refused to sit down. 'It was difficult to know which way the cat was going to jump,' she told me.

And there was a time when he practically destroyed Joan herself on the set. Lance Percival was there to hear Ken look at Miss Sims as she arrived on that boundary between the action and the production. They were sitting in their chairs behind the cameras. Joan arrived on set, freshly made up, her new costume fitted. Ken looked at her. 'My God,' he told her, 'you look awful.'

Nevertheless, she can now put moments like that totally behind her.

'I loved him and he loved me,' she told me. 'He was a very unique person and I saw him more deeply than I think other people did. I got to know the man behind the voices that people heard. When you saw Kenneth the real person he was very wonderful. Sometimes he drove you mad. But I loved him. He was a gentleman. If you sent him a present, he would reply immediately in that beautiful handwriting of his.'

When they first met up on a 'Carry On' set a couple of years before no one knew how strong that love would be.

To Gerald Thomas, however, she confessed the strength of the love. Ken, the loner and the camp actor who had never actually admitted his homosexuality, proposed marriage to Joan. 'But there won't be any of that dirty stuff,' he told her.

'Yes,' she admitted to me, 'it's true. He did propose, but it just wouldn't have worked. I had not had very successful relationships with people up to this time and I said no to him.'

She admits that she thought about it seriously enough. 'Kenneth and I would have been a marvellous companionship, but ...' She wouldn't finish that sentence. And she added: 'I saw Kenneth in many, many lights. Like me, he was a very private person.' And she repeated: 'Yes, I loved him – and he loved me.'

Ken sincerely believed that a separate-bedroom marriage would be the perfect relationship with someone for whom he cared so much. But it offered little to Joan.

After that, they didn't meet socially that often. At Christmas, Hattie Jacques would have a party and Ken and Joan were among the 'Carry On' team who would share the festivities and her very ample food selections. 'Hattie had the wonderful ability of taking people under her wing. She was mum, sister – everything to all of us.'

She also had the privilege of visiting the Williams home.

One day, Joan had the brave notion of asking for an invitation – or rather inviting herself. She and Hattie said they were coming around for a cup of tea. 'Kenneth was so astonished with this, I can't tell you. But we did get our cup of tea.'

Funnily enough, she doesn't think of Ken in terms of humour. That is not to say that she forgets the outrageous moments.

There was the time, for instance, when they had a love scene in *Carry On Up The Khyber* in 1968. Ken was in the midst of one of his severe pile problems and kept saying, 'I'm in such agony, I've got to blow off.'

But in the picture, he played the elegant Khazi of Kalabar. Joan was Lady Ruff-Diamond. 'He, to put it bluntly, broke wind in the middle.' Miss Sims, on the other hand, broke up. She told him: 'Kenneth how on earth can we make love if you keep farting?'

Ken looked at her, shocked. 'Valentino used to fart,' he told her. 'Yes,' she replied, 'but that was in the silent films.'

The all-talking, all-colour films continued to receive more praise than perhaps could have been expected. The exception was *Camel*. The *Evening Standard* said: 'It is something worse than totally unfunny. Even its efforts to be indelicate are dull.'

Anita Harris, who followed *Camel* with *Carry on Doctor* in 1968 – playing a nurse who looked more sexy in her cap and apron than she had as a belly dancer in the earlier film – suffered from being the butt of Ken's jokes in both pictures. 'He was awfully fond of ribbing people,' she recalled.

'I think it was just a mental exercise for him, his way of having fun.' But at other people's expense. Until he was sure that she was a professional actress, she was simply a new target, a figure of fun. 'I guess in a way, every comment from him was facetious. And that took a long time getting used to. I don't think it was bullying, simply in the old phrase, taking the Michael.' He would make disparaging remarks about her goose pimples. He looked at the copper bosom covers she had to wear as a belly dancer – and then at the less than fully-endowed nature of Miss Harris's bust and said cuttingly, 'Which way up are they supposed to go?'

The solution was to bring what she now calls 'some false bravado into play', to answer him back, giving the impression of a strength and security she really didn't feel.

'I knew there was a soft side to him,' she told me. 'I could tell that from the warm way Joanie Sims and Hattie Jacques spoke about him.' Then she added, as an afterthought which has subsequently been confirmed, 'I think he was actually in love with Joan. In fact, I am certain that he was.'

Anita Harris decided to try to play the game according to Ken's own rules, or at least give it a try. She pretended not to care, answered him back, and Kenneth Williams melted.

She might not now think of this as the action of a deflated bully, but the symptoms are classic.

'Basically, I was very naive. I was a convent-educated girl and he teased me mercilessly with a string of sexual connotations.'

In the queue for the Pinewood cafeteria, the loudest voice would be Ken and his innuendos. Few were allowed to escape. 'Oh look how your dumplings are wobbling,' he called to her and her tray shook along with the dumplings.

'In there, though,' says Anita Harris, 'there was such a marvellous talent and a marvellous brain. His use of the English language made me respect him. Even if he was trying to show off, I still respected him.'

As she said, for someone who was so lonely to be able to come to the studio at five o'clock every morning – picked up in a studio car, Ken had decided long ago he would never drive – and then play a very strong character, was worthy of that respect too. 'You have to be a very special person.'

Ken did, however, help Anita – with the ruby in her navel that kept falling out every time she did her belly dance. She tried double Sellotape, but every time her belly went in, the ruby popped out. Ken announced that he had a solution. 'What about some of that eyelash glue, duckie?' It worked. The ruby in her belly button stayed put.

But she adds: 'You don't get a fondness, a bond in a team like they had in the 'Carry Ons' unless there is something very real in their love of each other.' To the point that she herself felt distinctly out of things at first. 'And so did Phil Silvers,' her husband and manager Michael Margolis now remembers. 'They gave him a very rough time indeed.' But, she says, she did think that Ken showed him a certain degree of respect. 'As for me, I think he was tougher because I was a girl – one who felt that any kind of talkback would have just been out of order. I think he challenged me. If I responded, he would be on guard. I picked up the challenge, which he took very seriously.'

The medium of the films was a great escape for him. But he still took his work very seriously. Despite it all, he respected most of his colleagues. 'He treated her,' added Michael Margolis, 'in exactly the same way as he treated Phil Silvers. To him, they were both outsiders.'

Liz Frazer, who only made three 'Carry Ons', *Cabby, Cruising* and *Regardless*, remembers most affectionately of all the Ken who wasn't quite so serious. 'He was the only one of the *Carry On* team who was funny off as well as on film. But, as she added: 'They were all talented comedy actors, not comedians. There was no wastage of talent.' But she saw the intellectual side of Ken as well. 'When we had a quiz, as often we did in the caravans waiting for filming to begin, Ken always won hands down.'

Indeed, not only was there a tremendous rapport between the members of the company, there was also a recognizable repartee between them, led by Ken, which was so fast that unless he actually knew the language, a stranger was in foreign territory.

'I spent a lot of time with Phil Silvers talking about his family away from the others,' Anita Harris now recalls.

The biggest contrasts in Ken's behaviour – and indeed in his life – were seen by those who had worked with him elsewhere. Fenella Fielding, for instance, could contrast the sometimes obsessive manic figure of *Pieces Of Eight* with the more relaxed co-star in films like *Carry On Regardless* (she played a woman in search of a male baby-sitter who could take her to bed) and *Carry On Screaming* (a velvet-clad vamp). '*Carry On Screaming* worked because we both took that nonsense so seriously.'

Michael Thornton noted in the *Sunday Express*: 'Kenneth Williams is rather more subdued than usual, which is a pity. A bit of his nasal falsetto with . . . or "Don't be like that" might have enlivened the proceedings.'

Instead, when the monster loses an ear, Ken says: 'Oh well, ear today, gone tomorrow.' But Fenella Fielding survived it all and enjoyed the experience.

'There wasn't the awful competitiveness that we had on stage,' she told me. 'And we only did each take once.' Interestingly, she added to that: 'Every shot was like a first night.'

Consequently, he was more relaxed – and more funny. 'Sometimes, when people are funny all the time, they wear you out. Not him. He only stopped when he felt like it. When he felt he had said enough and made us laugh enough, he went back to his dressing room. It was as if he had tired himself out.'

Tiredness was frequently a good excuse for the moods in which he would be less than charming.,

'He was so moody,' Fenella Fielding said, 'that his moods were part of the difficulty of his genius – and his temper. There were on the film set few of the moments I had come to dread during the run of the stage show – when he'd slap me down, or even when he would encourage me, egg me on.'

He still had a low boredom threshold – which was why he was spending less time going to Equity Council meetings. 'He would only go occasionally now,' Fenella recalled. 'He would come in late and say very little. I really believe he couldn't stand the boredom of being in one place for a long time, listening to other people.'

Off-set meetings with others in the 'Carry On' organization were usually at their homes, certainly not his. He would spend Sundays occasionally with Peter Rogers at his home at Beaconsfield. 'At dinner parties, he would certainly liven the place up. He could keep the table in stitches.'

That was the risk one ran in inviting Ken to dinner parties. They inevitably became a stage for a Kenneth Williams one-man show.

He was at this time, a terrible gossip. 'But he would only gossip about people he was fond of,' Fenella Fielding told me.

'He would slag off someone terribly and you would think they must have had a terrible row. But no. They were still very, very good friends. He would say how fantastically bad someone was and would say they had no talent whatsoever. Yet when you bumped into that same person, they would always talk about him in the most loving way.'

This, however, was part of the unpredictable side of Ken's character. Sometimes, if they knew he behaved in that way, people would be unwilling to talk about him at all – for fear they would embarrass themselves by saying something sympathetic about a man they knew could just as easily assassinate their characters. Like them or not, one could never be sure what Ken did or did not mean.

The experience in *Gentle Jack* and the speech that caused all the problems in that play stood him in good stead. For as Peter Rogers remembers, he had 'a wonderful trick – of reciting Shakespeare that wasn't Shakespeare at all.'

What the Bard of Stratford-upon-Avon would have thought of his verse can only be imagined, but Ken adopted the Shakespearean metre to the subject matter on hand – the Government of the day, the state of show business or the food being served.

He would do it on the set, between takes, too. 'Sometimes, if he got bored he would just come up and start reciting. He did it so cleverly that you would think it was the real thing – until he burst out laughing. It was just gobbledegook. Some of it quite rude. But it was not vulgarity, just rudery – and he would do it for some very distinguished people we had on the set sometimes.'

They used to have sessions together, he and Rogers. 'We used to call it the Bitching Hour. He never bitched about other members of the team, but of people we knew.'

Sheila Hancock told me of his 'great disdain' for bad actors. 'He couldn't tolerate them,' she said.

Peter Rogers recognized Ken as being 'intolerant at some levels. But if he didn't suffer fools gladly, I must ask who would want to? There are some people who get bored who can just fall asleep, standing up with their eyes open. Kenny wouldn't do that. His mind was always too sharp. He would just start thinking about something else.'

That night, he would record his recollections of those who bored him. The following morning, he would tell Rogers: 'I wrote about that in my diary.'

The relationship between producer and star was so strong that Ken would reveal incidents that most people would keep to themselves. On more than one occasion, he told Rogers: 'I had a wonderful wank last night. Wonderful thing it was.'

As Rogers told me: 'He was outrageous to that extent. With anyone else, it would seem outrageous, but with Kenneth it was acceptable because he had that wonderful wit. I don't think Kenneth was trying to be outrageous at all. I think he had just got bored and was looking for something to do, so he sought to amuse.'

That would be his usual role at these parties. Sometimes, he took his mother with him. 'She was a wonderful, quick-witted little woman, hilariously funny,' Fenella Fielding remembers. 'She would hold court. She was also useful to Ken. He would use her as his excuse for never going to America to work – a prospect which always frightened him.'

Lou was everyone's idea of the cockney sparrow let loose to fly in a wider world than she had once ever known existed. They loved stories that tripped off her tongue as easily as other women talked about waiting in the check-out queue at Tescos.

'She was starin' at me so rudely,' Lou recounted one day, 'I very nearly said, "Wait a minute, I'll get a basin for your eyes".' On another occasion, she said: 'Posh? Spit in 'er eye and it wouldn't choke her.'

Gerald Thomas saw another side of Ken as well as the jovial clown. The depressions of Kenneth Williams even within the confines of the 'Carry On' set-up could be profound. 'They were never about his work, but about his health,' he said.

'He spent his life worrying about his health – terrified he was going to get cancer. He would constantly talk about it, constantly running to the doctor.'

He was more than just a hypochondriac. 'He couldn't stand physical pain,' said Thomas.

Once, the script required him to jump through a plate-glass window. The window was made of sugar glass, the substance adopted in a thousand movies to look like the real thing. Thomas kept trying to persuade him it was safe. To demonstrate the fact, he put his hand through the window himself. That did the trick – 'Of course,' recalls the director, 'I didn't show him that I had cut my hand in the process.'

If there were no problems with pain involved, Ken would happily do whatever he was asked. But he wouldn't want to be expected to do anything while he spoke. 'For an actor of his calibre,' recalls Gerald Thomas, 'and he was of a very high calibre indeed, he had the inability to play dialogue at the same time as he was handling props. He so concentrated on his dialogue – I never had to reshoot a scene because Kenny fluffed a line – that he couldn't do anything at the same time as he was talking.'

Thomas first discovered that for himself when he was shooting *Twice Round The Daffodils*. There was a scene in which Ken was playing chess with Andrew Ray. The director wanted him to move his Queen in the course of a deep conversation. He couldn't do it. In the end, the move had to be inserted, rather than filmed in master shot. Afterwards, Ken told him: 'Never give me dialogue and ask me to handle props at the same time.'

It took some time before the real Kenneth Williams came to the surface. 'He was very serious in the first of the pictures,' the director now remembers. 'He was too concerned to do a good performance to be really funny. Afterwards, he settled down and relaxed and became a little bit more impish. He could never feel sure that he was being accepted.'

The advantage that Ken offered the team was the ability to be able to pull off love scenes and other out-of-character poses without anyone ridiculing the whole thing. 'We didn't overdo or over emphasize Ken's neuterism because we had him make love or going after it, but we knew that underneath it all was another character.'

He would tease, too – telling people that Rogers sat all day in his office, counting the money, except on the occasions he made forays to location 'wearing a pair of green wellies' – which Rogers maintains, 'I have never worn in my life'.

He would tell the rudest stories out loud, when he knew that Joan Sims was within earshot.

The question of money would always come up with a team operation like the 'Carry Ons'. But not from Ken, Rogers maintains. 'He was always the one cast member who always stood up for me if there were any bleating from Equity members about them not getting their money from repeats, compilations and so on.'

After the third 'Carry On', the cast had been offered a profit-sharing scheme – and had all turned it down on the advice of their agents, who thought they would be better off getting increased salaries.

'Kenneth was always the one who reminded them that they could have been very well off had they accepted the offer, which they rejected. He was content with the money he earned, which was what the agents asked.'

'There were times when Sid James sowed dissatisfaction among the other artists by claiming that he was getting more than the others. They all came back through their agents and complained and I told them to forget it. It was just schoolboy talk. It never worried Kenneth.'

He never worried about scripts, either, according to Rogers. 'I would send him a script, but he never turned one down.' On the other hand, the company always knew which part would be his. The writers, Norman Hudis and Talbot Rothwell (who took over from Hudis with *Carry on Cabby*) wrote for Ken and knew exactly which part would be his.

He says that he always knew where he was with Ken. 'When he was in a reflective or depressive mood, you knew to leave him alone although his manners were such that if anyone came to him to talk, he would stand up to talk to them.'

Ken didn't want to be thought wanting by people for whom he had respect. 'He liked to be thought of as a man of the world,' said Gerald Thomas. 'That was why he dressed the way he did, always immaculate.' Thomas believes that he sipped his favourite drink at the time, Campari and soda, because he believed – in the terminology of the time – that was the 'with-it' thing to do.

In restaurants – his tastes were no more sophisticated now than before, but occasionally he would do better than the Corner House – he would still order at the top of his voice, still hoping to be recognized.

He could be outrageous in the most genteel Italian eaterie, as Gerald Thomas remembered for me. 'I don't have asparagus,' he would say as loudly as the way he had greeted the waiter, 'it'll make my pee smell.'

Other times, he would sandwich discussions about the menu with still more talk about the 'pain in my bum'.

'I don't think he would do it to draw attention, but I believe quite genuinely that he was trying to amuse me.' And it happened towards the end of a lunch or dinner. 'We always started seriously, usually discussing Louisa and perhaps her problems with her legs which stopped her doing her old-time dancing.' Then the mood would grow mellow and the bum stories would come thick and fast.

Once, during the shooting of *Carry On Regardless*, Ken was supposed to be at the Ideal Home Exhibition. He fell off some scaffolding and had to be taken to the studio surgery.

'I saw him lying totally naked on a bed,' says Gerald Thomas, 'while the sister, who was quite formidable, was applying Savlon to his private parts. I asked him how he felt, "Marvellous!" he replied.'

He would start expounding his theories on the cultural state of the nation. Gerald Thomas believes this was not so much his great erudition, 'but Ken's *superficial* knowledge of a lot of things'. In this, the director is at odds with most of Ken's other friends and associates, but he could be closest to the truth.

'I think he had a great superficial knowledge, but if you delved too deeply you would probably have felt that he didn't know so much. He had a very retentive memory. He learned a great many quotations which he would suddenly come out with. I doubt, though, if he knew the whole play. He was showing off. Everything he did, was showing off.'

Sheila Hancock agrees that a great deal of the Williams intellectual showing off was to rid himself of the 'Carry On' persona. 'He didn't like that image,' she told me. 'He didn't like people thinking he was an idiot. I think he should have been a monk or a professor. He admired knowledge, which was why he would lord it over you.'

'He was very upset about some of the work he was doing. He would rubbish it.'

'Load of shit, dear,' he would say to her. 'Load of shit. But, as she added, 'we all do that.' Nevertheless, despite saying so, she is convinced that his diary is full of entries about her. 'I loved him very much.'

He was as reticent about having people to his home as ever. If Gerald Thomas went to his flat to pick him up, he would be looking out of the window waiting for his car to arrive. When he saw it, he was downstairs, ready to get into the vehicle by the time it had stopped, and the director had got out.

It was a feature of life other characters in the 'Carry On' story would recognize. The series would go on until 1978 with Ken in the last, *Carry On Emmanuelle*, a spoof on the soft-porn hits of the age, as he had been in *Carry on Sergeant*, the first. He missed out on only *Carry On Up The Jungle*, *Carry On Girls* and *Carry On England*, the penultimate in the series.

In between, there was *Carry On Again, Doctor* ('Kenneth Williams and Sid James excel,' wrote Richard Barkley in the *Sunday Express*) and *Carry On ... Loving*, (Ian Christie wrote about this in the *Daily Express*, 'The only difference between this, the twentieth film in the ribald comedy series and the first instalment is that the key members of the cast are just that much older.'). Ken also made 'Carry On' ... *Henry*, *At Your Convenience*, *Abroad*, *Matron*, *Dick*, *Behind* and finally, the thirtieth in the series, *Emmannuelle*, (the film that Barbara Windsor refused to do because she said it was 'just one long nude scene'. Eventually, she just played a cameo role and Suzanne Danielle was the very femme fatale.) There was also going to be *Carry On Dallas*, a parody on the TV series. But in the end, there were problems about getting the requisite finance and the film was abandoned.

The formula never changed, although with *Emmanuelle*, the *double-entendres* left less to the imagination than did any of the other films. Women were seen to have complete breasts with nipples on them. Ken himself bared his behind seemingly whenever there was a camera to turn. As he said at the time: 'I've never been seen naked in any bed, never. In my own bed, yes, but then I usually wear pyjamas, but never in public.'

As the critic noted eight years earlier, Ken, like the others, grew a little more grey, a little more lined. But the people still came to the box office, paid the ever-increasing charges for admission, and stayed to laugh.

All the time, Ken was appearing on television, on radio or on stage. Some weeks, he would be doing all three and writing his letters, at the same time as making a 'Carry On'.

As we have seen, some of his work led to friendships – not all of which were uncomplicated. In the mid to late Sixties for instance there was the playwright Joe Orton. What happened in their relationship made a day on a 'Carry On' set seem to Ken like sitting in the audience at a pantomime.

FOURTEEN

Ken had a ringside seat for one of the most explosive and widely publicized bouts of homosexual love and hate in recorded British history – the lives and deaths of playwright Joe Orton and his lover, Kenneth Halliwell.

Orton was the writer of the naturalistic *Entertaining Mr Sloane*, and later on of plays like *What The Butler Saw*. They were highly acclaimed and immensely popular. None more so than the play he virtually wrote for Kenneth Williams – *Loot*. There can be no doubt that he rewrote it for Ken.

Ken and Orton had been introduced by Michael Codron in 1964. It was the time of *Entertaining Mr Sloane*, a play Ken didn't at first see himself. Codron produced it, but even his links with the producer couldn't persuade him to go to a play which 'sounded irreligious and immoral'. As he said, 'I am not an irreligious man and I am not an immoral man and therefore it struck me that it would be offensive. I don't want to come out of a theatre feeling disturbed and offended.'

But he went after a friend persuaded him and was glad that he did. 'I'd never seen anything quite as stimulating as this in the English theatre. If you'd said to me, this is a French play translated, I'd have agreed ... I was devastated by the evening, almost crystalline.' It made him think again about contemporary language.

At about that time, Ken asked Codron if he had anything for him. They talked about *Mr Sloane* and the producer suggested an introduction to Orton. 'I think you'll get on very well with each other,' he told him.

A supper was arranged at Codron's flat. Ken came and so did Orton and Halliwell. 'There's absolutely no doubt that Joe was totally smitten by Ken,' Codron told me. For all his sophistication, he was still a boy from Leicester and Ken saying outrageous things impressed him greatly.

Largely as a result of that introduction, they became strong friends. It wasn't long before the personal friendship became a working set-up, too. Not a partnership – strangely for someone so set in his own ways, Ken would be willing to do as he was told, as far as work was concerned. He accepted the writer's script and the director's instructions. Not always happily. He would complain as loudly as he would in the midst of a 'Carry On' situation, and he would talk about it endlessly, but he would do it. That, as we shall see, would be a situation that his association with Orton would change.

Later that year, when the writer was working on *Loot*, the idea first came up for the two of them to work together. Ken was busier now than he had ever been before. There were the 'Carry Ons', a new radio series with Kenneth Horne – *Beyond Our Ken* had matured into *Round The Horne* and was better than anything he had done on air before. Ken's own television series, *International Cabaret* had started making an impact, and he was a guest on shows like *Juke Box Jury* and *Call My Bluff*, on which he managed to get Joe to appear.

It was during the time the play was being crafted, and for years afterwards, that Ken was a witness to the bizarre happenings that made up this strangest of all relationships, a relationship which ended with Halliwell murdering Orton and then taking his own life.

Ken didn't actually witness either the murder or the suicide. But was a first-hand witness of so many of the circumstances that led to the deaths. He saw them at their home, talked with them, wrote to them, received letters from them – and all the time heard blow-by-blow accounts of their sexual activities, all of which a few years earlier would have had them rotting away in jail for life.

The behaviour whetted Ken's own appetite. For a time the celibate once more tried to end his own monk-like existence. He relished hearing the stories that Orton told of masturbatory sessions in public lavatories, of men he had picked up in the street, of having sex in shop doorways, of the sizes of his acquaintances' organs and of his experiences with venereal disease.

As Ken told John Lahr, author of the official Orton biography *Prick Up Your Ears* (Lahr also edited the Orton diaries): 'He (Orton) had this capacity to have a sexual adventure and tell you the conversation that went on as well. One wonders how he was capable of sustaining his own sexual performance. He had this tremendous desire to be thorough. His sexual adventures were recounted with such an eye for detail.'

On one occasion, Orton told about an old man who took him into a cave in Tunisia and asked him to feel his posterior. ' "Wonderful bum," Ken said, "Marvellous and working class to boot".'

Ken enjoyed his visits to Orton's flat, with its crucifix on one wall surrounded by pictures that Ken said were 'almost porno'. There were hundreds of pictures on that wall, forming a somewhat unusual collage.

Ken was a great observer at all times. He remembered how Orton used to sit slumped in a chair and Halliwell was always upright. It wasn't the only difference between the two of them. While Orton was promiscuous, always searching for new adventures, new partners, Halliwell was more keen on a stable, married-type relationship with Orton.

'Halliwell said that these sexual experiments can only lead to a dead end. My immediate response was to agree with Halliwell,' said Ken.

The writer told Ken about it all. But much of it he saw for himself. 'I was convinced of Halliwell's absolute timidity all along. I always said that Halliwell was too timid by half. The only time he seemed to be bold and at all resolute was in contradicting Joe's apparent errors. He had no fear with Joe in being bold. But with people he did.'

Orton wrote him letters, both serious and humorous, going into the most intimate details of his sexual encounters. He also sent him some of his famed fake letters in the name of 'Edna Welthorpe' – a character he invented for his own fun and that of the few chosen intimates who were allowed to receive them. They were addressed to people like the manager of the Ritz Hotel – asking if he had seen a handbag 'she' had left during a brief stay.

Then there was one from 'R. Ufricks District Postmaster' informing residents of his area that pillar boxes with two holes in them had been 'put to an improper purpose', which he spelled out in a way unlikely to commend itself to the Royal Mail.

Another letter was signed 'Uncle Whippity', which might have been sub-titled, but wasn't, 'The Joys of Syphilis'. It advised children on the ease of getting gonorrhoea, but said that while syphilis was more fun, it was more difficult to get. He also said that before anything else, a boy must first learn how to masturbate.

Ken said he found that one 'too rude' for his tastes. Only slightly less controversially, Orton also made up letters to newspaper agony aunts – 'What can I do because my boyfriend won't kiss me?'

They talked religion, too. 'Orton understood that his irreligiousness was entirely religious,' Williams noted.

'He could only talk like that because Ken was religious himself,' said John Lahr, who recounted many of the Williams reactions in *Prick Up Your Ears*.

Ken was in one of his most religious periods and so was Orton. But the writer couldn't understand the aristocracy of the Vatican and constantly said so.

'He understood the agony of the Crucifixion,' Ken told John Lahr.

'He was very much aware of the fact that many of our symbols had become clichés, banalities. He was very interested in restoring them to their proper significance. In the process, he felt he had to offend.'

So the stories proliferated, most of them true. Orton told Ken that he was totally anonymous in his affairs. He always said he was a lorry driver, a packer, a lithographer (no doubt an idea he developed from a conversation about Ken's own origins). Ken particularly liked the story Orton told him about a man he had picked up in a lavatory and asked him if he did it often. The man said he did – with some nice people who had LP's. Sometimes he got as much as what would now be £1.50 to go home with. He would write to Ken about his holidays in Morocco and going to see dancing 'by what turned out to be the Senegal National Shitpot Company'.

In another letter he wrote: 'I didn't see a cock the whole time – except my own and that glimpsed only briefly in a cracked mirror.'

Ken replied, Orton later wrote in his own diary, that he had had a similar experience in Beirut and had 'paid twelve guineas a night for the privilege.'

Orton wrote about Ken 'Sexually,' he said, 'he really is a horrible mess.' He said that Ken constantly referred to the 'guilt' that he felt. He recalled his telling him about the time he went into a pub when a man suggested having sex with him and pulled down his trousers in front of the assembled company. When Lahr wrote the story, Ken insisted on a line in which the man asked him to 'give me a fuck' being removed. He did agree to the sentence 'It's legal now,' being included. (A week later, Ken returned to the pub, but it was empty. Again, he said he felt guilty about it.)

Orton, on the other hand, told him that there was nothing to feel guilty about in a homosexual relationship.

He knew that Ken was incapable of any kind of real sex, with man or woman. That was why he needed to be funny with other people. It was an 'outlet' for him.

Otherwise, he was 'a very sad man'.

Ken insisted on a line in the diaries which quoted Ken as saying, 'I get no cock, you know. It's love I want,' to be replaced by, 'I have no sex.' There were other changes that he demanded. 'They illustrated a not very pleasant side of Kenneth,' John Lahr told me. One showed his racist tendencies. He took Orton to see his show. Afterwards, surrounded, says Lahr, 'by very BBCish company,' he gave a description of a fat black woman singing about 'mah chains'. Ken mimicked the singing of the woman – a 'dizzy cow' – who was dressed 'like a Nigerian priestess'. He couldn't understand why 'Negroes' who weren't in chains any more kept singing about them.

Ken talked a lot about suicide, but in Orton's company it had to have sexual connotations, as though he were constantly – and whatever the subject of his conversations – having to keep up with the Joneses, in this case Orton and his assorted friends if not specifically Orton and Halliwell.

A friend of Ken's had just taken his life after being given the choice of going to prison or a mental hospital. He opted for the hospital. Ken revelled in the story. ' "Well," she said, "there's all the lovely mental cock. I'll be sucking all the nurses off. I'm sure it'll be very gay".'

The man committed suicide after treatment 'to stop her thinking like a queen'. As Orton noted, Ken told a lot of stories about people who committed suicide – and constantly talked about death, but in a funny way. He also related them to his own state of affairs. He hated being alone, he told Joe, perhaps slightly envious of his relationship with Halliwell. Orton said that he himself enjoyed his own company.

Ken told him about a trip he had made to Spain with a friend whom he called 'Milicent'.

He saw a 'queen' in the hotel and decided to try his luck. But as Orton pointed out in the diary, as usual nothing came of it – not even after telling a man who tried to get in their way to 'piss off'.

Ken's favourite holiday spot was Tangier. In a letter to Orton from there, he wrote: 'Tangier is certainly the place for homos. Well, cheerio, keep your cheques and your legs crossed.' In 1965 he went to Tangier with Orton and Halliwell.

Ken himself was called upon to act as a kind of bodyguard for Halliwell – which is only part of the near-farcical side of the relationship between the three of them. The very idea of Kenneth Williams protecting anyone is so ridiculous that it is laughable, but Halliwell didn't see things that way. He asked Ken to walk him along the Rue Dante. He was frightened of being attacked by Arabs. Ken later said: 'I said, "This is ludicrous Kenneth. Nobody's going to murder you. You're not prosperous enough … This kind of timidity always made me feel that he was incapable of any violence. And when they rang me about the killing and somebody said, "your friend's been murdered," I said, "You're talking rubbish." '

In a letter from Tangier to Ken in London – Orton was known to write to him on toilet paper – he told Williams that 'Bill and Mike' kept Ken's picture on the bar for several days until replaced by a half-empty

Chianti bottle.

Ken loved it all and wrote letters back to Orton which the playwright said reminded him of James Joyce.

The effects of the Orton–Halliwell lifestyle became so infectious to Ken that he started breaking habits of a lifetime. He invited the two of them to his flat for tea or dinner, a practically unheard of thing. More importantly, he wanted to match exactly his accounts of meeting 'rough trade' in the street and bringing them back.

Once more, there is no record of his actually completing a transaction. But the Guardsmen he told Andrew Ray about multiplied now. There was a lorry driver who made excursions to the Farley Court flat and one evening when Orton was there, he introduced him to a Post Office telephone engineer called Clive – who later became part of the Orton set – and his flatmate Tom.

Ken kept pressing Clive to tell him of his sexual adventures on site. They were 'filth' but everyone appreciated the stories, he said.

Ken, meanwhile, told the most outrageous tales about himself and his views on sex – occasionally with Lou present. That was sometimes too much even for the equally outrageous Orton, who partly envied the relationship Ken had with his mother – he knew he couldn't talk to his own parent that way – and was partly disgusted by it, to the point of wanting to change the subject from sexual organs and sexual intercourse to something more inane. Ken, though, was in one of his devil-may-care moods and continued the chat about cocks, fucks and other parts of the body and their various functions.

When Joe told his story of making love in a cold doorway with his backside exposed to the street, Lou told him he was a fool. 'You might have caught double pneumonia.'

Lou, at this time, was very keen on that sort of talk herself. When one of Ken's friends told her he had just bought a new television set – a 17-inch console – she commented: 'Seventeen inches? That should console anyone.'

Lou talked about Pat being on holiday in Greece. 'She'll be getting the dick,' said Ken.

Lou told Ken afterwards how much she had enjoyed the evening and the company. She particularly liked Orton. 'What a nice fella he is. Really nice, isn't he? Not like most of the theatrical friends of yours who really don't listen, do they? Wanting to hear themselves speak. And he listens to you, you see. He's interested in people.'

None of the banter Lou heard, however, compared with the stories he told about mutual acquaintances – sometimes in the embarrassed and blushing presence of the people about whom he talked. One man was a 'queen', who deserved all that 'she' could get, and as Ken told the story the man prayed for the floor beneath him to open up. Ken didn't care. It was like the conversations he had on the 'Carry On' set, embroidered for an audience whom he knew could relate to it all. If he upset the people involved, why should that spoil a good story?

He loved his tales of the 'queens' – he said that one of his favourite occupations was sitting on a park bench, watching them, all of whom, in the parlance of the active homosexual, had to be 'she' and 'her'. Lou was doubtless bemused by it all and is convinced to this day her son was not a homosexual at all – 'thank God he was nothing like that', she says.

If in other company, he was constantly saying that he was asexual, in the presence of Orton and Halliwell he was one of them – and wanted it that way.

Orton's diaries record the time when Ken and a friend called Henry came to the writer's flat. Williams called Henry, 'Henrietta' and proceeded to detail a story that made the man blush and deny everything. But Ken proceeded just the same. The details were horrific. No words were spared.

The diary entry also added that Ken told Orton: 'I'm awfully fond of you, you know.' He was glad he had agreed to take part in the TV series *Call My Bluff* in which Ken was starring. He pointed out that he had originally wanted Robert Bolt, but his secretary said it was not the sort of thing he would do.

Another Orton diary entry referred to a man complaining about the TV show being a 'fake' – presumably because he could see they worked from scripts.

Moments of more serious theatre talk seem to have always been secondary to the outlandish sexual banter. He was happy telling his own stories or listening to Orton's. Ken told him that after a performance of *Call My Bluff* a woman approached him and asked, 'Any chance of a fuck?' He said he was quick to point out that he had no such intention.

Ken later felt the necessity to justify his joy in Orton's adventures, which he claimed met his disapproval. He said that as an actor he had to respond to stories which he found so funny.

The day after one such party at chez-Williams (whether Orton or Halliwell appreciated how privileged they were to take part in rare occasions like this is not on record) Orton wrote to Ken:

'I can't tell you how I enjoyed yesterday evening. It was v. pleasant meeting such nice people. But, as I've said before, you do have such interesting friends. And the filth, far from reacting upon me as upon a famous London impresario, added fuel to the fire of my enjoyment! I gave Tom and Clive my telephone number when we left ...'

Williams would always like talking about Orton, although he would publicly protest for years that it was so boring to keep going on about his relationship with the writer. As John Lahr told me 'He was very pleased to have been included in the books and he helped. He was loyal. God, I can't tell you how much I appreciated that.' But Ken more and more didn't want a lot of the bad language that passed between him and Orton and Halliwell to be included.

They saw his depressions, too. Ken believed that Orton was the man to whom to go when he was down. 'If we're talking about compassion, a sense of sympathy, I would say Joe had it. About humanity, especially with people like Halliwell ... a tremendous loyalty and as far as Joe was concerned a great love.'

Once, Ken told John Lahr, he was in the depths of despair.

'I was suicidally depressed,' he said − a phrase that was omitted from Lahr's book at Williams's request − and called on Halliwell at his home. He looked, he said, 'like a great boiled egg' − the once extraordinarily handsome young man was now as bald as one and the day that Ken called had left off his toupee. Ken though he was 'wet, full of goodwill and resolution'. But Williams wouldn't let Halliwell see that he thought so little of him.

Instead of finding consolation in Orton who was out, he stayed to talk to Halliwell − who couldn't understand why Ken would want to talk to him instead of the writer. Halliwell was cooking haddock at the time. Ken persuaded him to cut the portions he was making for Orton and himself into three.

After Orton's return, Ken said that he 'dropped my facade'. As he told Lahr: 'Up to that point I'd been brittle and arch with Halliwell, because I sensed his inwardness and his desire not to talk. And I sort of made him talk. After a while, I said, "I'm terribly depressed, utterly, sickeningly depressed. It all seems so utterly pointless, my kind of life".'

It was about the only time Ken opened up about his feelings about living in Farley Court by himself. Maybe this was principally why he had gone to Joan Sims and proposed. But it was to a totally different kind of person to whom he confessed his total loneliness.

It was, he told him, 'an unshared life. My predicament. My living alone.'

John Lahr spent a lot of time with Ken when working on his Orton books.

Today he describes the always dapper figure in the Burberry raincoat (over sharply pressed grey trousers and a tweed sports jacket) who would come at ten o'clock in the morning for his chats. He told me he knew that Ken would have been an impossible person to live with.

'He was far too hysterical a personality to cohabit.' He was always depressed. 'Always lovely, but always depressed.' But this time when he saw Orton – a man who was constantly telling Ken to enjoy himself sexually before it was too late and to stop feeling guilty about it – he was worse than usual.

Orton told him: 'Any time you feel this, always come here. Don't even bother to phone. I'm glad you came. It's murder to sit and brood. I know what it's like. Tell me ... tell me exactly what you did today. Why? Where did you go today?' Ken said that he found Orton to be 'the most marvellous counsellor. He actually got the adrenalin going, forced the pendulum which had almost stopped to swing again. He was a great activator. He had tremendous energy. I never met Joe in terms of no energy. I never met him when he was atrophied or drear.'

But it wasn't easy to get him to give sympathy. Joe told him: 'I must remain objective. I can't be involved.' That was the way he worked, too, Ken said. Orton's philosophy was to be 'a fly on the wall'.

He said that they both loved 'exposing the bogus and pretentious'.

Ken and Orton related to each other, not just because of their similar sexual proclivities but because of their backgrounds. They were both working class and somehow with him Ken could drop his own pretentions of what Alfred Doolittle in *Pygmalion* called 'middle-class morality'. He didn't affect his upper-class accent that a lot of people believed was natural Williams speak. He didn't talk of his intellectual aspirations.

'We did both love exposing the bogus and pretentious. I've always hated it ...: I've also had to face behind desks the same kind of pretentious people, what Shakespeare calls the "insolence of office". I loathe it. Joe loathed it, too.'

Loot was the obvious vehicle in which Ken and Orton could work seriously together.

It was Joe's idea that the part of the police inspector – posing as a Metropolitan Water Board inspector – should go to Ken. When Williams appeared to like the idea, Orton totally changed the part so that it could fit him, not so much like a glove, but like a well-crafted cabinet, one in which Ken could be displayed at his finest and with plenty of space to ensure that nothing got in his way.

It was early on in their friendship that Joe Orton realized that Ken was ideal for the alleged policeman, Truscott – a man he freely based on Det. Sgt. Harold Challoner, the policeman who planted evidence on innocent people whom he disliked and who was described at his trial as being 'quite mad'.

Orton told Ken: 'I want to make this detective much more you.'

In the original play, called *Funeral Games*, the nurse (to be played by Geraldine McEwan) was the centre of the action. Orton switched things around so that it was much more Ken's vehicle, as Williams said, 'He did, suddenly, get fired with the idea of writing a zonking great part for me.'

That, according to Michael Codron, was probably the problem. 'That meeting with Ken and his decision to make Ken's part big made it a sort of broken-back type of play. He developed Truscott in Ken's image, but it really wasn't Ken. I think that was to the detriment of the play, but was due to his absolute hero worship of Ken.'

Other parts were played by Duncan Macrae as the father MacLeavy, and Ian McShane as the son – both Scots, so Michael Codron asked Ken if he would like to play Truscott in a kilt, an idea that was not pursued. David Battley played the son's friend.

Loot was a farce, although it was not about people running in and out of other people's bedrooms, in and out of coffins more likely. Instead of a French maid, there was a nurse. Rather than missing lovers there were missing bodies, or to be precise one missing body – and a lot of missing loot.

By the time it reached London, what seemed to be missing most of all was the play itself. But by then, a lot of other things had happened.

The play began its provincial tour in Cambridge (it went all over the country, but when it came to including the play in Ken's career notes for *Who's Who in the Theatre*, he only mentions Cambridge, as though referring to the West End theatre of that name). The actors played one version and rehearsed another. At the end of the tour more than 150 pages of rewritten script had had to be learned by the company.

There were changes in the script right from the earliest moments. At first these were received by all concerned well enough. Michael Codron remained optimistic during the first rewrites. The play had still been called *Funeral Games* up to this point. But on 21 October 1964, he wrote to his star:

'Dear Ken,
Here is the exit Joe has re-written and which I think is very good.

He has thought of a new title: *Loot* . . .'

As Ken recalled: '*Loot* was an appalling flop, a great big flop. . . . It was like a ship that set out with the navigator doing one thing, the captain doing another, the deck hands doing something on their own. It never got concerted.'

Orton was drained. As for the cast, 'we were all exhausted. David Batley crying. Me angry with everybody. Duncan Macrae coming off the stage talking to himself.'

In Brighton, the then Sir Laurence Olivier came to see the show and called round to Williams's dressing room afterwards. 'The trouble, Kenny,' he told him, 'is that you haven't got a play.'

There were problems with local 'watch committees'. In those days, if a writer didn't get approval from the Lord Chamberlain, councils had to approve the plays being presented in their areas. In Manchester, they refused to allow a line in which Ken, as Truscott, asked one of the characters: 'Where do you do it?' and was told: 'On crowded dance floors during the rhumba.' There were even police standing in the wings ready to cart everybody off to the nearest station should the forbidden line be recited.

'I felt again and again as an actor that we simply were not gaining the audience's confidence. We never did establish that for the simple reason we were in a terrible quandary ourselves wondering which version was the right one. We were tentative – which is death for Orton. You must take the stage with enormous conviction and panache.'

The director, Peter Wood, made Orton – who had personally requested him to direct it – do the rewrites.

Rehearsals were hell – although not quite as hellish as the first performances in Cambridge. Lines were difficult to learn. They required considerable breathing practice. Ken said he saw the play in the way he saw all comedy 'like a ball being thrown from one place to another'. Orton told him he was totally right.

The play was produced in a stylistic fashion. Ken remembered a lavatory chain without a lavatory in sight. 'When *Loot* failed, we were all performing stylistically.'

Peter Wood put a metronome in the footlights. When Ken asked what it was for, he was told: 'This play is essentially stylistic and I want the dialogue to be delivered in a stylistic fashion.' As Ken remembered: 'We all had various arguments about it. Eventually, after the failure of the opening there was a management conference called. The director agreed that he'd misinterpreted the play. And we decided that from then on the performance should be naturalistic, which of course was the point of Joe Orton's dialogue.'

So they started rehearsing again – naturalistic in the midst of a stylistic set which, as Ken pointed out, 'contradicted everything that we were doing'.

Ken wrote in his diary (quoted by Lahr): 'My relationship with Wood is getting very strained. Today, when he asked me to alter dialogue I'd already learned once more – I refused. I dislike doing this as I'm well aware that defiance of authority is a bad example to the cast. There are occasions on which he forces one into rebellion simply because what he's doing is wasteful and futile.'

'Ken didn't like the director at all,' says Codron today. 'He didn't admire him at all. Ken thought he had got the idea of the play all wrong and I think in that I have to agree with Ken. John Lahr made the point to me that Ken became a kind of scapegoat for the problems of the play. Williams was bigger than Truscott. All the time he was on stage, it was difficult for audiences to think of him as other than the "Carry On" character or the voice they knew on the radio or now on television. The box has always had a lot to answer for. *Loot* gave it a whole lot of new reasons for guilt complexes.'

When the rewrites were presented by Codron and Wood, Ken was out of character again. He thought they were lousy – and said so.

'I shouldn't have set foot near this rotten mess,' he wrote in the diary.

Michael Codron – who shared his work with another producer Donald Albery, a man who had totally different ideas from his own – felt much the same way. 'We should never have toured, for one thing.' As he explained: 'It was not a play that should have toured at all. It was so outrageous. The regions – they have since come up to London – were miles away from that sort of thing. I'm not being sneery about it, why should they have wanted it? It was not a subject that should have been laughed at.

'People came to see Kenneth Williams and thought they would be watching a "Carry On".'

At one rehearsal Geraldine McEwan shouted: 'I can't go on with this any more. I can't go on.'

Towards the end of the tour, the show played at the Golders Green Hippodrome. It began badly but by Saturday night, it seemed that the audience was with them. The company felt better about things.

'After so many weeks of work, it seemed that we had got it right,'

Michael Codron told me.

If that were true, it was probably in spite of Ken, not because of him. Fenella Fielding saw him in the play there. 'He had a role, but he kept going from character to character, using a whole lot of different accents, cockney one moment, the voice of a high court judge the next.'

If this were a respite it was a shortlived one. At the Pavilion in Bournemouth there was a mass walk out of about 200 disgusted people. As *The Times* headline put it: 'Bournemouth old ladies shocked.'

But it was a short-lived respite. Ken remembered hearing a woman at his hotel tell a man: 'It was a good job you didn't come. The play was disgusting, absolutely filthy.'

The play got as far as Wimbledon and then seemed to die. 'People came out of the theatre and were shaking their fists at us,' said Ken.

One woman went up to Codron and Peter Wood and said just one short crisp sentence. 'It was Felicity's twenty-first.' 'In other words,' said Codron, 'we were responsible for totally mucking up this woman's entry into womanhood by letting her see *Loot*.' The Phoenix in London's Charing Cross Road, which was empty at the time, wouldn't take the play. The owner said that he would rather keep the theatre dark than offer such rubbish.

Codron tried to get it on at the Royal Court – on the face of things, an ideal setting – but it was turned down there, too.

If the cast had wanted to, they could have moved to the Lyric, Hammersmith. The members of the cast decided that no, they didn't want to. After fifty-six performances, it seemed that it was all over.

As Michael Codron told me: 'Ken remained very loyal to it, even though he was miserable about it. There were moves to recast the play, but I wanted to stay with Ken and believed that if we could have got it into London we would have had a success.'

Before very long, however, it did open in the West End. But it was a totally different version, with a different producer and without Ken. Orton wrote to Williams hoping he wasn't too upset.

Orton certainly was not upset. The final version of *Loot*, totally different from all the ones in which Ken had worked, was an instant hit. On 16 October 1966, Orton wrote to him: 'As you know by now, *Loot* has had an unqualified success. I hope this won't affect our friendship.' The play won the *Evening Standard* drama award for 1966.

Later, the film rights for *Loot* were sold for £100,000.

Ken wasn't exactly thrilled with any of this, although his anger was more against Michael Codron than Orton. 'After all the *Loot* misery,' Codron told me, 'we sort of went quiet on each other.'

Ken had to go back to his own life and Orton and Halliwell to theirs. It would also be their deaths.

The story was that Halliwell killed Orton in a frenzy, believing that the writer was going to leave him. Ken always thought that was untrue. He heard him say several times, 'I'll never leave him.'

Ken was sorry about it all, but he didn't let it interfere with his own plans, which were blossoming as usual.

FIFTEEN

Ken wore his homosexuality like a trade mark. It was an unforgiving label – simply because as far as anyone can tell, he never fulfilled any of his urges.

In one of her braver moods, Pat once asked him about homosexuals. It was all right for the active partner, but how did the other fellow get his satisfaction. 'It's down to J. Arthur...,' he told her. She worked that one out using the combined thought that J. Arthur had to mean the movie mogul J. Arthur Rank and that what her brother really was doing was using a convenient form of rhyming slang. With Ken, it was constantly down to J. Arthur.

Ken never thought of girls. He did continue to think of rough-hewn men, or boys with what he described as 'French bodies'. He tried to enjoy their company, but there was always that guilt.

He had an inferiority complex about his sexuality as about much else, which is probably why to some people he could be so rude. John Lahr told me of his astonishment at how unpleasant he could be to waiters at the Indian restaurant they visited together.

Yet when people were being positively rude to *him*, he took it all very much in his stride. He and Pat were walking through a London street when a red Royal Mail van shuddered to a halt beside them. 'Hello, Ken, you old poofter...' called the man behind the wheel. 'Hello,' Ken called back, feigning the appearance of what looked very much like a smile.

Pat, however, was shocked to the core. She ran cold all over. 'Why did you do that?' she asked Ken. 'Why answer him?'

Ken had no doubts about the reason. 'Do you know him?' he asked. 'Do I know him?' No, was the answer to both those questions. 'Will I ever see him again? Do I even know which depot he comes from? What's the point of worrying about him.'

Pat was deeply hurt, but Ken maintained a look on his face that seemed to be as shiny as the brown shoes he wore under those immaculately pressed trousers.

He was at times obsessed by his feelings for women. The only one he loved was his mother. He trusted Pat – despite the impression he seems to have given a lot of his friends and acquaintances – and enjoyed the company of people like Maggie Smith and Sheila Hancock. But the idea of going to bed with a woman revolted him. He wanted nothing to do with men who were bisexual. That notion, too, disturbed him beyond measure.

Pat saw just how true that was so the night that Ken was due to go out with one of his current close friends. The man was so shocked by what happened that he told Pat all about it.

Ken went to the man's flat before they were going out to dinner. He wasn't quite ready. Ken wanted to know why. The man said that he had been with a woman. Ken was furious. 'You,' he said, 'have you been to bed with her? Have you been touching her? Have you been playing with her tits?'

The man smiled. But Ken was not laughing. 'You're not going out with me after that, he said. 'Go and have another shower.' And for the second time in ten minutes the man showered. Ken didn't want to *think* there was any remnant of a woman's sexual smell on a man he had previously trusted as one of his own.

Pat said that until she heard that, she hadn't realized just how anti-women her brother was.

She had first had her suspicions years before when he had sent her a photograph taken on his twenty-first birthday. She was in Australia at the time and her then husband looked at the picture and said, 'Oh, he's a poof.' She denied it at the time, but soon she realized that those were his inclinations.

She once asked him outright if he were homosexual. He replied. 'If you mean do I prefer the company of men to women, then yes, I am.'

Once, Ken came knocking at her door. He had been at a 'knickers-off' party which he heard might be raided by the police. He didn't want to be incriminated. Pat herself felt much the same way about that after Ken's death. She came across boxes of photographs of Ken with boys in highly compromising positions. 'I tore them up and destroyed the lot,' she said.

For the same reason, she won't allow his diaries to be published. Not only do they include unkind and unflattering things about other people in the theatrical profession, they bear witness to their writer's sexual habits and name names. 'I won't allow those to go out,' she told me again and again.

If, however, her main dislike of Ken's sexual behaviour was the way it coloured his career, then she has perhaps cause for concern. Ken was the one for whom the word 'camp' could have been coined. Yet, despite all the evidence, she was not that easily convinced.

'I had never believed that Ken was a homosexual. I knew that a lot of his friends were. It was on one of the visits to her then home at Bickley in Kent which he used to make on summer Sunday afternoons, that convinced her.

'He used to sit in the garden and go to sleep or drink hundreds of cups of tea. He gave me a great long lecture on what homosexuals do. Then, he asked me, "Why did you ask me?"

'I said, "I don't know." He asked me how old I was and I said, "forty-five" or whatever I was. He couldn't understand how I had been married and been in the bloody Air Force and yet didn't know. I told him that I didn't mix with them and it never came into my life or my conversation.'

That was the point that she again asked him if he were homosexual. He repeated that he preferred men's company to women's. But now he added 'If you mean, do I participate then I am not a homosexual. So you can draw your own conclusions from that.'

She told him that the Bible indicated that thinking something was like doing it. 'That's what I say,' he replied. 'Draw your own conclusions.'

She followed that up with what seemed to her to be the inevitable question: 'Well, are you a virgin then?'

'Yes,' he replied. 'And I believed him.'

It wasn't easy to discuss sex with him. But several years later they did. Pat was having an affair – and in a crowded restaurant, he asked her at the top of the sentorian Williams voice: 'Well tell us about this man you're having the affair with then.'

Lou chimed in: 'Her having an affair! She'd run a blinkin' mile.'

Pat wanted to change the subject. 'No, come on then,' he called to her. 'Did you have the blinkin' dick?' That was the way he enjoyed talking about sex, a slightly diluted form of the conversations that were so much part of his connections with the Orton–Halliwell set.

But he said it loud enough for the whole restaurant to be convulsed and Ken to enjoy his audience at the same time.

Later he rang her up and said he had embarrassed her. She thought an apology was coming. Instead, he laughed, one of those raucous *Hancock's Half Hour* snide laughs. 'Well,' he said, 'that serves you right. It's what you get when you go round having the dick.'

Pat rounded on him: 'Well, at least I can say, "I'm not a virgin".'

Ken's voice changed. 'He got all serious,' said Pat. 'Yes' he answered. 'That's true.'

She asked him if he were still a virgin. He replied that he was. 'Well,' she said, 'I think that's sad.'

He told her: 'I daren't be otherwise – because if I were ever in a compromising situation, if the police raided or if someone kissed and told I'd be up the creek.' She didn't know at the time about the pictures that had been taken or about some of those activities in which he did take part.

She told him that she firmly believed he was missing an experience to be treasured.

He never, she maintains, missed not having a family life or the presence of children. And here is another one of the paradoxes of the Williams life, the closed compartments that ensured Ken was a different person to different people. Friends talk of how marvellous he was to their children. 'He didn't like children,' says Pat. 'No, not very much,' agreed Lou. 'But he was always kind to those who were around.'

But Pat remembers him saying to various children: 'Why don't you lay down at the bottom of the swimming pool for half an hour?' Or 'Why don't you go and lay down in the middle of Piccadilly Circus?'

Neither of them would know until his death, for instance, that he had a godson.

He became more and more secretive as the years went by. He didn't like to talk about money any more than he used to like spending it. 'It's not important,' he told his sister. 'You shouldn't love possessions. You should love people.' As Pat said: 'That was the Christian bit coming out again.'

Accordingly, the only outward sign of a certain limited degree of prosperity were his immaculate clothes, although he never had a Savile Row tailor make him a suit or went to one of the more fashionable outfitters specializing in foreign-made clothes. He patronized John Lewis and Marks and Spencer and usually felt glad that he did. (Pat describes a shopping expedition to John Lewis in London's Oxford Street with Ken, looking for a shirt. He called to her from one crowded floor to the other, 'Any luck?' As she said, everyone else seemed to think they were on *Candid Camera*).

All his suits were hung in the wardrobes in covers. Next to them, his assortment of sports jackets and then his dinner suits. His shoes were always brightly polished before being put away – echoes of childhood here – each pair with wooden trees inside them.

One side of his wardrobe would be his best ties; then the crocheted ties he wore every day. His underwear – 'very white, very neat, very tidy' – was in drawers. His socks were neatly rolled or folded. All his shirts were properly folded in three columns in his wardrobe, the striped shirts in one pile, the plain whites in another, the checks in a third.

But he always gave the impression that he cared much more about people than things – even if that meant falling, as Pat would have it, for the occasional sob story. She remembers the time he was coming out of his flat in the midst of a rainstorm and was approached by a young man who asked him for the price of a meal.

'What are you doing walking the streets in the pouring rain without a coat?' Ken asked him. The youngster told him that he had come from Wales to make his fortune as a pop singer. He had been seen in Wales by a DJ who had suggested that he look him up, should he ever come to the big city. The boy took this as an invitation to London.

Ken took the boy to his home, dried his clothes and gave him a meal. Now, Pat is convinced there was no sexual connotations to this kindness. 'It was his way of doing a Christian act.'

He told the boy, she says, to go back to Wales and save up the money which would allow him to come to London with a certain degree of security. He also gave him an overcoat.

'I can't go back to Wales,' said the youngster. 'I haven't got any money.' Ken bought him a train ticket, put some cash in his hand and took him to a nearby restaurant.

'Is there anything else you need?' Ken asked. He had in mind a newspaper or magazine to read on the train. The boy said, 'Well, I did notice in a shop window a lovely glittery suit that would look very good on stage.'

'Ken was disgusted,' Pat said. 'He was upset that the boy would try to tap him for that dreadful suit. He told him that if his voice was that good, he wouldn't need a glittery suit. He was very hurt.'

Said Pat: 'That would be Kenneth's way of doing a Christian act, let that boy get home in safety, instead of roaming the streets homeless.' Nevertheless, is it too far fetched to include this in the collection of stories of guardsmen, telephone engineers and building site workers who went to Ken's home? Almost no one else was ever invited back.

What is likely is that once more Ken did not follow through with his desires. Was it once more his conscience, his sense of guilt? Pat is certain it that it was not.

He was on happier terms in his favourite restaurants. In the Seventies he was a regular visitor to Joe Allens in Covent Garden where he went with his mother. Pat was with him the day a young woman approached him exceedingly politely while he was enjoying his veal – in one of his favourite Italian restaurants, Biagis, he would go for a filleted sole – and asked for his autograph. Ken looked at her and said, 'Fuck off.'

'He liked Joe Allen's because it was filled with theatricals, people whom he thought always minded their own business,' said Pat.

Needless to say, minding his own business was the one thing Ken was not able to do. Dining in one restaurant with Hugh Paddick, he got himself into a furious row with a woman doctor at the next table, challenging her views on life. 'He kicked up a rumpus wherever he went,' said Paddick.

It never seemed to matter very much to managements, however. In the midst of doing both the *Round The Horne* radio series and a couple of 'Carry Ons', Ken was cast as Napoleon in a BBC TV version of the Anouilh play *French Cricket*, with Robert Helpmann playing Fouche, the Chief of Police. It was a welcome break from comedy, but it wasn't noticed enough for there to be a great many similar offers. Not that he any more minded his own business now than he had before.

He would probably have maintained that minding his own business would never have got him anywhere, least of all starring on radio. There, he was above all an observer of life, carrying on – forgive the pun – those observations into the characters he played.

Round The Horne was Ken in his element, largely because Barry Took and Marty Feldman (the latter before long to make a huge hit in Hollywood) wrote as much for him as for Kenneth Horne. It was *Beyond Our Ken* refined and restructured. The old elements were essentially the same, but the refinements made the weekly shows not just entertaining, but addictive, compulsive listening.

He played a wide selection of roles again. Even as the sidekick to Kenneth Horne – 'I'm an old panhandler ... I was huddling over my pan looking for gold,' said Horne. 'You won't find any there either, duckie,' replied Williams – he was a favourite.

He played an old salt – 'Aah ... aah ... aahh. You all think I'm a raving madam.' That was a misprint in his script about Moby Dick. 'Madam' should have read 'madman'. 'Oh ... yeees,' he agreed when co-star Betty Marsden pointed out the misreading of the misprint. It went out the way it was recorded. As Hugh Paddick told me, 'it was never rehearsed'.

But there was no one more popular than Rambling Sid Rumpoe, the folk singer, who would at the drop of a mangelwurzel sing 'The Runcorne Splodcobblers Song', sung by the splodcobblers of Runcorne as they thump their cordwaggle bellow afore cobbling their splods.

Or the Oriental gentleman, Chou En Ginsberg, MA (failed). He, together with J. Piesmold Gruntfuttock would have kept Ken gainfully employed had he done nothing else.

They were all different, their voices varied. Yet one always knew which one was Kenneth Williams. And when he and Hugh Paddick joined together for their Julian and Sandy routine – bravely supposedly using the names, and names only, of Julian Slade and Sandy Wilson (writers of *The Boy Friend* and *Salad Days*) – Williams and Paddick were giving new meaning to that word 'gay', especially when they talked about the figure-hugging black number they had bought in Carnaby Street.

He loved that role, Barry Took told me, because it was a way of being quite open about homosexuality and taking the mickey out of it was safe.

Julian and Sandy were a reaction to Rodney and Charles, but less cliché-ridden. At one time, they were dropped because Took and Marty Feldman were bored by them. There was such a protest from the cast that they were reinstated.

They were a tremendous send up of 'camp' characters years before their time, two 'glaring queens', as Paddick pointed out. The idea was thrashed out at a lunch given by Kenneth Horne. Marty Feldman, whose idea it was, came out with a great deal of language that no one else seemed to understand. Paddick was supposed to use the word 'lallies'. He refused. He thought it meant breasts. Feldman told him it was an old-English name for legs. The word stayed in. On a later occasion, Hugh was supposed to do a tap dance. 'Come on then, show us your lallies,' called Ken.

There were problems about so blatantly exposing homosexuality on the air. The smoke in Broadcasting House offices blew through long meetings on the subject of Julian and Sandy. Ken was to tell John Lahr about his discussions with Marty Feldman on the subject. 'I don't care,' Feldman told Ken. 'I want very much to establish two comic homosexual characters and they can revolve around a figure of the establishment like a Richard Dimbleby character – decency, Establishment values.'

Sandy would say to Julian: 'Oh, girl, your patio's gorgeous, shove a couple of creepers up by our trellis and we'll have this place going.' To which Kenneth Horne would add: 'I quite agree.' As Feldman told him: '(It was) making it obvious that the Establishment and the outrageous could meet on some level.'

Ken added: 'Marty's angle was not to be afraid of anti-feeling, because we're making people laugh and in laughter we're making a kind of sanity.

It's like going into a dark room and being afraid. Then when you put some light on, it's not a big deal.'

Both Ken and Hugh Paddick just had to feel the same way.

'We were always very, very friendly,' Paddick told me. 'We got on terribly well together.' Once more, they respected each other's work. And they saw each other out of work, too. They even went on holiday together. It was in the middle of the Sixties, half-way through the eleven-year run of the two shows.

It was one of the few BBC radio shows which played to full houses.

Paddick had just finished his run as Col. Pickering in *My Fair Lady* at Drury Lane. Ken had the memory of *Loot* still burning his ego and both agreed that simultaneously they needed a break. They decided to fly to Gibraltar and then to tour the south coast of Spain – with Paddick at the wheel because Kenneth still wouldn't learn to drive.

'We were supposed to be travelling incognito, but a "Carry On" film was showing on the Rock at the time, so he was mobbed and we were whisked through customs very quickly. Then at the hotel, he was recognized and before we had been there for five minutes Radio Gibraltar was down to interview him. We ended up doing a "Rodney" and "Charles" routine about the Gibraltar apes.'

The next morning, the crowd scenes were repeated in the shoe shop to which Ken had gone to buy a pair of sandals. Paddick had had enough of this and insisted on moving on. They went to Malaga, where Ken was upset about not being recognized and then left because after raising his voice he was being pestered by autograph-hunters. It was time to move on. Ken wanted to go to Tangier – 'He had been there with Orton and all that jazz and I wasn't interested.' In fact, he said by now they had begun to get on each other's nerves. 'I'd be on the beach sunbathing and he'd be sitting there in a suit, collar and tie and black shoes. Not really my idea of how to spend a holiday.'

They reached Cannes, where Ken got into the spirit of things again much to Paddick's embarrassment. The sole entertainment in the restaurant to which they went was a violinist 'with three strands of henna'd hair from left to right.' Ken couldn't speak French, but insisted on requesting a tune – by humming it out loud, at the top of his voice.

'We had to share a room because we couldn't book two singles. He took pills to get to sleep. I lay awake all night worrying about the chaos he had caused.'

At that point, they decided it would be best for everyone if they went home. They stayed up all night before the flight back. 'We both got terribly drunk. Me on whisky, he on gin and tonic.' They had a row.

'I really went for him and felt rather sorry for it afterwards. He said, "How is it you know so much about me?"' Paddick told him it was because he had watched him at work for so long.

'I then went on holiday by myself.'

He was never invited to his flat, apart from a drink in the Farley Court flat before an evening at a restaurant. 'It was a monk's cell. But a spotless, pristine monk's cell. He gave me a drink. After the drink, we went into the kitchen. I am sure it had never been used before. After that, his mother came in to wash the glasses up. He smoked himself, but everything, all the ashtrays, were immediately put away.'

'I don't know whether it was like Howard Hughes and cleanliness, but it was going on that way.'

He was fastidious in other regards, too. Punctuality was by way of being an obsession – although once he missed a recording session with Barry Took altogether and all but flayed himself for his lack of professionalism. During the run of *Round the Horne,* Ken had found himself – probably reluctantly – hosting a meeting at Farley Court of Horne and the rest of the cast. It was due to begin at eleven am, Bill Pertwee told me. 'We arrived at 10.55 and rang the bell. There was no answer.' Then, there was a voice from inside. 'I know who you are, but it's not eleven o'clock yet,' Ken called. On the dot of eleven, he opened the door and allowed everyone in. They were served coffee. By now, though, no one was allowed to smoke.

In restaurants, Ken and Hugh Paddick had meals together where there was inevitably the same story of not being recognized and then having to move because too many people were pestering him.

Ken always seemed to respect Kenneth Horne – 'a father figure to all of us,' as Barry Took put it. But he would have sport even with him. The two Kenneths were walking up Regent Street, on the way from a Broadcasting House meeting to a Paris Cinema recording. Ken suddenly left him and went into a doorway of Hamleys, the big toy shop. He made all the movements of a man apparently answering a desperate call of nature. As he walked away again and up to Horne, he fiddled with his trousers and said, 'Ah, that's better.'

To the principal female interest in the series, he had another trick. When Betty Marsden positioned herself in front of the microphone, that was the moment he chose to touch up her bottom. 'Just putting you at your ease,' he said. Since she must have known he had no sexual interest in her, she didn't complain too much.

Monkey business in *Carry on Regardless*, 1960

The seadog in *Carry On Jack*, 1964

A menacing Bernard Breslaw and Ken the potentate in *Carry On Up The Khyber*, 1968

Carry On Spying with Barbara Windsor, Bernard Cribbins and Charles Hawtrey, 1964

Joan Sims at her sexiest, with Ken as the commandant and an apprehensive Charles Hawtrey in the background in *Carry On – Follow that Camel*, 1966

Not quite a wedding – Sid James, Joan Sims, producer Peter Rogers, director Gerald Thomas, bride Barbara Windsor, Charles Hawtrey, Ken, Hattie Jacques and Jim Dale in *Carry On Again, Doctor*, 1969

Director Gerald Thomas offering Ken advice while a white-coated Jim Dale looks on in *Carry On Again, Doctor*, 1969

The scene no one expected to see – least of all Ken. With Suzanne
Danielle in *Carry On Emmannuelle*, 1978

In production, *Carry On Abroad*, 1972, Ken leading the tourists and talking to Peter Butterworth

The ageing of Kenneth Williams – 1970, 1975, 1986, 1988, (the last photograph)

In conversation, he could be very rude about his colleagues. In the studio, he would talk about people in the show, 'being very brutal,' said Pertwee. 'If anyone stood up to him, he would deflate. But he would never talk badly about Kenneth Horne, or about the writers.'

And yet Ken kept very much to himself. 'People say how sad it was that he had no relationships. I think that was the way he wanted it.'

He went into hospital to have his piles sorted out, but nobody knew anything about it until the treatment was over – and then there were more Williams 'bum' stories. Barry Took heard them all – and a few more besides.

Once more, he was telling the same jokes before a show went on the air or was finally taped. It was as though he were acting as his own warm-up man.

His favourite was about the man who told a doctor: 'Yes. You see I was having a pee – and my dick came off in my hand.'

The doctor asked to see the fallen member. 'I've got it in my tobacco pouch,' said the patient, undoing his pouch and showing the contents to the doctor. 'This isn't a penis,' said the medical man. 'It's two ounces of Ready-Rubbed Old Holborn shag.'

'Oh,' the patient replied, 'I've smoked my cock.'

It was an old joke, but he told it beautifully. 'It wasn't the joke, it was the ritual – to get himself psyched up for the performance.'

Took discussed this with Marty Feldman – told him what jokes Ken would tell and in what order. He was in form. The same jokes in the same order.

'He could mould the characters,' said Barry Took. 'Our trick was to put them in different situations. Once we got into the swing of things, it took no time at all.'

Once, Ken invited Took and Feldman for lunch. He wanted them to write a television show for him. They came up with a mock chat show programme in which Williams was being interviewed by Clement Freud, as lugubrious-looking then as now. The BBC commissioned it instantly. But before he had seen the script, Ken changed his mind, he didn't want to do it. Eventually the script was used for Marty Feldman's own show later on.

Another show they did included a sketch in which Ken is one of two men discussing a third, now deceased, called 'Funny He Never Married'. The obvious inference after a time is that the man was homosexual – and that the men talking were, too. Again, Ken withdrew.

A series that was to have featured Ken was later done with Terry

Scott instead.

Ken was as unclear about what he wanted to do as to how he was going to fulfil sexual urges which he inwardly knew would never be satisfied. He told Took about a consultation he had had with a doctor, who told him: 'What you ought to do is to get yourself a retired petty officer to look after you.' The implication was obvious. 'He was far too fastidious,' said Took. 'It became a mania, that fastidiousness later on.'

He was constantly concerned about both his backside and his nasal passages.

It took a particular mood for Ken to talk about his sexual problems. 'He needed to be in a docile mood after a show to be able to talk. He told me about himself in a cab after a show.'

If he upset people, he would write to apologize. Once, Bill Pertwee – again a staple member of the cast – remembered for me, Kenneth Horne made him write to the wife of an executive he thought Ken had insulted at a party given by the BBC for the *Round The Horne* cast.

Ken hadn't wanted to go, but Horne had insisted. He told him: 'These people provide our bread and butter and you've got to go.' Ken's solution was to be outrageous. He cornered the wife of the then head of BBC radio and told her: 'There was this man. Opened his raincoat to me, he did. And there it was, all hanging out. You could see all his pubics.' The woman looked dumbfounded at this strange man in her presence and walked away. Ken was warned by Horne never to do anything of the kind again.

Sometimes, the offence was seemingly less severe. On a TV *Wogan* show, Ken would pay tribute to Marty Feldman for writing *Round The Horne*. Barry Took was deeply upset. Ken wrote asking to be forgiven for being 'a foolish old man'.

It wasn't the only letter he wrote to the Took family. Once, Barry's daughter asked him for an autograph. 'Go away little girl,' he said. Later, when he discovered the identity of the child, then thirteen, he wrote to apologize.

Despite all that, Took remembers him as being 'very generous of people's ability. He respected talent.'

But Ken didn't always respect his own talent. 'He didn't see the difference between *Beyond Our Ken* and *Round The Horne* or between *Carry On* and *Just A Minute* – in which he was quite brilliant.

But it was the sophisticated talent of his radio work that lingered. It was just one aspect of the continuing legacy of *Round The Horne*.

'At his best, he was as great as Peter Sellers, although he had a humility that Sellers never aspired to,' Took now says. 'He wasn't uniquely gifted, he was just better than anyone else in my view.'

Years and years after the series finished, it is still being played on BBC World Service and abroad. It is a favourite in Australia and in Los Angeles. Perhaps more than anything else he did, it represents the real Kenneth Williams.

SIXTEEN

There were times when Ken resembled a shadow boxer. A flyweight, to be sure. A flyweight who never looked as though he were ready to face anything more severe than his shadow in the ring. Yet there was more ambition in him than some of his closest friends realized.

That was why he was constantly on the look-out for new plays. At the root of it all was not an over-riding thirst for the sound of applause or for the feel of greasepaint on his face. It was more to salve his own conscience, those feelings of inadequacy which so often overwhelmed him.

Despite what everyone seemed to think, he did want to try to lay the ghost of *Loot* and to bury for good all that had happened in *Gentle Jack*. He could be better than that and he wanted people to know it. Also, there was that nagging belief that no one would think he was capable of anything more strenuous than the latest 'Carry On' vehicle.

All these were good reasons why Ken accepted the lead in a play called *The Platinum Cat*. He had every reason to wish that he had never done any such thing.

Beverley Cross first approached Ken with the idea of playing Bernard, a man so obsessed with business that his marriage was falling apart at the seams. Cross was going to direct and Ken had every confidence that here, at last, was the sort of play he had been looking for. It was a serious role, but one that was replete with the sort of comedy at which he was so skilled.

He took the task so seriously that he dieted, bringing what little weight he had down to what his friends decided was practically nothing. He said that he had lost twenty-one pounds.

He looked as though he had just returned from a penal colony – the sort of place critics all over the country might have been hinting Ken should join for the 'crime' of appearing in the play at all.

His co-star was Caroline Mortimer, daughter of John and Penelope, but she couldn't help matters along any more than could Kenneth. In fact, the whole business left such a bad taste in her mouth that even now, almost a quarter of a century later, she has no desire to talk about it.

The opening at Brighton made the performances of *Gentle Jack* in the Regency resort seem like a total triumph. In Oxford and in Birmingham, Ken and the rest of an admittedly undistinguished cast were wishing they were back in Brighton again. By the time the play finally opened at Wyndhams on 16 November 1965, the looks on the faces of practically everyone Ken knew and cared for, said it all. All, that is, except the sounds from the audience and the gasps of the company when they read the first notices.

For the first time in his life, Ken was booed by *The Platinum Cat* audience. It was to have a lasting effect on him. The critics were more easily dismissed, or so he thought.

They were quite merciless. One of the kindest things said about the play was the headline for Herbert Kretzmer's review in the *Daily Express*: 'Alas! Even Kenneth Williams Is Adrift'. As the critic wrote: 'Devotees of Mr Kenneth Williams's bizarre vocal mannerisms may derive some scant, fleeting pleasure from the new comedy at Wyndhams in which Mr Williams is currently immersed. ... Mr Williams is no fool and he has clearly elected to indulge in all this vocal grotesquerie to compensate for the lack of any real wit or humour in Roger Longrigg's text. It must be a long time since a comedy as resolutely uncomical as *The Platinum Cat* has exposed itself to public view in the West End.'

The respected W. A. Darlington wrote in the *Daily Telegraph*: 'Kenneth Williams is a comedian who beguiles me, but I failed to get much beguilement out of him last night at Wyndham's. He worked hard enough – never harder – but I just could not get myself interested in his antics.'

Nor could anyone else. On 11 December, the show was closed. The official reason for the closure was that Ken was ill and the management accepted that he was the 'big draw' and without him, it was hardly worth continuing.

Ken actually was ill. He had flu. He felt faint to the point that he couldn't focus – a state of affairs not helped by all that dieting. At the London Clinic, he was diagnosed to be anaemic and there was the possibility of a shadow on his lung. It was all Ken the hypochondriac needed to hear. He was panic-stricken and decided to go away on holiday.

His destination was Beirut – it was a few years before the city became a total war zone. Stanley Baxter joined him and the company of his close friend cheered him up immeasurably.

He was thus in a better frame of mind when he returned. The year 1966 had to be better than 1965 and there was sufficient evidence to indicate that this might be so. *Round The Horne* had been a huge success. The 'Carry On' films were not only very good box office – more than one was the top moneymaker of the year – but they were developing a cult status among an ever-growing group of people. The set who patronized the boutiques in the King's Road and Carnaby Street couldn't get enough of them. Not only that, the crowd who twenty years later would be called 'Yuppies' were 'Carry On' crazy.

When Ken wanted to look for something extra, Peter Eade came up with an answer that he was prepared not to argue about – television. Not another play, not another comedy spot, but taking part in a chat show.

Ken was as scared of those programmes as he was of anyone bigger or more powerful than he was himself. But he was persuaded to join singer Shirley Bassey and comedienne Dora Bryan on the Eamonn Andrews show, a forerunner of today's huge BBC success *Wogan*.

Instead of the show being a disaster, Ken was a great success. It was just his forte – an opportunity to spout forth on practically anything he thought people would find interesting, and since he was constantly convinced that people would always find everything he did interesting, he took to it like a cat faced with a saucer of cream. He lapped up response from the studio audience – to say nothing of that of his host and his producer.

The only one who didn't like the show was Lou. 'He used terrible language,' she remembered for me. 'I never thought that was necessary – and on the telly, it was very embarrassing.'

But the powers at the BBC Television Centre were not so easily disturbed. In fact, they liked it so much that on the strength of the Andrews show, they offered him his own series. Now this really was a departure.

In *International Cabaret*, Ken was not playing a role, and was definitely not playing the fool. He was ostensibly there to introduce other acts – a singer from France, an acrobat from Italy, a boys choir from Holland. Not the sort of thing that came easily to a man who liked to show he had great pride in what he did, using clever words. But the producer Tom Sloane convinced him he could do it.

The strength of the performance was the opening monologue, carefully scripted for him by John Law, tailoring opportunities for long, meandering stories, using all the voices and gestures that Ken believed were the strength of his repertoire. As a result of the first test for the show, he was offered a series.

It is now remembered as one of the most successful things he ever did – although even that provided cause for more than a few 'Disgusted' letters from viewers who thought that both his words and his gestures were too direct by half.

There was, for instance, the story of the woman accordionist who kept getting her breasts caught in the folds of her instrument. 'You must have pleated tits, I told her.'

People seemed to like it and the series was extended well into 1967. That, and appearances on shows like *Call My Bluff*, meant that Ken really now had a new career. Television audiences were discovering a different kind of Kenneth Williams and seemed to be enjoying the discovery.

'I didn't like his TV image,' Val Orford told me. He loyally continued to watch everything his old friend did, but found it as difficult to stomach the things he did on the small screen as he had never really enjoyed Ken, the 'Carry On' star. That was a pity for him. He rarely saw his former Stanfords colleague now and letters were few and far between. If he ever thought that Ken had grown too big for those shiny shoes of his, he kept that sentiment to himself.

Meanwhile, *International Cabaret* seemed as big a hit as *Round The Horne*. One series followed another – while Ken made LPs of his 'Rambling Sid Rumpo' character.

Peter Spence, who was to write for Ken a short time afterwards, told me about the great success of *International Cabaret*. 'People would watch the show just to see Ken. Previously, they thought that he was just a wild man. Yet here was something very new for them.' Here was also something very vibrant.

The Press were equally interested in the new TV show. Writing in *The Observer* George Melly noted:

'Most of the programmes on BBC 2 are better for colour but only incidentally. Variety shows glitter more but it isn't the colour that makes Kenneth Williams's Molly Bloom-like introductions to the acts in *International Cabaret* so inventively outrageous – or helps that splendid comedian Dick Emery to overcome his rather poor material.'

In the *Sunday Telegraph* it was reported: 'International Cabaret is a very proper showcase for the occasional pop singer it engages. Kenneth Williams is so enmeshed in some high camp monologue (last week the saga of the apple turnover) that he has no time and probably less inclination to do anything more than name the performer and skip aside.'

Ken wouldn't have any of that. In his autobiography, he noted how much effort he put into introducing a whole series of acts with whom he had no rapport whatsoever. Undoubtedly, no one noticed that he wasn't as thrilled and excited having those people on his show as he seriously expected the millions watching the programme at home to be.

It was all very successful indeed. There were more Eamonn Andrews shows – and more frowns from Lou – who had now left her Kensington flat and gone to live at Osnaburgh Street, not far from Baker Street and a favourite sister. At the back of her mind was the fact that other people could be watching the show, too, and they might say unkind things to her when she went to her old-time dancing sessions.

It all seemed to be going so well that David Frost invited Ken on to his show four times. Plainly, Kenneth Williams provided an untapped vein of talent.

A young BBC radio producer named David Hatch certainly thought so. In September 1968, he invited Ken to appear on an edition of his show, *Just A Minute*.

SEVENTEEN

It was a lesson in a far-off school which Kenneth Williams had never visited which was primarily responsible for one of the greatest successes he ever had.

A small boy was caught not paying attention by a teacher. He was ordered to stop wasting his and everyone else's time, but to talk with a purpose. 'I want you to tell me what I've been talking about for one minute without repeating yourself and without deviating from that subject.'

The boy's name was Ian Messiter. He had been staring out of the window of a classroom at Sherborne School in Dorset during a Latin lesson. 'Suddenly, there was a whack on my desk,' Messiter now recalls.

He remembered the incident and that moment of inattention which was to serve him extraordinarily well a generation later – to say nothing of the benefits enjoyed by Clement Freud, Peter Jones, Derek Nimmo, Nicholas Parsons and Ken.

By then, Messiter had made a career for himself as a writer and as an inventor of radio and TV shows – 'devised by ...' was to be the official credit accorded him.

A television producer asked him for an idea for a show and he remembered the event at Sherborne. The show *A Minute Please* came and went, but then someone in Broadcasting House came to him with the suggestion of adapting it to radio. It would require much more in-depth conversation and none of the visual aspects of the TV show. And it would be called *Just A Minute.*

The show was broadcast and did reasonably well – BBC terminology for a few furrowed brows at Broadcasting House. During the break after the first twenty or thirty programmes, Ken was booked for two episodes of the second series. He recorded one and he and the show sounded no better than any that had gone before it.

It was a chastening experience for Ken. He thought this was just another flop to add to what seemed like an ominously lengthening list of failures – in moods like that, he didn't even think about *Round The Horne* or any of the other successes with which he was still being identified.

But he was persuaded to stay with it. It took off instantly. Ken used his voices. He was bombastic. He complained loudly to Nicholas Parsons, the question master, about the way he was being treated by the other participants. He seemed to take it as a personal affront when other members of the team broke the rules. Messiter had never intended the show to take that form, but he was delighted that it did.

'Suddenly, the penny dropped that by attacking Nicholas Parsons and the others, to say nothing of the audience, he was doing very well,' Messiter told me. Equally suddenly, he found he was enjoying the experience. Instantly, he was booked for the next series.

The show began in 1968 and is still running today. For the rest of his life, Ken would be its most notable performer – he had to be; no one could mistake his voice.

Not everyone liked his style. Ian Messiter's mother once asked him: 'What's that awful man doing on your show?' 'I replied,' he told me, 'that the figures showed he was a very big success.' He certainly was. Those figures – ratings in TV terms – demonstrated that more people regularly listened to the programme now that Williams was a part of it.

They wanted to hear him wipe the floor of the Playhouse studio with Nicholas Parsons. 'Chairman? Call himself a chairman! He's more like ...' Frequently the ultimate insult was lost in audience reaction.

Or he would say: 'That's the subject we're supposed to be discussing, you great big fool. I haven't come all the way from King's Cross to be made a fool of.' It was a line that would be repeated for the next twenty years, although it would be adapted to 'I haven't come all the way from Great Portland Street.' He wouldn't reveal his exact address, but the location was good enough.

He became so important an ingredient in the *Just a Minute* recipe that if he were ill, the edition that was recorded without him would be inserted in the middle of the series so that his absence wouldn't have as much impact as it would if he were not heard either at the beginning, or the end, of a season.

He made as big an impact on the team as he did on the audience. The man who is now Sir Clement Freud put it to me like this: 'He was the reverse of a chameleon. The mood Kenneth Williams was in dictated how everyone else felt. If he were depressed, a grey cloud descended on the studio as a whole. If he were happy, we all seemed to be happy.'

'He dominated it all,' said Ian Messiter. 'Freud did, too, but in a very different way.' The lugubrious features of 'Clay' Freud were enough to put the fear of God in any radio performer.

To Ken it was just another job of work, but one in which he could excel without having to sweat blood. 'His philosophy,' said Messiter, 'was that you work or you starve.'

He wasn't tied to a script, but neither was he expected to improvise in a theatrical sort of way. For him, *Just A Minute* was a radio version of all those raised voices he affected when the veal was overdone or the dover sole burnt in one of those restaurants, or discussing an Old Bailey murder trial at the Corner House. Freud, Nimmo, Jones and particularly Parsons were waiters who allowed the soup to get cold.

Even so, as Ian Messiter told me: 'Ken always did it in a very funny way. He could be rude to someone without giving offence, in a sort of Noël Coward way.' (Ken would have appreciated the comparison.) 'He wouldn't make a cutting remark unless he could make it funny at the same time. He could be funnily disarming to people.'

He was also able to 'spout' about all the matters on which he had either knowledge or strong feelings – and be paid for it. The French Revolution or whatever it was he was currently reading about suddenly had a new outlet and was no longer a topic simply for conversation at the round table at Pinewood.

He could even give not-too-subtle commercials. Asked to speak about 'rules', he said: 'I went to a restaurant called Rules in Maiden Lane ...' (There is a real restaurant called Rules.)

Sometimes, he got so carried away in these radio conversations that he resorted to the kind of language Lou didn't always like hearing in public from her son. The more outrageous Kenneth Williams was edited out of the final broadcast. 'But he was very brilliant,' Ian Messiter remembered.

The one thing which his *Just a Minute* colleagues never really came to terms with was the fact that they wouldn't be invited back to his flat. 'We knew he was frightened that we would want to sit on his loo,' said Messiter.

But he was never frightened of mixing business with pleasure. An irregular regular on the *Just A Minute* team was Lance Percival. It was during a break from the show that Ken took Lou on holiday to Portugal. He knew Lance was working near Lisbon, so made sure that he and his mother would call on him. On a day off, he went with them on a tour of an ancient monastery. 'This monastery was built in 1589,' said the guide. 'Yes,' said Ken,' his nostrils flaring, 'smells like it, too.' It was an amazing contrast to the Williams whose erudition floored most of the company on *Just A Minute*, but was the sort of comment he might be expected to make if a cutting edge was called for.

'It depends how you took it,' said Lance Percival 'If you thought what he said was cruel, it was cruel.'

You also had to know something about him before coming to conclusions about the degree of friendliness he showed. Derek Nimmo put it like this to me: 'He was the least tactile of people. He never really showed affection. He would hardly use a handshake, almost. Some people on the programme would get a bit huggy. Kenneth would hug to shock. He could hug Clement Freud on the programme, kiss him – which the audience loved very much. The view of Kenneth sitting next to Clement Freud was a sight to behold. Clement at his most lugubrious, Kenneth at his most flirtatious, running a finger up his trouser leg, was wonderful to see. The audience loved it and it would have been wonderful on television.

Sheila Hancock maintains that with the *Just A Minute* set as with almost everyone else in whose company he was he used to see just how far he could go. 'He knew there were some people who would be shocked just to hear him say, "shit", so he would say it.'

When Lance Percival appeared on the programme, he was given special instructions by the producer: 'Don't worry about Clement or Derek at all. But if Kenneth gets going don't press the buzzer, because what ever he says you can guarantee you'll get a laugh. With the others it doesn't matter, so press the buzzer. Kenneth would create a great entertainment about talking for a minute, so why spoil it? Part of the programme is not just scoring points and buzzing. If he gets into full flow, let him flow.'

It was an instruction everyone understood. It was as if there were an electric current going from one table to the other – two members of the team on one table, two on another and a third occupied by Nicholas Parsons and the scorer and Ian Messiter.

Ken would turn to the audience and appeal for support for his case, over the head of Parsons.

His wrath was, of course, manufactured – as was his indignant surprise at some of the subjects about which he was expected to speak. According to Lance Percival (but denied by David Hatch, the first producer of the show) team members knew at least what the theme of their own subjects would be before the recording started – and it wasn't difficult for the others to find out, too. It was necessary not just to talk for a minute, but to be funny for a minute, so there had to be a degree of preparation. (Ian Messiter always chose subjects for Ken himself that would match what everyone – Williams included – considered to be his erudition. If a subject on famous portrait painters was selected for instance, it would go to Ken.

'He was very arrogant about his own knowledge,' Sheila Hancock who appeared on numerous *Just A Minute* programmes told me. 'He could lord it over you and if you interrupted him and happened to know a bit about that subject he would get very pissed off and would do all he could to get the subject back again. '*She* doesn't know what she's talking about.'

Again, he would say, 'I'm going to put you in my diary.' As she said: 'I just know his diary is full of terrible diatribes against me.'

He would tell stories about the wild affair Sheila had had with a gigolo in Blackpool. The truth was that back in their touring days, they had shared a lift in a Blackpool hotel. They hadn't been talking since entering the elevator and simply to make conversation, she whispered to Ken about the waiter who had just got in. 'He's good looking,' she said. 'And for the rest of his life he made up this outrageous story about me having this affair in Blackpool.'

There was possibly a deep-seated reason for it all. 'I think if he had had a happy sex life, then maybe the obscene talk that he was capable of might have, not been so relevant, I don't know.'

He got at her on the air, too. 'They shouldn't have women on this show,' he would say. 'He was a kind of genius on that show. A lot of it was cut out, but once he got on to his fantasy level, he was marvellous. Had he been born in America, they would have built a TV show around him. No one really knew how to handle him. He was a total original.'

The team knew that his rude outrageous stories were going to be cut out, 'but we just loved it all and fell about. The audience were in hysterics. The most extraordinary people worshipped him, but it was quite frightening to be with him on *Just A Minute*. "I know a lot of women who said, 'I'm not going to be on that show again with that awful little man'". People have been known to cry, Sheila said. 'Because it was always half real. There was venom in him, always a lot of anger. All his humour was based on a huge anger. God knows what it was all about. But I think he was not happy about himself, particularly about his own sexuality. He was so incredibly clean and that gave the impression that there was something he couldn't get to grips with.

'I think the real Kenneth Williams was a lonely, sad, desolate individual,' she added: 'He was absolutely destroyed by *The Platinum Cat*.'

Sheila Hancock tried her best to comfort him, to say that he would be well advised to have treatment as she herself had had. 'But he would never do that,' she told me.

'He was afraid that if he did, he would lose his gift. He knew about people who had gone into analysis and had stopped being funny or being clever. He maintained that it was his madness that made him funny.'

As she said: 'In a way he was almost happy as this tortured thing that he was.'

When he was very depressed, he shut up. He wouldn't talk to anyone. 'I didn't think that was unusual. I'm like that myself. I just thought it was more honest than trying to cover it up. Like a lot of performers, what you feel is what you project. If he were in a bad mood, you'd feel it.'

There were times when he would arrive at a *Just A Minute* recording and everyone there would know that he was feeling bad. 'He would just not speak, do the show and go home again. Another time, he would fall about and stay behind. When he was with you, he was capable of great kindness and love.'

He could talk politics at the slightest opportunity, usually revealing without using so many words his belief that the Conservative Party was a Communist front.

Writer and broadcaster Barry Cryer was in *Just A Minute* too. 'His simulated rage could terrify me. He would pretend to be angry, but he liked it if you were able to fly back at him. There was never any malice in him. He was one of those people who believed that the best form of defence was attack. Yet he was always very kind, considerate and very funny. The paradox is that he was a shy man who put on a great front. If there were a lot of people in a room, he would gather a small group together and shamelessly hold court. He could handle that. But in an intimate gathering he was lost. He was frightened of getting into any long-lasting relationship.'

Nicholas Parsons said that his own relationship with Ken was based on 'being professionals. We never met socially. If I saw him in the street, it was like taking up a conversation as though we had been with each other for a long time. But he could be very abrasive to people he didn't like and could be very scathing. Yet he was a very kind man who gave a lot to his public.'

People couldn't understand how they could do anything but hate each other, the way Ken spoke about Parsons on the programme. 'We were very great friends, but Ken was an extrovert who could get away with ruderies and insults the way no one else could. But if you listened to the way he did it, it was always with great fun – in his own camp way.

I don't think people would have laughed at his insults the way that they did if they didn't know that Ken was doing it with fun and that I could take it. Sometimes, he would give me the greatest compliments. "Oh, what a marvellous chairman!" That was very nice.'

On the other hand, he would say: 'Poor old thing. Bring on his wheel-chair.'

In a way, this was a British version of the American 'Friars Roast', when an entertainer would be literally taken to pieces if not roasted by his professional colleagues. Ken was not happy when someone was funny at what he took to be his expense – like the time he was sitting on a stool at a party and was introduced to a famous American choreographer. It appears that Ken had his feet wrapped around the stool leg so firmly that he couldn't get off. The American looked at him and said, 'Don't say "I can't walk". Say "I *will* walk".' Ken didn't enjoy that at all. On the way home, other guests saw him walking out the door and called out, 'See! See'. He was not happy.

'He was only happy when he was in control,' Barry Cryer said. 'He didn't like being topped.'

If people laughed at him rather than with him, on the air, he was equally miserable. The team usually had their tactics well planned. They could work out their strategy as to when would be the best possible moment to interrupt and how they would cope if left to complete the minute. Anyone who successfully interrupted, in other words when Nicholas Parsons accepted they were justified in their challenges, was expected to carry on speaking about that subject for whatever amount of time was still elapsing.

Lance Percival for one never thought Ken was simply showing off. 'He had a marvellous vulgar twist to everything, which is where the fun came from. He was a master at pricking big balloons. He yearned in one way to be straight and presentable, but in the other he just loved to prick balloons. You could be talking about something very serious, and then Ken would come in with the most terrifying remark.'

David Hatch, now managing director of BBC radio, and the first producer of the show (in some of the earlier episodes he shared the job with Simon Brett), said: 'We brought Ken in because we both concluded that what we really needed was having somebody who would being automatic fizz whenever it was required. Having Ken on a show was like having a supercharger.' Until Ken's arrival the strength of *Just A Minute* had been the 'almost Frank Muir-Dennis Norden cross relationship that existed between Clement Freud and Derek Nimmo, which worked wonderfully right from the pilot, a crossing of those two minds. But later there was an opportunity to put in other ingredients. We then needed an up ingredient. We also needed someone to puncture all that and come in underneath, which is why we brought in Peter Jones. When they were all firing on all cylinders, it was wonderful to behold.'

He used to sit in the production booth of the Playhouse cinema, looking directly at Ken on the left-hand side of the panel. If Hatch gave him a visual signal, he would go into one of his 'Portland Place' or 'Great Portland Street' tirades. 'He would go berserk,' David Hatch told me. Another signal and he would be back on an even keel. 'He was one who could quite literally pick up an audience at will – within seconds.'

In the early years, the chairman's job was swapped around. Ken was largely responsible for the job being permanently in Nicholas Parsons' hands. 'He was the most appalling chairman,' David Hatch told me. 'He was so authoritarian and rough and aggressive with them – so different from when he was a member of the team and wanted all the compassion that the chairman could give him. As a contestant instead of the boss, he was very different, as chairman, he quite liked the power.'

In his autobiography, Ken disagrees. 'I'd shrunk from the offer initially saying I'd be no good as a figure of authority, but in the event I was business-like, quick as a Coward and as sagacious as a Solomon.'

Hatch had worked with him occasionally before, when he was under-studying the producer of *Round The Horne*, John Simmonds. 'He was the most wonderful performer. But even when he was depressed, there were jokes.' But then, as he put it, 'Ken was not paid to be down, he was paid to be up and was quite tiring, really. I suspect that a lot of the depression came from having given so much energy going up, he had to get some back coming down.'

Simon Brett, on the other hand, now looking back with the benefit of all that has happened since, believes that Ken's fear of his own mortality was responsible for so many of those down periods. A fear of death that Brett is convinced he frequently considered putting into operation himself.

'I was very much aware that Ken was always talking about suicide, usually about that of other people, like the RSM who took his own life by drinking prussic acid and took three days to die. He would get into one of those sequences of anecdotes about that period in his life. He told it as a joke story, but it was one he kept coming back to. One knew that Ken, if not a depressive, was one whom we were not seeing all of on the surface, someone who needed to retreat into his private self.'

That could, of course, be the reason why Ken dressed the way he did – seemingly nondescript sports jacket and trousers, or the raincoat and cap brought down firmly over his eyes. 'The result,' Brett comments, 'was that it made him stick out even more. You could see him from the back and it was so clearly Ken. His raincoat, which was meant to be anonymous, was always just that little bit too long. You always knew it was him.'

It was another symptom of the now old story of Kenneth Williams never wanting to be recognized but dreadfully upset when he was not.

This was not a subject he would discuss on the air, but everyone involved in *Just A Minute* knew about it. When they heard about his visit to a bank, it was virtually impossible to keep faces straight – even Clement Freud's – at the one time when they should have been immobile.

This was when Ken went up to a cashier and asked to draw some money from his account. Before he could write a cheque, the cashier said: 'I know you, you're Kenneth Williams, aren't you?'

Ken smiled slightly embarrassed. 'Yes, you are,' repeated the cashier. 'You're Kenneth Williams. I'd know you anywhere. I've seen all your films, heard all your broadcasts.' At which point she introduced him to her colleagues.

'What would you like?' she asked him finally.

Ken showed her his cheque. 'I'd like to draw £50,' he said.

'Right,' she replied willingly. 'Have you got any identification?'

That was not what he expected. Even at the end of the seeming idolatory that had brought the bank virtually to a halt, he was expected to dominate the room. As David Hatch told me: 'You could see that when he walked into a room, that was what he was expected to do.'

That was why the signal to start was frequently Ken's own definition of a warm-up. Or perhaps it should be a walk-up, as before, pacing up and down the stage, sticking his bottom out. Most people in the audience seemed to love it – particularly Lou, sitting in her regular seat in the front row of the Playhouse. Derek Nimmo told me he was convinced that Ken 'played every line' to his mother. 'The more cheeky he was, the more she laughed.'

Most people reacted in a similar way to the various Williams voices, all of which found expression in the programmes. 'There was a kind of gear change in those voices,' Simon Brett recalled. 'He went in and out as he paced his audience.'

The crisper the voice, the more Nöel Coward it sounded, the more you knew that Ken was displeased. 'Right,' he told Brett on one occasion that he was given directions he less than appreciated. 'I will do it your way if you want – or do you want me to do it right?' On the other hand, he could be very kind, particularly to a young very inexperienced producer as Brett – who was now best known as the writer of the *After Henry* radio and TV series.

Yet, he seems to think there was very little malice in what he said. 'There was a great deal of bitchery, in a theatrical sort of way, calling other actors 'she', and that sort of thing.'

He loved his anecdotes, talking about Orson Welles and name-dropping like the best of them. And there were always the sexual stories. 'I think he told them to me to shock me because I was so young. I was about twenty-three or twenty four and he would go into an anecdote that would contain words like, "I told him to just suck the tip, just the tip ... oh wonderful!" This was in the midst of a crowded tea room. Ken's reasoning went rather deeper. He was probably simply registering his power over the young man. 'He would push things just to see how people would react. He wanted to know how far he could push me.'

Those *Just A Minute* shows were tense in themselves. 'There was a clash of some quite formidable personalities.' And always there was the feeling he was trying to shock.

Sometimes, he was so used to hearing people fawning over him, according to Sheila Hancock, 'he went in search almost of someone who would turn to him and say, "Fuck off".'

In fact, says Derek Nimmo, Ken sometimes shocked himself when he went over the top. 'He had a deep interest and a lot of faith in Christianity and he was much given to quoting from Biblical passages. Just before a programme, you might have heard him speaking quite seriously about the Bible, but then he'd hear the name "Kenneth Williams" announced and he'd go on, sticking his bottom out and go for the laugh. Then, he'd come back and continue the conversation as though nothing happened. He had rather shocked himself. I think he was a puritan at heart.' That was Nimmo's verdict on the way Ken lived in his spartan flat.

His verbal jokes were sometimes attempts – usually successful ones – at topping those of other performers. David Hatch recalled going to a pub at lunchtime with Stanley Baxter when Baxter was in the series *Brothers In Law*. 'Ken was in there, too and between the two of them there was the most wonderful hour of cabaret. Stories, exaggeration and wildness. The whole pub, the Sherlock Holmes, came to a halt while their show was on.'

Ken frequently wrote to his producer, thanking him for his help on shows, responding to comments. He would talk politics with him, too. 'I was producing the *Week Ending* radio programme, a satire show, at the time and Ken told me he thought that satire was very dangerous, was likely to unhinge the state, and by attacking the great institutions of the country, making them vulnerable. When the mood took him, he would attack anything.'

Derek Nimmo has no doubt that *Just A Minute* was 'the perfect programme for Kenneth, because the thing about him was that he was so difficult to cast. It suited his very curt and singular talent. He had his own outlook on life combined with his great erudition. He had extraordinary recall. He may not have read a poem for years, but if something triggered it off, he could recite it perfectly and at great speed.'

Nicholas Parsons believes that *Just A Minute* was just right for Ken because 'when he could combine his erudition with laughter, he was very happy. He was unique because he could develop a rapport with an audience in a way I have never seen anyone else do.'

Nevertheless, Derek Nimmo is one of those people who think that Ken miscast himself. 'I think he would have been happier as a university don because he was a natural scholar and communicator. It would have given him the greatest pleasure to be able to pass on the knowledge he had acquired to a new generation.'

But then maybe he would not have been anything of the kind. As Simon Brett pointed out: 'Ken was not a relaxing person to be with at all. It was frequently very tense. There was just so much energy there. He would come into recordings of *Just A Minute*, come in very quiet into the upstairs tea bar at the Playhouse Theatre and then he'd start his stories, with an edge of unwholesomeness, talking about Joe Orton and North Africa.'

'His sexual anxiety you could see in his face. He would say that sex was not all that people claimed it to be.'

Lou sat and heard them all. Sometimes Ken told stories which were allegedly about her. 'There she was, sitting at this café when a whole lot of young men came milling around us. "What are they doing here?" she asked. I told her to be quiet. "They're rent boys," I said. "Rent boys?" "Yes," he explained. "They give sexual favours for money." "For money? I thought I was going to get it for free".'

At the end of the show, Ken would give Lou a parcel – his week's dirty washing which she would do for him.

The shows were and remain a huge success. During his nineteen years in the series he was the most successful part of them. 'I always thought of Ken during those shows as being a glove puppet,' says Simon Brett. 'There was only one other person there – the audience which was the hand in the glove. When you took the hand away, he fell apart.'

EIGHTEEN

In 1969, Kenneth Horne died. John Simmonds, *Round The Horne's* producer, had to come up with a successor for the show. He decided it had to be based around the one character who might have been seen to challenge Horne for the starring role in the series – Ken.

It was, on the surface, a sound move. Everyone who knew Kenneth Williams knew that he was much more of a multi-talented personality than any of the 'Carry On' films revealed, although it was still that series of crazed nonsense with which he was identified by most of the general public. It was also known by the moguls at Broadcasting House that of all the media, it was in radio that he excelled.

Just before he joined the *Just A Minute* team he had joined with Joan Sims in a radio satire at first entitled *A Bannister Called Frieda*, and later changed to *A Tribute To Greatness*, based on a hundred-odd tributes to personalities of the Victorian era. It was an historic event – a comedy programme on the normally highbrow Third Programme (later on called Radio Three) which made such an impression that the people then controlling Britain's broadcasting destiny were determined to give Ken his own series. The result was *Stop Messing About*.

It wasn't another *Round The Horne*, despite the fact that Ken used many of his voices and had the company of Hugh Paddick and Joan Sims, once again showing the same kind of rapport she had established on radio with Ken in the *Bannister* show. It went into a second series, even though it was not particularly brilliant.

What it did was establish once more Ken's old catchphrase from the *Hancock's Half Hour* days. Annette Kerr, who still occasionally saw Ken, told me of the time they were in a cab – 'it was raining, otherwise we would have walked' – totally immersed in a discussion on Gibbon's *Decline and Fall Of the Roman Empire*, which they had both been reading. She was one of the few people allowed into the sanctum of the Williams flat and when they reached Farley Court, they were still talking about the book in general and about the Emperor Tiberius in particular. They talked as Ken paid the driver, who had overheard the entire conversation.

'Mr Williams,' he said, 'would you do me a favour?' Ken, his mind very much still on the subject of the conversation, idly said he would if he could. 'Would you say, "stop messing about" for me.' 'Oh,' said Ken getting into full character, 'oh, stop messing about.' The cab driver thanked him, gave his change and Ken and Annette walked into the block, with him speaking at the top of his voice, 'Now about Tiberius again ...'

It was one of the last trips to Farley Court. He was finally driven out by fans – not the kind clutching autographs books whom Ken considered to be a plague but the whirring electric kind that were placed all over the building as an attempt at air-conditioning. Ken couldn't stand the noise they made.

He rented a flat that Stanley Baxter owned in Bloomsbury, but he also found that too noisy, and was soon away again.

Seemingly his only contented professional moments were on *Just A Minute* which continued happily enough. There were not many projects, however, that made him happy at this time. He was also still making films, *Carry On Camping*, in 1969, followed in 1970 by *Carry On Loving* and *Carry On Henry* (in which (Ken played Thomas Cromwell) and *Carry On At Your Convenience* Ken played Mr W.C. Boggs, a manufacturer – guess what he manufactured). And he was busy on television, too. He took the place of Kenneth Horne on the small screen as well – as a *regular* member of the *Call My Bluff* team. There were regular Williams appearances on the children's programme *Jackanory*, in which he told short stories, using all his best voices.

More important in the Williams story, was the series called simply *The Kenneth Williams Show*, basically a series of sketches which were to have been written by John Law, following the generally-recognized hit, *International Cabaret*. Law, however, was taken ill early on and Ken did much of the writing himself with Austin Steele. It didn't do much for Ken's reputation, but it kept him extraordinarily busy. In 1971, there was a better series which was more than vaguely reminiscent of *International Cabaret – Meanwhile on* BBC 2. Ken wrote his own material for this and most people seemed happy enough with it, if not happy enough to repeat the series. He did, however, enjoy the discipline of writing and it seemed to meet many of his needs – writing *and* appearing on television, while making films and radio programmes.

If one didn't know the complications in the life of Kenneth Williams, there would be the distinct impression that he was a happy man. Especially when he was invited to appear on stage again – and with Ingrid Bergman.

The play was *Captain Brassbound's Conversion*, which opened in Brighton and had a box office success for six months at the Cambridge Theatre – even Ken admitted that this was solely due to Miss Bergman's drawing power. It would have been unheard of for that classic beauty to flop, even though Ken said she didn't pronounce her words properly and the mysteries of Shavian drama seemed to elude most of the other people involved – except for he himself, of course.

He, however, was totally under her spell – like Judy Garland, Ingrid Bergman had an immense following among homosexuals – and was flattered beyond all measure by her invitations to dinner at her hotel suite. She even took Lou to dinner with Ken. 'Oh, she was lovely,' Mrs Williams told me, 'Just lovely.'

She was certainly kindness itself to Ken and to his talent. 'I want you to direct my next play,' she told him. 'You have such wonderful ideas.' Certainly, Ken was directing himself much of the time and his asides about the way the production was going were more powerful than most of the speeches he had to recite on stage.

As he said at the time: 'I don't feel typecast by having appeared in twenty 'Carry On' pictures. I see the whole thing as acting. And if you cannot get a laugh out of Shaw's scripts, it doesn't matter what the public thinks. The sole criterion is to get the audience's attention.'

He was probably more than a little inhibited by Miss Bergman. He kept firmly to the book and allowed himself not even the slightest hint of a snide 'Stop messing about.'

In the meantime, *Stop Messing About* itself was killed off. The general feeling was that the series died because it was successively near the knuckle. The BBC denied they took it off because it was too rude. 'The only reason the show came off was that it had finished its established run. There was no question of bad taste being involved.' But neither was there any question of the show being given a second season. Ken said he had been told that 'rudeness' was the reason. 'I don't think it was crude,' he said. 'Shakespeare is much dirtier. I was told that the show was getting into a rut and there were too many complaints that it was dirty.'

'I myself thought it was a very good series and expected it to come back on the air this year.'

John Simmonds, before his death, told me that he couldn't understand how Ken had come to that conclusion. 'Ken was talking nonsense and he knew it. We just wanted to rethink the formula.'

There are others who think that the big mistake was building a series around Ken himself. Simon Brett put it like this: 'He was a wonderful support character and needed pacing.'

Ken was decidedly unhappy about it all. He had put a lot into the series, partly because he saw radio as his real future. 'I don't like TV,' he said in 1971 – speaking entirely as a performer. 'The work involved hardly even seems warranted by the results.'

He didn't like television as a viewer either. He still didn't have a set of his own and never would. But when he wanted to see himself, as for instance on a Christmas special, he went to his mother's flat to watch.

There was, however, another radio series in the pipeline, which is precisely where it should have stayed. It was a parody of the Simon Dee TV show and was called the *Betty Witherspoon Show*. It was an unmitigated flop. Ken said the reason was that it was recorded on Monday mornings at the Paris cinema, which was a terrible time to expect audiences to get into the spirit of a comedy programme – and if they couldn't get into that mood how could the players?

It wasn't entirely Ken's show. There was Miriam Margolyes, a wonderful comedy actress who put most people into a great mood when she arrived at the studio, late and flustered, and apologizing because she had had a late night before, talking to a group 'and there aren't any other Jewish lesbians in Golders Green'. There was also Ted Ray, who was a marvellous ad-libber (he was offering grace at a show business lunch once when someone from the back called out to him to say it louder. 'I'm not speaking to *you*,' said Ray.)

With Ken, too, everything seemed to work well for the series – except that the parts were much better than the sum. The idea for teaming up Ken and Ted Ray had come after both were guests on a *Michael Parkinson* TV show. They had got on so well that it seemed the most sensible thing to team them in a series of their own.

It was David Hatch's idea, but it didn't work marvellously well. 'I think the series was doomed from the outset,' said Simon Brett, who produced it. 'It was a kind of doomy series. I remember I used to stagger into work on a Monday morning spreading gloom all around.'

Thirteen episodes of the series were made – and then pared down to ten, which was very unusual indeed.

'What was wrong with that format was that Ted wasn't Kenneth Horne. Kenneth Horne never tried to vie with the funnies. After each recording, or as each script arrived, Ted would take me aside and say that he hadn't been given enough funny lines. He was cast as the straight man while Ken was the extravagant one. Ken worked on it very professionally. However, I think he regarded it as a bummer from the start.'

Sadly, it was another one of those times for bummers. He was about to embark on one of the worst stage experiences of his life, a play called at first *The Fat Dress* which, when it opened at the Globe Theatre, had turned into *My Fat Friend*.

His co-star, the fat friend in question, was the extraordinarily lithe and beautiful Jennie Linden, who was plainly no one's idea of fat. She also became no one's idea of Ken's friend. Or Michael Codron's either for that matter.

Jennie Linden had recently caused many a man's heart to flutter extravagantly in the film *Women In Love*, in which she starred with Glenda Jackson opposite Alan Bates and Oliver Reed – probably the only picture in which nude men overshadowed the women.

The play was anything but a happy experience. On the whole the notices were very, very good. But Herbert Kretzmer wrote in the *Daily Express*, 'Jokes about fat girls and homosexual men lie thick on the ground in Charles Laurence's comedy which brings Kenneth Williams swinging back into view in his well-known camp style. If you don't find jokes about fatties and fairies all that hilarious – and I don't – the evening will lose much of its charm.'

The thinness of the play, as Mr Kretzmer intimated, was one of the main troubles. Ken was a homosexual [at that time he was constantly referred to by critics as 'queer'] tax inspector living in the same house as a hugely fat girl (Jennie Linden, padded out with a mass of cushions) who falls in love with an oil prospector the day before he leaves for Iran. She determines to slim in time for his return and does so – only to discover that the man is kinky about fat girls. Ken tries to console her. Mr Kretzmer reported that he was perhaps alone in his dislike for the piece which opened on 6 December 1972. '... all around me people appeared to be enjoying themselves like kids at Christmas.'

That was certainly not the way most of the participants in the drama off-stage – by *all* accounts much more exciting than that on it – saw it all.

It ended by what seemed at the time to be the final breaking of the friendship between Ken and Michael Codron which had only just recovered from *Loot*. Codron produced the play and today virtually shudders at its memory.

'Ken went into it with relish, although I don't think he had very good rapport with the director, Eric Thompson, whom I thought was very good.'

The box office was initially fine. In fact, as Codron told me, 'we started off with a very big success'. But, as he added, it started to tail off. Ken wasn't happy with Jennie Linden and made it very clear that he wasn't. He didn't think she was getting the right laughs. 'And then,' as Michael Codron put it to me, 'he got quite ill – or, rather, he made himself quite ill.'

This time, it was what he thought to be a stomach ulcer rather than his posterior that was causing him many of the agonies of which he complained. But what he was really complaining about was the play. 'Most extraordinarily,' he told Codron, 'I dread going on every night with that opening line.'

The line was 'I'm a queen, not a camel.' It was an outrageous line which he carried off perfectly and, at the beginning of the run, apparently very happily. He said it as he tried, without success, to get into the communal lavatory in the lodging house where he and Jennie Linden were supposedly living.

'It was a terrific opening line, but he kept saying, "I can't say it".'

In the end, Ken said he had to go off – on the advice of a surgeon who diagnozed an inflamed colon – and the play closed. 'Obviously, I felt very let down,' said Codron who thought *My Fat Friend* would be a useful bridge in their relationship after the failure of *Loot*.

Ken has said Codron accused him of being 'self destructive'. 'The trouble with Ken was that he didn't trust any director or any management.' Peter Eade had told him that if he did the play, he had to take direction – even though he complained there were too many words in it, too many words combined with too many actions and he could no more handle props and speak lines in *My Fat Friend* than he could in a 'Carry On' picture.

To make things worse, Ken later wrote in his autobiography Codron accused him of trying to cheapen his play by making it vulgar. There was constant rewriting, during the out-of-town tour in Brighton and Wilmslow, before opening at the Globe – which Michael Codron says was not a happy choice of venue. It was next to the Queen's Theatre where Maggie Smith was playing in *Private Lives* and Ken looked enviously at the smash business being done there. He also envied the notion of having Maggie Smith to play opposite him.

Jennie Linden is the first to admit that they were not suited to each other.

She had never met him before they gathered for the first time at a rehearsal room off Piccadilly Circus. He came along straight from a *Betty Witherspoon* recording, which didn't put him in a great mood. This was not lost on Miss Linden, who had given up a chance to be in *There's A Girl In My Soup* on a South African tour to make what was to be her star debut.

'You didn't forget Ken when you met him,' she told me. 'His talent was very special and very highly strung – which meant that it was difficult for Ken to accept the framework of a play. He wasn't happy with a script. You could see that he found the framework of the play and the discipline of the dialogue something he almost had to force himself to do. His imagination was huge and words would suggest jokes – and there were a lot of jokes that he put in the play which weren't in the Charles Laurence script.'

This was hard on her. 'I'm not sure that it wasn't right, but it was hard.'

Particularly hard was the fact that he would leave the stage in the middle of the play and would frequently go down and talk to the audience. 'He didn't do it every night, but he did so when he thought the play was falling flat, when he lost faith in himself and in the play. But the audience loved it. I had to accept the fact that people came to see Kenneth, not me and not the play.'

'It stopped the show and with all the knicker jokes he was marvellous. The audience enjoyed that more than the play.' But even though he broke away from the script, he didn't change any of the cues. He would come back and say, "Now, where were we." 'I must say I found that a shock,' she says. 'There were two media fighting each other, a straight actress fighting a comedian.'

She agrees that he found the play 'a tremendous pressure on his particular talents.'

He was very nervous, she remembered for me. 'He was nervous when he thought he was being undermined. He had wanted to do the play very much, but he knew *how* he was going to do it, and that wasn't the way Eric Thompson wanted him to do it. Eric was the new hot stuff and was getting full marks at the time for doing what people thought was right for the play.'

His illness wasn't helping – his stomach problem combining with teeth trouble and he was frequently off, leaving performances to an understudy in his twenties who tried to do a Kenneth Williams performance. When people realized that Ken wasn't performing, many of them demanded their money back.

She admits that there were times when she was less than happy by Ken's comings and goings. 'It was wonderful sometimes when Ken came out and did a joke or two, but not when he didn't turn up. There were nights when we wondered whether he was coming on or going off, whether or not he was going to come out of the dressing room. It was terrible in that regard.'

She remembers wondering whether she could cope with his behaviour, 'but afterwards I did'.

But she did suffer from him. 'Ken wasn't nasty to me, but I wouldn't say he was nice. He was extraordinarily difficult to know. I suppose at certain times he was irritable to the straight actor.'

He was intolerant. 'But he was never unkind about my work, although *personally* he was. He would make extremely painful remarks, which were very hurtful.'

He would 'make a great meal' out of his criticisms for the dresses she wore. If he didn't like a dress, he wouldn't stop telling her so. If he didn't like a perfume she wore, he was vicious in his comments about it. 'And if I had put it on at the beginning of the show, it was difficult not to have it on all through the performance. He would make a great meal out of that, too. Those personal things could be upsetting. I knew he wasn't joking. I knew he was going to make an unholy fuss. I couldn't say anything to calm him.

'He would let fly about the perfume, but was really saying things about the way he felt about the play or about me.' He looked at the dress she wore after a show once and said, 'those colours go well don't they!' Meaning that they didn't. 'But he wouldn't let go, he would nit pick and it was enough to make me blush, particularly when he did so in company.'

His behaviour warming up for the play, she remembers, was 'almost manic.' In the wings, he was at times virtually insufferable. 'He would leap about a lot, getting all the energy going, doing the mad performance, a lot of big eyes, a lot of vocal sounds, a lot of farting. He would explode – sometimes because he didn't like the play, sometimes because the audience didn't seem right for him.'

But you couldn't molly-coddle him. 'You couldn't say, "everything will be all right, Kenneth." He would say simply, "Get off!"' Sometimes, she told him to try to be quiet. He virtually told her to mind her own business. 'Sometimes he was almost grey, like ice. I wondered if he would go on at all. But I would have to say that his best performances were when he was buzzed up, the evenings when he would often go into the audience. Sometimes I looked at the man and could almost see him tied to the chair, as though the script was straight-jacketing him. You don't see that with straight actors, because they are used to it. But he longed to embellish. That was his way. And the audience always loved him.'

206

Once an old lady went to the box office and asked simply: 'Is Kenneth Williams live?' Frequently, it almost seemed as though he were not.

As Jennie Linden said, 'He felt ill. He lost faith in the play. And he lost faith in himself.'

NINETEEN

Ken never recovered from the *My Fat Friend* disaster. His illness had been largely diplomatic, although diplomacy was not a Williams talent and his decision to leave the play didn't enlarge his name in London theatre circles. He just had to leave and if a sympathetic doctor was the route, then so be it.

In truth, he was scared – yet he was left with a taste in his mouth that seemed to be summed up in one word, failure.

What he was really happy with was writing. The few scripts he had written had whetted an appetite that he always thought he had but, until put to the test, he could never really be sure. He wanted to do much more about it.

There was another thing he had enjoyed doing. Reading poetry. A couple of years before *My Fat Friend*, he had done a complete radio programme, reading verse, and had been amazed by the reaction.

As he told Annette in one of his affectionate letters at the time, he had been astonished at having to work on this in front of an audience. And yet, 'when I walked on to the stage of the Playhouse Theatre, they all tittered and I thought, hello! *they're* not going to want to hear poetry! But after a few minutes, the atmosphere became right and I stopped being apprehensive about a third of the way through!'

In 1974, he repeated the experience, with another programme of readings. This one was called *The Crystal Spirit*, the title of a George Orwell poem which he included. David Wade wrote in *The Times*: 'It was a slightly bizarre experience listening to Kenneth Williams's forty-five minute solo, *The Crystal Spirit*; here was the voice, which, try as it may, cannot entirely shake off all those inflections which in other circumstances breathe innuendo, the snorted vowels and the nasal twang which calls to mind at once the characteristic Williams nose.'

There was a satisfaction in that sort of thing that he didn't get from much else. But when other work came, he took it – like a boxer hearing a bell ringing, knowing that the time had come to stand up and pretend he liked being punched in the face.

He was, though, determined not to go back to the stage – for the moment at least. He didn't want to learn more scripts – certainly not other people's scripts. *Just A Minute* continued and that was fine. But with a second series of *The Secret Life of Kenneth Williams* he was much less content. If he had to read other people's words, he needed a safety valve, a means of exploding from his pressure cooker – which was why *Just A Minute* was so important to him. It was also why he joined up with Lady (Isobel) Barnett, William Franklin and Nanette Newman in a new series of that old staple of black and white BBC TV days, *What's My Line?* David Jacobs was the compere.

Lou says today that he would do anything with Nanette Newman and if she was willing to do a show, there was every reason to go into it, too.

Certainly, she enjoyed being with Ken – particularly on the train journeys from London to Manchester where the twenty-six editions were made.

'He was quite outrageous,' she told me. 'He would start doing the crossword, which I admired tremendously because I could never do them myself – and telling the most hilarious stories at the top of his voice. He knew he was giving a performance.'

So did the businessmen who, in those days, sat in the First Class compartments of the London–Manchester Express wearing their heavy dark suits, bowler hats in the racks above them, trying to pretend that no one knew they were there – and that no one else was there, either.

One morning, Kenneth was determined that no one would be in any doubt that he himself was there – and in charge.

He put his head between one of his fellow passengers and his copy of *The Times* and said, 'You're listening anyway, why don't you sit back and enjoy our conversation.'

The man blushed behind his newspaper like a schoolgirl. But he did as he was told. By the time the train drew into Manchester's Piccadilly Station he was close to hysteria.

As for Nanette Newman, wife of author and film actor Bryan Forbes: 'When I laugh a lot, I tend to cry. I got to the hotel with my hair all over the place and mascara running all over my face.'

Sometimes, things were even worse during the recordings. On camera and in front of a live audience, Ken started passing notes to Nanette.

'I thought they were clues about the participants. But they weren't. I undid them to find he had written the most terrible, obscene things about other people on the panel – they really were dreadfully rude. I meanwhile had to sit back and pretend that it was all terribly relevant to the contestant who was trying to stump the panel.'

Ken's practical jokes were legendary. Others in the team tried to find ways of topping them, but could never come up with a sufficiently exciting idea. Until, that is, David Jacobs thought he had the answer. The time had come – he laughed to himself at the thought, and so did everyone else on the panel when they heard his idea – to repay the compliment.

The response he got was anything but appreciative.

In fact, all these years later, David Jacobs still looks back on the event with a mixture of horror and indignation.

The precise details of the joke are still so raw that Jacobs is determined to keep them to himself – and to the other surviving members of the panel who likewise shudder at the thought that turned the usually pixie-like Kenneth Williams into something out of movies like *Whatever Happened To Baby Jane*. Ken's reactions to it all were not dissimilar to the effect of having a dentist drill into an exposed nerve.

Everyone else on the panel certainly knew about the joke and none of them anticipated the result. But in a way, that only made it worse. 'It backfired and it was dreadful,' David now recalls. 'His face went green.' Ken's only words that he managed to splutter out were something like, 'How dare you?' He then went to his dressing room, locked the door and refused to come out on to the set.

Jacobs made a statement to the cast re-emphasizing that it was all a joke – 'although by this time some of them were beginning to wonder whether it was true or not' – but still this was not enough.

'Eventually, I had to go to his dressing room and I had to plead with him to accept my apology and admit that it was one of the most despicable things I had ever done.

'He really put me through it. He made me eat the most hateful humble pie I've ever eaten in my life.'

But there was no alternative. 'I had to get him on to the set. Generally I'm a pretty sincere fellow, but after a while I felt so sour at falling into a pile of my own making – and felt so angry.'

The show had to go on and with half the series still to be shot, it was no easy thing. Ken was never less forgiving. A few years later, he and David Jacobs were sitting opposite each other at a lunch, on a beautiful summer's day, in a garden in the heart of the Surrey countryside. 'We were just about to start eating a plate of the most delectable smoked salmon when a lady opposite me asked if anyone minded if she smoked. I said, "Well, yes, I do." It didn't seem right. We hadn't started to eat yet and the smoked salmon looked so wonderful. But that was not a good enough reason for Kenneth Williams. 'Disgraceful," he called. "That's the most appalling ungentlemanly behaviour I've ever seen".'

Jacobs pointed out that he wouldn't have said anything if the lady had not asked if he minded. But, like before, Ken was not to be mollified. He, in truth, was still trying to get his own back on his former colleague. As David Jacobs told me: 'As you will gather, Ken and I did not appear to get on.'

Ken didn't seem to get on with many newspaper critics either. In 1976, he did venture back on stage at the Comedy Theatre in a Feydeau farce called *Signed and Sealed*. As was all too apparent, the fate of this play was signed and sealed almost before anyone sat down and certainly as soon as the curtain went up.

It was the story of a bridegroom who challenges the mayor of his village to a dual the night before his wedding. As a result, the mayor, who conducts the civil ceremony, marries him to his mother-in-law, played by the ever-formidable Peggy Mount.

Jack Tinker wrote in the *Daily Mail*: 'I must confess at the risk that some elf or pixie might drop dead at the Barriesque heresy, I do not believe in Kenneth Williams. He has equipped the groom with such an artillery of mannerisms firing on all sides that it is difficult to imagine all the possible social contretemps that could cause such a virago of petulant eccentricity.'

The play played and then closed and no one seemed desperately sorry that it did.

In many ways, this was crisis time for Ken. He was upsetting a lot of people, more than he was upsetting himself. Protest as he did, he was distinctly not content with the way his career was going in the mid-Sixties and there was not a great deal that *was* right for him.

This, too, was good reason for his jumping at all possible chances to write. There was a weekly column called 'Preview' in the *Radio Times*. This gave him an opportunity to turn tables and act as something of a pundit as well as performer. Magazines were asking him to write articles. He liked that, too. They were times to show that he wasn't just another man's puppet.

Then in 1976 came a new radio show, called *Oh Get On With It*. This was more like *Round The Horne* than anything that Ken had ever done on his own – which is perhaps one of the reasons it, too, went wrong. According to Simon Brett, who produced the series, Ken was still not suited to being a central character. 'Again, the pacing wasn't right.' Ken was marvellous, but he seemed to get faster and faster – to the extent, it seems, that overkill took over.

As Brett put it to me: 'For anarchy to work, there has to be some sort of government to oppose. Here, there was just anarchy.'

Some of it, however, was very funny anarchy indeed. Ken was a hundred different things in the show – a gardener in one part of the programme and a sports commentator in the next. In this role, he gave graphic details of the short-sighted competitor in the men's three-legged relay race who didn't quite grab the right baton.

And in every episode, he was also Sherlock Holmes – whom he insisted on playing as Noël Coward.

'That was his idea,' says the writer Peter Spence (best know later on for the TV series, *To The Manor Born*).

'He said it would give everything legs. And it did.' Spence appreciated Ken's participation. 'Everything took off when Ken came into the studios on a Thursday,' he told me. 'He knew when to go over the top and when to ad-lib.'

In fact, there were marks on the scripts where he was going to use his own words, if he so chose. Sometimes, he did. Sometimes, he didn't. 'But we never had retakes. He was so brilliant – on the button all the time.'

Spence is the first to admit that Ken could be difficult. But he had profound regard for the writers. 'He never stopped saying, "God, how I respect you guys." We were very young and comparatively inexperienced. But he never pulled rank on us.'

Ken was comfortable with the show as on the whole, he was comfortable with radio. After all, he didn't have to bother with manoeuvring props when there was just a mike between him and his audience. And, as always, there was an audience who were willing to appreciate him outside the studio as inside. In restaurants, immediately after a recording session, he would regale all around with more stories, usually about his army service and particularly about the sergeant-major's suicide. Before long, every story had been heard a dozen times already, but since Ken embellished every one differently each time, they always sounded fresh. Besides which, listening to Kenneth Williams, at any time when the mood was right, was an entertainment.

Inside the studio, if Ken thought the audience needed warming up, there was more reason to do the walk with his bottom sticking out.

Peter Spence was so fascinated by Ken's knowledge of history that he wondered why he didn't do TV programmes on the subject. 'There is a profound difference,' Ken told him, 'between an interest and what one does professionally.' There was probably a doubled-edged reasoning in that statement. On the one hand, he was expressing a regard for those who made their money from the subject, on the other, he was also suggesting that humour was a job for the professionals, too. Like every other comic actor, Ken was constantly being button-holed by people who asked, 'Have you heard the one about ...?'

What he was doing on radio, professionally now seemed to be very good indeed. 'He was,' says Spence, 'a lovely, lovely man. Beautifully gentle and pleasant. And never camp. He was perfect to work with. So perfect, I couldn't believe it was happening.'

A certain ingredient to it all was his relationship with the two other leading performers in the series, Lance Percival, to whom he was still a mentor, and Miriam Margolyes, returning probably more happily than before, to the relationship established in the *Betty Witherspoon* days, 'He loved Miriam,' says Spence.

She certainly appears to have returned the compliment. 'He was extraordinarily generous to other performers,' she told me. But that generosity was confined to performers he liked, who appreciated him, who wouldn't argue with his latest *Just A Minute* catchphrase, 'I'm a cult,' which, mischievously, he would sometimes mispronounce.

He liked the effervescent Miriam and would agree with her even in the highly-charged political atmosphere of Equity Council meetings – despite the fact that you couldn't get more left-wing than she, or more positively reactionary, should he feel that way, than he himself.

Ken didn't like the right-wing chairman, Marius Goring. On principle, he would disagree with everything Goring said. She didn't have much difficulty in following suit. None of that, however, gave her the impression that he was happy. 'On the contrary, he was an unhappy person, a worrier.'

There was a party at this time to mark Ken's fiftieth birthday. Miriam gave him a biography of Georges Clemenceau, the French leader in World War I. She says she knows that Ken was flattered to be given a serious book. But the party gave him less satisfaction. 'He was highly embarrassed by it. But very gracious. I know he was a very, very lonely man – but one who wanted to be lonely.'

And, even in their relationship, if he felt that loneliness – not to be confused with privacy – was compromised, he could be very 'spikey'.

The actress found him equally spikey about sex. 'He used to tell the filthiest jokes, and yet he could be quite prudish about someone else doing it. On the other hand, he loved hearing me talk about sex. He loved salaciousness.'

There was about him, as often others had noticed too, that continuing inferiority complex − which itself added to the prickliness. The blame for the failure of his plays he may have put firmly on the heads of managements and co-stars. Inwardly, he blamed himself. As Miriam told me: 'He had a very low opinion of himself.'

That was why he enjoyed intellectual stimulation − as if he were inwardly telling himself that there were some qualities he possessed after all ... weren't there?

It was when those doubts surfaced that he was in his worst moods. 'You knew when he was in a bad mood or one was coming on,' she told me. Like an unhappy cat, he wouldn't want to be touched. He would get snappy. 'On the other hand, there were times when you became conscious that he didn't mind being held, which was nice for someone as tactile as I. But I am afraid, more than ever, I realized he was capable of black despair.'

As the Seventies wore on, that despair seemed to get ever blacker.

TWENTY

Ken looked for new projects, but once found, most of them were quickly abandoned, as Barry Took had found to his cost. And then, he worried about not having enough work to do. It was a continuing story that fitted so well into the character of the man who asked for a quiet table at a restaurant and was then frightened that no one in the place recognized him.

It was at moments like these that he took on work that he might otherwise have declined. He liked to think that he was fussy about what he did – 'Carry On' films apart. They still paid his tax bills as they always had. But they, too, were reaching the end of their run. After six others in the series for him that decade, in 1978 he made *Carry On Behind*, and the year later, *Carry On Emmannuelle*, which as we have seen dropped most of the double entendres in favour of entendres that were definitely single. But somehow people preferred the hints to the bare facts and *Emmannuelle* was the last for Ken and for everyone else.

He still talked about never wanting to go on stage again. Inwardly he was still frightened of doing so. Outwardly, he still made excuses. 'Eight performances a week!' he told his sister. 'Sod that!'

His language was as expressive and rough-hewn as ever. When he and Pat did crosswords together, he was disturbed if she found a solution to a clue that had been stumping him. 'Oh fuck!' was his usual succinct comment. 'Oh, fuck! you're right.'

They were seeing more of each other now and consequently arguing more. In the mid-Seventies they were arguing more than before about religion. Once again, Pat's reaction to Germany and the Germans were the cause for a religious dressing down by her brother. She talked again about 'Krauts' and he rounded upon her.

He went with her one day to buy a coat. It was Ken who found the one that he thought would look best on her. She had to agree that it was the nicest in the shop. She was going to buy it – until she saw the 'Made in Germany' label. He argued furiously with her over that. 'It's very un-Christian of you,' he told her. 'Jesus says in Matthew 35 that ...'

She tried to call his bluff. 'How do you know what chapter it is?' she asked him. 'Look it up in the Bible, dear,' he said, 'and you'll see that I'm right.' She did – and he was.

He wasn't so right in succumbing once more to the West End stage in the autumn of 1979. More than a little reminiscent of Orton's *Loot*, he played an undertaker in Trevor Baxter's play, *The Undertaking*. It opened in Greenwich to distinctly lukewarm reviews, but because it had Kenneth Williams as the star, the management took it on to the Fortune – a total misnomer if ever there was one. The play, set in a funeral parlour, hardly lasted long enough for the manager to turn off the light. One of the few good things about this farce was that it teamed Ken with Miriam Karlin, an actress frequently as underrated as Ken himself.

Ken's friend, Gyles Brandreth, says that he wanted to do this play because it gave him intellectual stimulation of a kind for which he had been vainly searching for years. If it did, it didn't give much stimulation of any other kind to anyone else.

'In recent years,' reported *The Sunday Telegraph*, 'Kenneth Williams has seemed inimitable, so skilful has he been at imitating himself. But in Trevor Baxter's *The Undertaking*, he gives a performance as a genteel, eloquent, increasingly sinister undertaker, that is a gem of understatement. Unfortunately, the gem is not the Koh-i-noor – one wonders why an actor of his eminence should have accepted a part so small.'

There were nicer things said about Miriam Karlin and the other actress in the piece. 'There are also two, delightfully contrasted performances by Miriam Karlin, the acme of sophisticated chic, and by Annette Crosbie, the nadir of dim-witted dowdiness. But as in the case of the car-journey from London to Greenwich in the rush hour, one seems at the end to have experienced a great deal without travelling very far.'

Ken explained his reasons for participating in the venture. 'I'm a cross between Freud and Merlin. Of course, it's all about death, but there are some pretty sharp comments on today's morals, too.'

One night, walking out of his dressing room, coat collar turned up, flat cap pulled down, he listened for audience comments in the old Charlie Williams tradition. He heard one old woman say: 'It makes you feel better about going.'

Ken himself wasn't feeling better about much – particularly about going, a time which in those blacker moods seemed to him very close indeed. When *The Undertaking* closed, those moods were blacker than they had seemed for years.

He was rescued from them by two factors – a new play and a chance to do more intensive writing than he had ever done before. The new play was in fact an old one. But he wasn't going to act in it and, in fact, was never to appear acting on a stage ever again.

In the autumn of 1980, fifteen years after the death of Orton, Ken was directing *Loot* at the Lyric Hammersmith Studio. He enjoyed the experience and followed it almost immediately afterwards with his own concept of *Entertaining Mr Sloane*. More than anything, he saw it as an opportunity to pay tribute to Orton as well as to get a directing bug out of his system.

His writing proved more satisfactory – certainly to his bank balance. He could thank Gyles Brandreth for that. Brandreth, an entrepreneur who was also an actor, a theatrical producer, a TV game presenter and a publishing 'packager', had had the idea for a book by Kenneth Williams.

What he wanted was a presentation in book form of much of the gossip with which Ken had been delighting people in his outrageous stories for as long as he had been in show business. The one about Noël Coward and Gertie Lawrence. What Groucho Marx told his host at a dinner party.

Ken was not at all enthusiastic. 'Utter rubbish,' he told Brandreth when he first put the idea to him. 'Publishers have been after me every year for a book.'

Eventually, Ken was persuaded to meet Brandreth to discuss the idea. There was already a publisher, Dent, waiting in the wings of what could turn out, Gyles thought, to be an entirely new stage for him.

Ken went to the Brandreth home in Notting Hill Gate and was talked into the project. Soon, he was going there almost every day, travelling by Tube, always wearing the same Burberry raincoat, the same shiny brown shoes, the same neatly-creased trousers under his brown sports jacket.

Brandreth's idea was simple. He would get a researcher to come up with stories and Ken would tell them in his own words. The daily meetings, fuelled by sandwiches supplied by Gyles's wife Michele, with whom Ken immediately struck up a very close relationship, resulted in Ken's discarding at least half the stories and supplying some himself.

In 1980, the book had a name – *Acid Drops*, and was a huge bestseller. Ken was delighted. He was not only able to see his work in print, between hard covers, but he was instantly on the publicity trail, spouting forth in the way he was happiest to new radio and TV audiences. Radio Four's talk show, *Start The Week* with Richard Baker was never more popular and he was invited back again and again.

Ken liked the publicity spots and the signing sessions that followed automatically.

'Sorry you didn't turn up at Selfridges,' he wrote to Pat in August 1980, 'but I'm signing at Menzies bookshop in the City on 7 August – the Tube from Euston Square to Moorgate takes you outside. Off to Croydon now and tomorrow is Nottingham. Love Ken.'

Relations with his family were now closer than they had been for some time.

After moving out of Stanley Baxter's flat, he bought his own in Queen Alexandra Mansions, Hastings Street, Bloomsbury, part of the Duke of Bedford's huge estate. He worked hard and spent a great deal on getting it the way he wanted – still no expensive furnishings, but a comparative fortune went on soundproofing the walls and ceilings. It was then that a woman moved into the flat below and 'entertained' all her neighbours by practising the piano – seemingly day and night. Ken could stand it no more – he certainly was not now going to soundproof the floor – and sold up.

That was when he heard that a flat was available next to his mother's in Marlborough House, Osnaburgh Street. So he took that one for himself – even though Pat tried to advise him against it. Living next door to his mother was a responsibility as well as a comfort. But he thought he could keep an eye on Lou without her being a pressure on him. What was more, there was a reason for being in an area like that. Ever since the time he overslept and missed a performance, he was determined he would never allow himself to be dependent on transport to get him to a theatre. If the alarm clock didn't go off, he wanted to know he could always walk.

It was convenient for him. He could have breakfast with Lou and she could cook dinner for him, too. And he would take her with him on his shopping expeditions to Marks and Spencer, picking up there St Michael packaged foods they both enjoyed, like lamb casserole.

Ken was equally impressed by his mother's laundering prowess. Every night, he would hand her his washing – knowing that she would wash, iron and fold it to his own exacting specifications. 'I never minded,' Lou told me. 'I had a washing machine and a spin dryer and I had a little balcony to hang it out to dry afterwards.'

Ken bought her the machines as well as a TV set and kept her regularly supplied with watches when he went abroad on holiday, and there was always a bottle of perfume for her, too.

His own flat was furnished in the traditional spartan Kenneth Williams style. He still insisted that he didn't want possessions. When he wanted to watch television, there was still always Lou's set sitting in its place of honour with his photograph on top.

Occasionally, however, he admitted he did like the additional touches in life.

'Meant to tell you when I saw you last week,' he wrote in another letter to Pat, 'every time I use the heavy glass ashtray you gave me (years ago) it exudes opulence and luxury. Quite the ritziest feeling.'

He was still good about writing – although in another letter to Pat in January 1981, he reported: 'Lou said to me yesterday, "Well, I *am* surprised at you for not wanting to thank Pat for those gloves." So this is to apologize for any tardiness.'

If there were tardiness in other respects about Ken's life, it could possibly be explained by the modes of transport he used. He still went almost everywhere by Tube, if not by bus, and there were few stars that did that. Sometimes, though, it brought perks.

In another letter to Pat in January 1981, Ken wrote to thank her for a 'very nice tea', to compliment her on her 'drawing room (that) looks stunning' and to report on what happened when he left her that evening.

'On the way to the bus, they were bawling, "Hello, Kenny! Carry On!" etc. and the conductor refused to take my fare. I suppose he thinks he's being generous, but alas, it's other people's money and, of course, totally corrupt.' One could hear the indignant sound in his voice as he muttered that to himself, writing the letter.

But there were more important things to think about. His letter continued: 'Got back to the flat and tried cleaning up around the base of the loo where the plumbing has left awful marks and tears away the tiles. Went to bed at about eleven o'clock and didn't wake until eight-thirty. V. good, I thought and realized I'd got a headache. The traffic lights are out of sync in Osnaburgh Street. So cars are HOOTING like made the whole time. Phoned the police, but no reply. Disgraceful!'

Ken's sense of decency told him that if people complained, there is a need to do something. That's what he appreciated in people and that was what kept his faith in humanity, or so he seemed to say.

In the late autumn of 1980, Hattie Jacques died. Ken spoke at the memorial service in her honour at St Paul's, Covent Garden, the actors' church. 'She was as sweet as a kiss on a winter's day,' he said.

The language was more flowery than some he used in his book – or in the one that followed. This was *Back Drops*, which was all his own work. Again the publishers were Dent – 'he was intensely loyal,' says Brandreth, 'so Dent it had to be – and again Gyles worked with him on it. 'He needed a sounding board,' he explained.

The book was not – almost inevitably this, with sequels – as big a hit as the first, but it did well enough. It was based, Brandreth told me, 'on Ken's diaries – with fabrications'. He told stories about his own life on stage and of some of the people with whom he had worked. As Brandreth said, it was not completely true, but it once more provided Ken with opportunities to give forth about his philosophies on life.

He even thought he would like to write a book on philosophy – a sort of *Williams on Wittgenstein*, but Brandreth persuaded him to do an autobiography instead. This was *Just Williams*, which gave a very scanty picture of Ken's life indeed and ended in 1975 – in the hope that there would be a sequel. There never would be. There was also a children's book, stunningly, beautifully illustrated by Beverlie Manson. It was a poetry book, called *I Only Have to Close My Eyes*, the title of the first verse in the slim volume:

> 'I only have to close my eyes
> And I can quickly see –
> A castle reaching to the skies
> That no one knows but me.'

That said a lot about Ken's life. There was a lot about him that few realized. Not many knew, for instance, the identity of one of the people to whom the book was dedicated, Robert Chiddell. Not even Lou knew that Robert, ten years old when the book was published in 1986, was Ken's godson.

But he kept a great deal to himself. He had friends that not many knew about. He would go shopping with a neighbour called Paul Richardson and spent a great deal of time with the head of the giant Reed employment agency, Michael Whittaker.

One of his favourite occupations was going to dinner at friends' houses, although he would never return the compliment, and no one ever expected him to do so.

Giles and Michele Brandreth were frequent dinner hosts. Once they entertained film director John Schlesinger to dinner with another friend. The conversation turned to Ken. Schlesinger and the other man said they hadn't seen Ken for years – in the case of the director not since their army days together. Brandreth said he would invite him to meet them.

Ken came and he and Schlesinger hugged each other and went in for supper in the Brandreth kitchen. 'It was wonderful,' Gyles remembered. 'Ken was on wonderful form. It was easy and Ken was telling great stories.' The sequel was not quite so marvellous. Schlesinger decided to have a replay. There was dinner at his house – in the impressive elegant dining room, not supper in the kitchen. 'Ken was a lot less at ease.' But because he was Kenneth Williams, he decided he had to entertain. 'He took over – and wouldn't let anyone else get a look in.'

Ken enjoyed dinners where he could impress people. At another at Brandreth's home, he was engaged in conversation with a Greek gentleman. 'He was very deferential,' his host told me. 'But afterwards, I had great difficulty in explaining to him that the man was not King Constantine.'

The Marchioness of Dufferin and Ava told me of one evening she had dinner with Ken at Derek Nimmo's home. 'I was amazed at his grasp on so many topics,' she said.

If he could have had a firmer grasp on his own life, things might have gone better for him.

TWENTY-ONE

Ken had reached a watershed in his life and found it difficult to decide on his new direction.

'Sod that,' still encompassed his attitude to going on the stage again, yet every day without a signed contract in his agent's office was a day which undermined his self-confidence. He went to book signings if the mood took him. If an unsuspecting purchaser asked for more than a signature Ken's answer was invariably 'fuck off'.

His co-performers in *Just A Minute* took it all as a matter of course. 'Oh, Ken, how could you?' Sheila Hancock might ask, but there was no ready answer.

In a way, Ken was lazy. He wasn't interested in taking on any new long-term projects that required hard, sustained work. He was really like a small boy faced with competition from a newcomer who suddenly jumped to the top of the class. He obviously wasn't at the top anymore and it disturbed him. He showed that disappointment in his remonstrations to people when he thought they were too demanding.

Just A Minute apart, he was increasingly fulfilling the role of chat-show participant. Parkinson, Russell Harty, Richard Baker, they all wanted him for what they knew he could give – a supposedly unrehearsed monologue that required neither a script nor serious production.

After being a regular guest on *Start The Week*, he was frequently invited to chair the weekly Radio Four chat show.

It wasn't the money that Ken sought. He was more well off than most people who knew the spartan lifestyle he adopted could have imagined. His money was carefully invested and he knew the state of his shares as well as he knew his Shakespeare.

And yet it was money that caused more upsets in Ken's life than almost anything apart from sex. Over the years, the untrue story has got around that he and his sister Pat were enemies. They may not have been as close now in the Eighties as they had been in the old OG days, but there is no question that they still felt for each other. In fact when, in 1981 Pat retired from her then job as a senior executive with ICL, Ken attended her send-off party and immediately penned one of his notes, saying how glad he was to realize she was so well-liked.

'Well, if evidence was ever needed apropos popularity, you certainly got it last night! It was a superb gift they gave you and everyone's testimony was glowing.'

He certainly felt at least equally fondly for his mother – an understatement without any question – but he even criticized her. In that same letter to Pat, he wrote 'Thought Louisa was looking like the wreck of the Hesperus! Couldn't believe the hair! But in fact, I think she was very tired. Lately she ain't been in high spirits, I don't know why.'

But that sort of thing caused no problems whatsoever. 'The only rows we had were over money,' she told me. It was, in some ways, the classic story of boots being worn on wrong feet, of misunderstandings that should not have arisen.

Ken told her that he was taking the advice of his accountants and making himself into a limited company, inviting Pat to become a director – with director's fees. She was thrilled. 'I always wanted to call myself a company director,' she told him. He said he was pleased to offer the opportunity.

However, there would be restrictions. He wanted the right to be able to tell her where the money should be spent – like on a holiday. She turned the offer down. 'I've been subject to rules and regulations all my life and I knew I would be breaking them,' she told me.

More seriously, he advised her that he was going to abandon his practice of sending her both birthday and Christmas presents. He was going to give her money instead. 'Thank you very much,' she replied. 'But,' he asked, 'will you still love me? Will you still give me presents?' She told him that she probably would – on both counts.

He gave her £100 a year. Eventually the £100 would go up to £800. But there was still a catch. He demanded a receipt for the cash – stating that it had been paid to her for answering the telephone, dealing with fan mail (which she had always done on his behalf), for taxis and other travelling expenses. Suddenly she was switched from simply being his sister to a deductible business expense item. 'It did me no good at all,' she told me. 'It put me into a new tax bracket.'

There were other causes for financial disharmony between them. Soon after her retirement, Pat told Ken that she wanted to make him a monetary gift of her own, 'Oh, yes,' he asked seemingly slightly ungratefully, 'how much?'

She told him that the figure she had in mind was £10,000. 'I didn't until that time know whether Ken had money or not. I thought I was offering him a fairly substantial amount.' Ken's reply seemed to indicate that he did not share that feeling. He was less than impressed. 'What would I do with a piddling £10,000?' he asked her. It was not an answer calculated to induce sisterly affection. But then it was often difficult to judge the mood of Kenneth Williams or how he would react to different situations.

There was still a great deal of affection for Ken in the public's judgement. In 1982, he was invited to take part in a massive BBC enterprise to mark sixty years of radio light entertainment. He played several of his old roles in a reconstruction of *Round the Horne*, with Barry Took playing the old Horne part that he had written for so long. The programme was produced by Richard Wilcox, now head of Radio Two comedy.

'He was so nice, so kind, so funny,' Wilcox told me. 'But the funniest moments were after the show – in the pub where he held centre stage all the time, mostly talking about Noël Coward.'

Moments like that didn't mean now any more than they ever had that Ken was secure about himself. Even though he didn't want to do any more work than he was doing, he still worried when there were not people begging him to come out of what they might have considered his semi-retirement.

Two years or so after the *Round The Horne* reprise, Ken again saw Richard Wilcox, this time outside Broadcasting House in Portland Place.

'I'm not getting much work these days,' he told him. 'Have I done something to offend?'

Wilcox assured him that he had not – and very soon afterwards, as if to prove it, arranged for him to get some work. 'But he was, it has to be admitted, getting harder and harder to cast.'

The work the producer gave Ken was hardly in his usual line – a member of one of the teams in *Pop Score*, a quiz about pop music, just the sort he never listened to and always professed to despise. 'He was terribly funny,' Richard Wilcox told me. 'Of course, he knew nothing about pop and we fed him several of the answers.'

It added a few pounds to his bank balance and restored, temporarily, his self-confidence. In truth, he had no reason at all to worry about money – money that would have been enough to keep him in reasonable comfort if only he had been willing to spend it on comfortable things. Apart from his shopping expeditions to Marks and Spencer and John Lewis, most of it just went into the bank and other investments suggested by his accountant.

There were no more 'Carry On' films for Ken. But he was kept busy by *Just A Minute* and his various other peripheral activities, including more and more to-camera children's stories in the BBC's *Jackanory* series.

He also had the opportunity for one of the best things he ever did on television – a show called *An Audience With Kenneth Williams* in which he entertained for an hour, most of which was taken up by answering not always serious questions from friends and showbiz contemporaries in the audience – always the hardest of audiences and one which Gyles Brandreth told me many of his friends worried about, but, in the event had no reason to do so.

Ken was ever loyal to those friends. When Brandreth organized an all-night speaking marathon in aid of the National Playing Fields Association – 'the world's longest after-dinner speech' – Ken came along in the early hours of the morning (the very early hours) to make his own speech for the fund.

Scripts continued to pile up, but he still said he was not interested in any of them. He had a new agent now. Peter Eade, who had steered his career right from his earliest days, had died and the new man was his friend and fellow refugee from the old Margate and Eastbourne repertory days, Michael Anderson.

Anderson was now a senior agent for the London branch of the American firm ICM. They had met one day near Anderson's West End office. Ken said he was looking for a new agent. 'You can be the one,' he told him and that was that. For the next few years they had a perfect agent–client relationship. Anderson suggested ideas and Ken chose the ones he was going to do – and would not do, and when the cheques came in, Anderson passed them on to him.

'I don't really think he wanted to do much more,' he now remembers.

They got on well, although they didn't mix very much socially. Derek Nimmo didn't find that at all strange. He didn't always enjoy social chit-chat with people with whom he worked. Although, he did add: 'I think he quite enjoyed going to ordinary, boring dinner parties.'

There were sometimes limits to his contributions to those parties. 'The main topic of conversation was usually the one about his anal complaints of one kind or another, and unless you were particularly interested in haemorrhoids, I don't think one was able to show the same sort of enthusiasm as Kenneth.'

Despite what Nimmo said, Ken thoroughly enjoyed the elegant dinner parties at his *Just A Minute* colleague's Kensington home; evening dress affairs with a footman in livery to show guests to the table. And there were the occasional other parts of his anatomy Ken would talk about – like the time he was in animated conversation with an elderly titled lady. He talked about the unfortunate occasion a stewardess collided with him on a plane. 'And she spilt a glass of gin on my cock,' he told her apparently in all seriousness. 'Of course, you haven't got a cock so you wouldn't understand.'

It was part of the contrast in the Williams character that he could talk like that one moment and amaze his fellow diners with his knowledge of say, the French Revolution the next.

In the spring of 1984, Pat Williams had a stroke. Ken came to the hospital twice with Lou, but when she was considered well enough to leave, it was a friend and the friend's husband who took her home. From that day on, Pat looked after herself, hobbling around her flat in London's Camden Town, making her own cups of tea, doing her own cooking. Neither Ken nor Lou came to the flat to see her. 'He didn't like being around illness,' said Lou. 'Yes, I suppose that's true,' agreed Pat. 'You only had to sneeze near him and he'd go mad.'

For the next three and a half years, he and Lou never went to see her. The only time they were together was when Pat took a taxi to Osnaburgh Street on their occasional meetings for lunch.

Meanwhile, every Sunday, Ken took his mother to lunch at the Joe Allen's basement restaurant in Covent Garden, a place where he thought he wasn't going to be disturbed by autograph hunters – 'although,' said Derek Nimmo, 'it was just the sort of place where he was most likely to be recognized.'

Lou continued to go to *Just A Minute* recordings. When friends called round to Ken's flat to take him for lunch, she only had to hear the bell ring to be outside her own door – and say, 'Hello, where are we going? I'll get my coat.' To them both, apparently, it seemed the perfect relationship.

There wasn't much doubt that the perfect relationship as far as his career was concerned was with producers and audiences in his chat show activities.

In 1986, he deputized for Terry Wogan on his top-rated BBC talk show, *Wogan*, where he had appeared many times as a guest and had virtually taken over the show. When Wogan had a holiday, Ken took his place.

Peter Estall, the executive producer, thought he would be able to cope – he had worked with him before on radio, producing one of his poetry programmes and the *Start the Week* shows that he presented. But there was, nevertheless, always the worry that he wouldn't allow the guests to get their own words in – not every guest could be depended upon to dominate the way Ken had when he was sitting on the other couch.

To cope with that difficulty, Ken was persuaded to do a monologue at the beginning of his shows – which he was not totally thrilled to do. 'In the end, we persuaded him to bring old *Round The Horne* scripts which he would adapt and we'd put on the autocue for him. Once he got going, he didn't seem to need them and they merely served as a base for him.' Ken was asked to bring the scripts to the Television Centre with him. 'Sometimes, he would forget them – and we had to send him back in a car to his flat to get them. He wouldn't allow anyone else to go inside the flat.'

Estall and he got on very well – and as with so many other people, the relationship was largely cemented via children, in this case Estall's young sons to whom he presented a Kenneth Williams one-man show. 'He was very rude. And they were highly flattered that an adult was taking such an interest in them, keeping them amused with quite sophisticated schoolboy humour, telling them elaborate stories.'

Sometimes he could be rude in other ways. 'He could be quite cutting about people I would have assumed were quite close friends.

'He would suddenly come out with things about people he had worked with which made me think, "I wonder if you have any friends at all". He would be very, very bitchy, very cruel about women in particular, pick out a certain trait that one had and describe her in the most appalling way, which was very funny but quite cruel. He was, of course, the master of the *double entendre.*'

And he demonstrated that in front of the *Wogan* cameras. 'No one could take any offence. He would get away with it. There was always another meaning. But he couldn't bear not being the centre of attraction. You knew he would always perform.'

Once in Joe Allen's, Ken saw an American whom he knew, sitting at an adjoining table. He spotted Estall sitting there with his family. 'And he proceeded to bring the place down with an impromptu story, while all I wanted to do was crawl up.'

The producer also experienced the strange rules that Ken imposed on himself. Once they went to Cambridge together for an outside broadcast. He and Estall met in Ken's room to discuss the script.

'He suddenly stopped smoking, but he got increasingly fidgety. I said, "For god's sake, why don't you smoke?" He almost physically attacked me for suggesting that anyone should smoke in a bedroom.'

Barbara Windsor, Derek Nimmo and Stephen Fry were guests whom

227

Ken particularly wanted on the show. 'He made a very good job of it,' Peter Estall now remembers.

In 1987, Ken was a guest on a chat show, hosted by the American comedienne Joan Rivers. It was a show most memorable for Ken's contribution – but not one that he would have wanted to be remembered. Ms Rivers got Ken on a raw nerve. 'Is sex important to you?' she asked. Ken flushed and then appeared to go green. 'No,' he replied, so firmly that it took on far greater importance than might originally have been intended. 'No. It never has been. I ought to have been a monk.' For the first time, Ken was uncomfortable in front of a camera and even worse in front of an audience. You almost saw his stomach churn up. You did see him wriggle in his seat.

When he wasn't working, Ken went out with his friends, kept in correspondence with them. On his birthday, Val Orford still sent him presents and Ken replied warmly, telling about the things that had happened to him. His tastes hadn't really changed, although he was being taken to better places – about which he still complained.

'There was a birthday lunch in advance at the Ritz. I've never seen such prices in a menu. Courses BEGINNING at twenty-eight pounds. I mean ... Marie Antoinette Land.'

It was an interesting letter, written in February 1988 with constant stress on his age. 'This morning an idiot on the radio was telling all and sundry that I was sixty-two and in Marks and Spencer EVERYONE knew. Someone gave me Edmund White's *The Beautiful Room Is Empty*. You've never read such shameless stuff. Sex on every page. Incredible how this sort of pornography gets respectable coverage ... doing the *Just A Minute* programme last night at the Paris in Lower Regent Street. RAN OUT after, 'cos I couldn't face more autograph-hunters. Breathless up the street. Phew. Age takes its toll all right. Interesting you enjoyed *King and I*. I haven't been to the theatre for ages. Wouldn't dream of going for pleasure ... all those people ... oh, I'd just want to run. Anyway, I can't leave Lou for long. She's over eighty-six now and you have to keep an eye on her. Yours, Kenneth.'

Writing so warmly to Orford was, seemingly, a gesture to ensure that he was still liked. In the same way, he sought to mend fences. Ken met Michael Codron again and went to his home for dinner parties. They now became close friends once more.

Codron didn't like to persuade him to do another play for him. Like Wilcox he said: 'He was getting harder and harder to cast.'

He didn't look healthy any more. He had his usual collection of ailments to talk about, some real, some apparently not so real.

Every five or six weeks, Ken would take Lou to a chiropodist's surgery in Baker Street. Both had feet problems and Ken would sit in Nigel Tewkesbury's rooms where both he and Lou would regale the chiropodist and his assistant Sylvia Reed with stories, Ken going into character all the time.

'They were repeating old shows from *Round The Horne* at the time and he'd do bits of them for us,' said Sylvia Reed. He would talk about things he had seen on the stage. Despite what he wrote to Val Orford about never going to a theatre he'd say, "Have you seen ..? I saw it last night dear. I thought it was terrible. Terrible."'

Out of Lou's hearing, he would talk about her. 'Oh, she does fuss me,' he told her. Lou had a similar theme. 'Mustn't fuss him,' she would say, as though she were perhaps a little afraid of him.

There were, though, more serious problems in the life of Kenneth Williams and his health. Ken collected sundry medical specialists the way art lovers collected paintings and painters. He rarely bothered with a general practitioner. In April 1988, he was seeing a man who specialized in stomach disorders. He had serious abdominal pain and went into hospital.

In a letter to Michael Codron – in which he had commented on the death of an actress aged fifty-one – on 8 April, he wrote 'Yes – the ulcer is back with a vengeance. Made me give up the fags.' The man he saw at the hospital told him that if that didn't do the trick he would have to have an operation – and the surgeon added. 'Sooner the better, because let's face it, you're no chicken ...' 'They kept me in the Cromwell for two days – tests etc. – oh! how I HATE these places!'

He wrote a similar report to Clement Freud, if in somewhat more detail. 'After the gastroscopy and sonic scan in the Cromwell, the surgeon said, 'It's the third time the ulcer has recurred. You must STOP smoking.' So I have. They think that if [the cure] doesn't work (in six weeks) they will have to operate.'

Michael Anderson had plenty of work on hand for Ken. There were voice-overs and radio commercials. Miriam Margolyes with whom he did several of them said she knew he hated them. 'I'm sick of it,' he told her. 'I've had enough.'

He was due to make a promotional film for Esso – which Anderson had rescheduled to allow him to go into hospital.

Ken was no less funny, despite his problems. Just after coming out of hospital, he met Sheila Hancock in Portland Place. 'He called after me and we talked for ages, leaning up against a parking meter.'

She knew he was depressed, despite the laughter. She had learned how to sense that. 'As with a lot of actors, you knew how his mood was going to affect what he did. He projected what he felt. Sometimes on *Just A Minute*, he would come in and not speak and go home again if he was angry or depressed – there would be this big atmosphere around him. I just took it as Kenneth. Now I question whether I should have asked if he needed help.'

He possibly did, that day early in April 1988. He was more expansive about himself than was usual for him in a public place. She had got out of her car and Ken had shouted after her.

'Normally, he would walk right past and not speak, even though we were friends. He knew that if he stopped, people would recognize him and stare at him. But on this occasion, we talked for hours leaning on that parking meter.'

'He was talking about his pain, but being so funny about it.' To Ken, of course, it was his favourite topic of conversation and Sheila took little notice as he had her falling about while he spoke. 'It's the bowels dear, the bowels. They've got to gouge this whole part out . . .'

As she now says: 'If I had known it was more serious than usual I would have done something about it. It was one of his most manic moments and what I think now he was saying was, "Christ, I'm in agony".'

On the night of 14 April 1988, Ken was feeling worse than ever. The next morning, he and Lou were due to go to the Tewkesbury surgery. 'I'll see you at half-past-ten tomorrow,' he told his mother. 'I'll just go and listen to the nine o'clock news and go to bed.' He went into his flat, took some pain-killers and his regular sleeping pills.

Ken was always punctual – sometimes, to the point of causing despair among his friends who might have wished for an occasional moment of respite. But on the morning of 15 April, he did not call at Lou's flat, as promised, at ten-thirty.

When he didn't come, Lou used her own key to get in next door. 'Oh come on, son,' she called. 'We've got to go and get our feet done.' There was no movement from his bed.

Lou called Sylvia Reed at the surgery. 'We were supposed to come in this morning, but I can't wake my son,' she told her. Sylvia suggested that she call the caretaker, but she said that she knew Ken would be annoyed. 'He'll be cross if I disturb him.' Nevertheless, she did call the caretaker. The man went into Ken's flat with Lou and saw him lying still in bed. He was cold – and dead.

EPILOGUE

The coroner recorded an open verdict. He couldn't be certain that Ken's death was an accident. On the other hand, he couldn't be sure either that it was suicide. What *was* sure was that he had taken an overdose of barbiturates. And what he did say caused a flurry of anger among Ken's closest friends and the family.

Could the pills have been taken accidentally? Dr Christopher Pease, the coroner, said: 'It is possible but not likely.'

However, there were others who said that it was possible, but not likely, that at sixty-two Kenneth Williams took his own life. As Clement Freud said: 'For a two-packets-a-day man to give up smoking on medical advice is not actually a normal course of action for someone contemplating suicide. I knew Kenneth. I know he would not have deliberately taken his life while his mother − whom he loved above all things − remained dependent upon him.'

Ken wanted his body left to medical science, but there had been too many pathologists' examinations, too much time had elapsed for that to happen. He was cremated − in a quiet ceremony attended by many of his closest friends, like Stanley Baxter, Gordon Jackson and Barbara Windsor.

None of them were mentioned in the will, in which he bequeathed property worth more than half a million pounds. Nor was Pat. 'I never expected I would be,' she told me. But neither was Lou mentioned − although the accepted view is that he never expected her to outlive him. But it was an untidy state of affairs for a man who always arranged striped shirts in one pile and checks in another.

He left his flat to his friend Paul Richardson and his godson Robert Chiddell. The royalties from his books and on his radio and TV shows − although not from films; there were no residuals from those − went to Michael Anderson. The rest − including Lou's home − became the property of Michael Whittaker.

To paraphrase Derek Nimmo, it was frequently impossible to know what was going on in the other rooms. Soon afterwards, Lou moved into Pat's Camden Town flat and Michael Whittaker made her an annuity.

If that will surprised the people in Ken's life, it was nothing compared to the mystery of what happened that April night in 1988, a mystery that still puzzles his friends.

'I hope to God he didn't commit suicide,' Sheila Hancock told me. 'Surely not,' said Derek Nimmo, 'he would never have left Lou. He was not a cowardly man – except perhaps concerning the scalpel.'

Yet Miriam Margolyes saw the depressions and wonders. 'He was so depressed so often, so mercurial, I think it quite possible he could have committed suicide.'

Michael Anderson, on the other hand, thinks that suicide was unlikely. 'Had he planned to take his own life, I don't think he would have gone to such trouble planning and rearranging his work schedule.'

His mother would not contemplate her son taking his life any more than she thinks he was a homosexual. In an offguard moment, as she thought of being left out of his will, she could mutter, 'the little sod'. But she says: 'I loved my Ken, of course I did.'

Pat says that she is not surprised at the controversy. 'To some people, he could be a right bastard, but on the whole we got on very well.'

These are passing thoughts mingled with the affection they felt and he gave. Explain his behaviour? Perhaps it was all part of what was, after all, a very strange carry on.

Stage Plays

Debut in Combined Services Entertainments
Various repertory company roles
Slightly in *Peter Pan*, Scala Theatre, 1952
Dauphin in *Saint Joan*, Arts, and St Martin's, 1954–5
Elijah in *Moby Dick*, Duke of York's 1955
Montgomery in *The Buccaneer*, Lyric, Hammersmith and Apollo, 1955–6
Maxime in *Hotel Paradiso*, Winter Garden, 1956
Kite in *The Wit To Woo*, 1957
Green in *Share My Lettuce*, Lyric, Hammersmith and Comedy and Garrick,
    1958
Portia, the Ugly Sister, in *Cinderella*, Coliseum, 1958
Various parts in *Pieces of Eight*, Apollo, 1959
One Over The Eight, 1961
Julian in *The Private Ear and the Public Eye*, Globe, 1962
Jack in *Gentle Jack*, Queens, 1963
Truscott in *Loot*, on tour, 1965
Bernard in *The Platinum Cat*, Wyndham's, 1965
Henry in *My Fat Friend*, Globe, 1972
Barillon in *Signed and Sealed*, Comedy Theatre, 1976
The Undertaker in *The Undertaking*, Greenwich and the Fortune, 1979

Films

Trent's Last Case, 1952
The Seekers, 1954
Carry On Sergeant, 1958
Carry On Nurse, 1959
Carry On Teacher, 1959
Carry On Constable, 1960
Carry On Regardless, 1960
Raising The Wind, 1961
Twice Round The Daffodils, 1962
Carry On Cruising, 1962
Carry On Jack, 1964
Carry On Spying, 1964
Carry On Cleo, 1964
Carry On Cowboy, 1965

Carry On Screaming, 1966
Carry On – Don't Lose Your Head, 1966
Carry On – Follow That Camel, 1966
Carry On Doctor, 1968
Carry On Up The Khyber, 1968
Carry On Again Doctor, 1969
Carry On Camping, 1969
Carry On Loving, 1970
Carry On Henry, 1971
Carry On At Your Convenience, 1971
Carry On Abroad, 1972
Carry On Matron, 1972
Carry On Dick, 1974
Carry On Behind, 1975
Carry On Emmannuelle, 1979

INDEX

18; family life, 9–15, 22; 'our game' with sister, 9–10, 11–12, 17, 35; believes himself a prince, 12; in school play, 15–16, 17; training in lithography, 18, 21; possible first sexual experience, 19, 21, 40; realization of sexual orientation, 19, 21, 24, 40, 51; poems, 20, 30, 33–4; employment as map draughtsman, 22, 23, 24, 26, 44, 46; first theatre visit, 23; self-education, 24–5; in amateur dramatic group, 25; autobiography, 25, 64, 74, 132, 185, 194, 220; Army service, 25–43; popularity and nickname, 27, 28; broken nose, 28; concert performance, 28; and communal living, 30; transfer to map-printing, 31, 35; in India and Far East, 31–43; in Army entertainment, 36–43; first stage appearance, 38; 'crisis in my life', 42; return to civilian life, 43, 44; determination to become actor, 44–5, 46–8; contemplates conversion to Catholicism, 46; in repertory, 48–55, 57, 59; debut, 49; as Burton understudy, 52; film debut, 57, 58, 59; television debut, 58; first London appearance, 59–61, 62–3; on tour, 61–2; first reference to 'camp', 62; return to repertory, 64, 66; unemployment, 65; success in Shaw, 67, 69, 71; radio debut in *Hancock's Half Hour*, 67, 68–9, 71; 'stop messing about' catchphrase, 69, 91, 92, 94, 96, 105, 199, 200; spartan life-style, 70, 80–1, 111, 112, 140, 178, 219, 222; acid comments on other actors, 70; arouses Hancock's jealousy, 71–2, 92; ability to do serious work, 73–5, 92; lost chance to see New York, 76; brief stardom in musical, 76–7; dislike of father, 77, 84, 127; later stage work, 78–9, 81; concern with homosexuality on stage, 79–80; move to own flat, 80; revue success and confirmation as star, 81, 82–7, 90; favourite restaurants, 86, 116, 125–6, 174–5; start of *Carry On* career, 88–91; joins *Beyond Our Ken*, 91–4; increasing success, 94, 109, 112, 132; in pantomime, 94–5; playing of love scenes, 97, 152; return to revue as star, 99–104, 109; ad-libbing, 102, 110, 123, 143; warm-up routine for studio audiences, 107, 195, 212; desire to leave comedy, 119, 120, 121; return to straight theatre, 120–5, 127; frustration with parents, 124; and father's death, 129–30; holidays abroad, 130–1, 160, 177, 183, 189; moves to new flats, 133, 200, 218; stage failure, 133–8; return to *Carry On* films, 138, 139–55; concern with tax, 139–40; proposes separate-bedroom marriage, 146, 163; contrasting behaviour, 149; as dinner guest, 150, 151, 221, 225; and pseudo-Shakespeare recitations, 150; immaculate dress, 153, 164, 173–4; further stage failures, 165–8, 182–3, 203–7, 208, 211, 216; new radio series, 175–7, 187–98, 199–200, 201–3, 209, 211–13; search for new plays, 182; chat shows, 184, 222, 226–8; new television series, 184–6, 200; domination of *Just a Minute*, 188–9, 192–4; stage success in Shaw, 201; stomach trouble, 205, 229–30; loss of faith in himself, 207, 208; poetry readings, 208; victim of practical joke, 210; as author, 211, 217–18, 220; increasing despair, 214, 215, 216; fear of going on stage again, 215, 217, 222; as director, 217; watershed in life, 222, 224–5; financial upsets, 222–4; difficult to cast, 224, 228; as Wogan deputy, 226–8; in hospital, 229; death, 230; possible suicide, 231–2; his will, 231; *Characteristics*: artistic ability, 12, 17, 18, 21, 24; bad language, 118, 175, 184, 189, 190, 215; bodily contact, dislike of, 40, 117; body functions, preoccupation with, 5, 130, 131, 141, 180; 'bum' talk, 103, 107, 153, 179; business acumen, 140, 222–3, 224; 'camp' image, 62, 83, 91, 120, 140, 172; children, attitude to, 111, 115, 126, 173, 227; cleanliness, obsession with, 4, 5, 117, 178; depressions, 48, 56, 67, 116–17, 124, 138, 141–2, 151, 163–4, 191–2, 194, 216, 229–30; erudition, 118, 149, 154, 189, 191, 197; families, interest in, 111, 126; friendships, 11, 14, 22–5, 27–30, 32–3, 38, 40, 46, 49–50, 52, 53, 64, 75, 114–17, 127, 130–1, 145–6, 147, 156–69; handwriting, 4, 22, 29, 55, 146; health, concern with, 95, 107, 151, 183, 204, 205, 225, 228, 229–30; history, interest in, 8, 9, 12, 116, 212; homosexuality, 19, 21, 24, 40, 46, 51, 79–80, 104, 136, 146, 157,